Christianity
and Animism
in Melanesia

"Break down their altars, smash their sacred stones and burn their Asherah poles in the fire; cut down the idols of their gods and wipe out their names from those places. You must not worhip the Lord your God in their way. But you are to seek the place the Lord your God will choose from among all your tribes to put his Name there for his dwelling."   ~ Deuteronomy 12:3–5, NIV

———

"When I preach, I encourage people to hold on to kastom . . . The house of prayer should promote *tupunas* [sacred stones] and *tamafa* [incantations]."   ~ Joshua, a pastor from Tanna

Contents

Note on Vernacular Orthography

Many vernacular terms in this book are represented in the Southwest Tanna orthography. Special characters are explained below. (Note that Appendix A contains a short glossary of vernacular terms that appear frequently throughout this book.)

ə   Schwa; sounds like the "u" in "cut."
ɨ   High central unrounded vowel; sounds like "e" in "roses."
g   Voiced velar nasal; sounds like the "ng" in sing.
v   High central unrounded semivowel; sounds almost like "w" in "we," but unrounded.

Abbreviations

AG   Assemblies of God
CCC   Campus Crusade for Christ
LDS   Latter Day Saints
LMS   London Missionary Society
NT   New Testament
NTM   Neil Thomas Ministries
OT   Old Testament
PCV   Presbyterian Church of Vanuatu
PRC   Presbyterian Reformed Church
SIL   Summer Institute of Linguistics
YWAM   Youth with a Mission

Foreword

THIS book deals with issues that are of great concern to missionaries and local peoples across Melanesia and the world at large. While the focus is on the Island of Tanna in Vanuatu, the issues are the same across the length and breadth of Melanesia, stretching from Fiji in the east to the Moluccas Islands (in Indonesia) in the west. Understanding traditional experience in contrast to the missionary response to spirituality is a crucial missiological issue in our day. Despite over a century of mission dominance and an apparent acceptance of the gospel message, churches throughout Melanesia quickly become nominal and people continue to rely on traditional sources of power. Therefore, it is crucial to understand how contemporary churches can maintain a dynamic interface of culture and biblical awareness. Dealing with Scripture in the contemporary reality of living life as God intended provides the rationale for the case study in this book.

On Tanna, as in much of Melanesia, two religions now reside side by side; traditional animism and missionary-introduced Christianity (Tippett 1967; Trompf 1987). Both religions reflect the cultural environment that spawned them; thousands of years of interaction with spiritual forces and their influence on enabling people to survive in their physical, social, and psychological world; and two thousand years of Christian expansion structured to reflect Greco-Roman philosophy in categories that reflect missionary understanding but have little relevance to local peoples. It is this tension between local and Western worldviews that structures Dr. Ken Nehrbass' excellent book. Sadly, the missionaries encouraged people to abandon kastom and embrace Christianity. This forced people to make unfortunate choices resulting in "split-level Christianity" (Hiebert, Shaw, and Tienou 1999, 15ff). This dual perspective creates a dynamic syncretism which enables people to separate Christianity from the way they live their lives. The result is a lack of understanding of Scriptural perspectives—God's perspective. The Bible is all about God enabling people with whom he communicated to worship him appropriately in contrast to performing ritual to get something they want. God gave Israel many "kastoms" all with the focus of acknowledging and worshiping him. Nehrbass clearly presents this development in Chapter 1. This is closely juxtaposed with an anthropological understanding of animism as a "religion" of the people in Chapter 2. In focus, then, is how people respond to God as a product of their beliefs and values, not which worldview (local or Christian) they subscribe to. How people steeped in the reality of life process Scripture is far more important, for them, than the ideas the missionaries brought, as Trompf has made clear (1987, 5–6).

In our contemporary, globalizing world, the people of Tanna and Melanesia in general cannot—must not—ignore the rest of the world. Like missions in the past, a ubiquitous "globalization" now frames most things people do. However, they still live their lives in a particular context endued with their traditions and lifestyle expectations—kastom. This is the context within which all outside influence must be evaluated. It is this understanding of context and the role of the gospel, encased in Scripture, that Nehrbass seeks to make sense of. Both are critical to the well-being of people who come to church whenever the bell rings and maintain their identity in the context of a spiritually, socially, and emotionally charged reality.

The overall thesis of the book is that "kastom is more than a set of superstitions and rituals; it is a fully developed worldview. If missionaries wish to transform the worldview of people from animistic backgrounds, they first need to attain as thorough an understanding of the particular form of kastom as possible" (25). In one sense, this book is about the problem of syncretism, with four approaches to gospel and culture that reflect on the situation missiologically. But there is another important sub-theme—the problem of missionaries not taking cultural issues (local folklore, etiologies, social relationships, worldviews) that create "kastom" seriously. Instead the history of missions shows largely untrained foreigners relying on their own cultural knowledge to recreate "Christendom as a Western cultural tradition" rather than "Christianity as a belief system" (Whiteman 1983, 411). Sadly, too many missionaries, despite their enlightened perspectives, are not really interested in what drives local beliefs and values. Rather than being curious about animism, they write it off as something of the devil rather than a dynamic of a peoples' cultural understanding. Raising the need for cultural awareness drives the author of this book and provides the impetus for strongly encouraging readers to engage people and their ideas about spiritual issues. Today's missionaries, perhaps more than ever before (because of our globalized world), need to do the hard work necessary to acquire spiritual knowledge. This is not to minimize the need for cultural knowledge in general, but spiritual awareness is crucial to an effective presentation of the true gospel in contemporary contexts. Nehbrass clearly demonstrates the importance of connecting with Tannese in order to present the gospel in a way that makes sense to them.

The book is a nice blend of ethnography (especially in Part 2) and missiological reflection that draws on a wide literature and historical issues especially as they pertain to the development of the church on the Island of Tanna. The historical background enables the author to frame the development of a model that suggests both the state of the church in its integration of the gospel in culture and the type of interaction that best reflects how people go beyond the church to meet social obligations. Can the people be Tannese while at the same time being Christian? Is that possible? There is no quick-fix-gospel, no easy way to gain awareness of their viewpoint short of hanging out with them and understanding what drives their existence. A study of the function of animism (Chapters 3–9), the history of local missions (Chapter 10), and an awareness of local attitudes toward animism (Chapter 11) is essential for engaging a study of missions in an animistic setting (Chapter 12). In such circumstances people are encouraged to see themselves from God's perspective and apply that understanding to their lifestyle. In doing so, missionaries are able to gain ap-

preciation for what they lack because their perspective is so different. The gospel then becomes a two-way enrichment focused on knowing God—everyone gains new perspective
because of what the other brings (Shaw and Van Engen 2003, 209ff). Nehrbass' presentation of four approaches to the gospel enables him to show how the parameters of a new
model make sense for the ongoing development of the church in this island environment.

The focus of the book moves beyond contextualization to the implementation of relevant Christianity for a people who have moved away from God's intent for them. Much
of their kastom reflects the enemy's ensuring they maintain a search for salvation (Strelan
1977) rather than recognizing God's loving care and desire to fulfill their heart longings.
Christ came to fulfill culture, not marginalize his followers. To be followers of Christ implies culturally and spiritually fulfilled believers who acknowledge the call of God who
made them in his image and desires the very best for all of creation (Jn 10:10). Nehrbass
rises to a new level in missiological writing and anticipates recognition of new methods
and thinking that will encourage people to know God in the midst of their circumstances
—in their kastom! The missiological value of this book is the author's reflection on local
culture, how it has been approached historically (with "mixed" results), and what can be
done as local people apply his model to transforming their communities in culturally appropriate ways. Understanding how God can fulfill their lives and enable Tannese expressions of ritual and ceremony to bring honor to God while maintaining social responsibility
will make them better Tannese as well as better Christians. Enhanced cultural awareness
applied to knowing God will reduce syncretism (Shaw and Van Engen 2003, 144, 166).

May those who read this book engage in the study of local religious beliefs and practices that enable people to develop biblical theologies in their context. This, it seems to
me, is much more effective, and reflects biblical intent far better, than the historically inadequate contextual theologies that have populated the missiological literature (Shaw 2010).
Readers of this book can use its insight to transform members of their own societies in
order to realize God's intent for them. Enjoy the read!

R. Daniel Shaw
Professor of Anthropology and Translation
Fuller Graduate School of Intercultural Studies
Pasadena, CA
January, 2012

REFERENCES

Hiebert, Paul.G., R. Daniel Shaw, and Tite Tienou. 1999. *Understanding folk religion: A Christian response to popular beliefs and practices.* Grand Rapids: Baker Book House.

Shaw, R. Daniel. 2010. Beyond contextualization: Toward a twenty-first-century model for enabling mission. *International Bulletin of Missionary Research* no. 34 (No. 4): 208–215.

Shaw, R. Daniel, and Charles E. Van Engen. 2003. *Communicating God's word in a complex world: God's truth or hocus pocus?* Lanham, MD: Rowman and Littlefield.

Strelan, John. 1977. *The Search for salvation: Studies in the history and theology of cargo cults.* Adelaide, South Australia: Lutheran Publishing House.

Tippett, Allen R. 1967. *Solomon Islands Christianity.* London: Lutterworth Press.

Trompf, Gary W. 1987. *The gospel is not Western: Black theologies from the Southwest Pacific.* Maryknoll, NY: Orbis Books.

Whiteman, Darrell L. 1983. *Melanesians and Missionaries.* Maryknoll, NY: Orbis Books.

Preface

IT is unusual to find Sigmund Freud and John Piper quoted in the same book. And it is probably surprising to find postmodern theories of anthropology discussed alongside some famous missionaries and martyrs of the nineteenth century. However, it really shouldn't be that surprising. A book on Christianity in Melanesia, such as this one, is undoubtedly going to delve into anthropological theories of so-called primitive religion, mission history, and contemporary missiological strategies. While I focused on a fairly narrow topic—animism and Christianity on Tanna Island—I ultimately found myself knee-deep in the study of cargo cults, totems and taboos, kava intoxication, shamanism, pedagogy, theories of atonement, cross-cultural leadership, and even ecclesiastical architecture. While I have covered a broad number of topics, my primary aim has been to understand how churchgoers from an animistic background process the Christian faith to make it their own.

Traditional religion (called kastom) in Vanuatu comprises a number of elements that are characteristic of animism. There is an extensive cosmology and mythological corpus; and islanders engage in sorcery, divination, sacrifice, and a particular system of totemism. Early missionaries to Tanna deemed Christianity to be incompatible with their traditional religion and attempted, with limited success, to displace it with Christianity. However, with the rise of cargo cults, nationalism, and the enculturation of the church in the mid-twentieth century, many Tannese began to consider Christianity and traditional religion as two roads to the same end. More than a dozen denominations have since arrived, each idiosyncratic in its response to traditional religion. Some denominations have leaned toward syncretism; others have dismissed outright much of the indigenous culture, proscribing practices associated with animism, but not attempting to address the underlying animistic worldview. Still others have made a more conscious effort to contextualize Christianity, avoiding both separatism and syncretism.

Here, I have attempted to uncover how Christians from animistic backgrounds decide which aspects of traditional religion kastom to relinquish and which to retain. What do they find appealing about the churches that promote a clean break from animism? What distinguishes kastom-retainers from kastom-relinquishers? Alternately, what is the allure of the churches that are more accepting of traditional religion? In a largely homogeneous society, how is it that there can be such diverging attitudes about the relationship between animism and Christianity? To answer these questions, I conducted interviews with members of numerous denominations in order to discover factors that contribute to Tannese attitudes about gospel and kastom. Ultimately, I synthesized these interview responses into four ecclesiastical approaches toward animism on Tanna: mixing, transplanting, contextualizing, and separating.

This study is part of an ongoing discussion among church leaders about animism, syncretism, and contextualization. While missionaries on other continents may find that Tannese Christians' responses toward animism diverge from their own contexts, I anticipate that the model for integrating gospel and culture in this book will help church leaders develop their own context-specific approaches toward animism.

Acknowledgements

MY friends in Yanemilen village, Tanna, have been extraordinary hosts to me and my wife Mendy and our four children for the past nine years. They have done a fantastic job patiently teaching us their language and explaining their traditional religious system called "kastom." Chief Jenry wanted to document kastom for future generations, and hopes this study of animism on Tanna will equip missionaries as they spread the gospel of Jesus Christ among animistic peoples. I am indebted to the chief and church leaders in Yanemilen and the twenty-five men and women from Tanna who participated in this study.

Mendy helped me think through every concept in this book. Dr. Doug Hayward, Dr. Tom Steffen, and Dr. Doug Pennoyer provided guidance for my research. The following people also helped by proofreading a chapter or more of the manuscript: Phil Brigandi, Dr. Jeff Morton, Dr. Dan Nehrbass, Dr. Richard and Marilynn Nehrbass, Dr. Kevin Pittle, Michael and Danielle Smith, Dr. Richard Starcher, Ross and Lyndal Webb. Thanks to SIL workers on Tanna who provided input about kastom on Tanna: Greg and Bethann Carlson, Erik and Michelle Stapleton. Rev. Malcolm Campbell, Lori Ellison, and Rev. Ken Calvert gave input on the history of missions on Tanna. I appreciate the help from the following people who tested the appropriateness of the Gospel-Culture model (Chapter 13) within the context of their own fieldwork: T. A. (Iraq), Jeff Batcock (Vanuatu), Keith Benn (Philippines), Alan Canavan (PNG), Tom Feldpausch (PNG), Bill Eckerman (PNG), David Healey (Vanuatu), Hansung Kim (Korea), Leigh Labrecque (Vanuatu), Paul Minter (PNG), Stephen and Laura Payne (Senegal), Erik Stapleton (Vanuatu), Dr. Rich Starcher (Congo), David Troolin (PNG), and Ross Webb (PNG).

Thank you to Charlotte Barnhart for the initial format checking, to Brad Koenig for copyediting the manuscript, and to the team at William Carey Library for their part in editing, designing, and publishing this book.

Introduction

ONE thousand five hundred miles north of New Zealand lies a volcanic island called Tanna.[1] A brown, jagged coral reef runs along coastlines of black sand rich in volcanic ash. A mountain ridge three thousand feet high runs down the center. Standing at the highest peak, Tukwasmera, one can see all the contours of the twenty-mile-long kidney-shaped island, which is completely covered with the wild vegetation of a tropical jungle. Those who are familiar with the tropics would be able to distinguish the jungle from the small isolated hamlets of bamboo huts, the smoke of cooking fires, or the garden plots on steep mountainsides where the inhabitants cultivate taro, yam, sweet potatoes, and plantains.

Tanna is in the southern hinterlands of Vanuatu, formerly the New Hebrides. The nation is an archipelago of around eighty islands that gained its independence from France and England in 1980. It is a developing nation with a population of only 235,000, and with limited natural resources. Undoubtedly its most valuable resource is its people, who have maintained their tribal languages and customs for centuries. To this day, inhabitants of Vanuatu (called ni-Vanuatu) live simply—their days are occupied with subsistence farming, feasts, exchanges, and the rituals of traditional religion.

In the past one hundred years, the Christian church has experienced tremendous success in Vanuatu, as it has throughout the whole Pacific. However, the manifestation of Christianity in each of the islands in Vanuatu is nuanced, as islanders integrate the church with their traditional religion, called kastom. Many Tannese attend church and yet continue to identify with kastom. They observe clan totems, perform magic to ensure good crops and health, and observe taboos about territorial spirits. Others, however, have experienced a rather drastic worldview transformation. While they maintain social ties, they do not engage in practices associated with traditional religion.

MALCOLM: A "KASTOM-RETAINER"

"Malcolm,"[2] a Tannese man in his mid-thirties, is entrenched in both church and kastom. As the leading elder of the Presbyterian church, he preaches as often as twice a day, at 5:30

---

[1] The indigenous name for the island is *Iparei* (inland). Supposedly, when Captain James Cook arrived in 1774, he pointed to the ground and asked "what is this?" They responded *tana* which means "dirt."

[2] All names in this book are obscured, except in Chapter 10, where an accurate history of Christianity on Tanna requires the use of actual names.

a.m. and 7:30 p.m., in the small church building made of wild cane and coconut leaf thatch. He is also the oldest son of the taro *tupunas*—a "taboo man" who performs sympathetic magic on his clan's totem to ensure a good taro harvest for the rest of the village. As the heir of the taro stone, the "big men" of his village expected Malcolm to learn the intricacies of kastom. This presented no conflict for him; other church leaders in his village are actively involved in kastom. For example, the elders see it as their duty to their ancestors, both living and dead, to drink kava with the other men every evening. Also, "Leaf-Armlet," an elder in the church, opens his Bible on his lap as he prepares magical remedies under the influence of a spirit named Karwas.

Church leaders in Malcolm's village have been incorporating traditional religion and Christianity since the church was planted in 2000. However, kastom and the church could not coexist peacefully indefinitely. Ecclesiastical schedules, finances, and polity are, at times, at odds with traditional religious life. For example, manipulating magical stones involves a series of taboos, and the *tupunas* must go into seclusion for several months to perform his magic. When the chiefs said it was Malcolm's turn to go into seclusion and "work" the taro stone, he had no choice. The harvest of the whole village depended on it. How would he continue his preaching responsibilities if he was in seclusion? Was it even right for a church leader to engage in magic? Wasn't magic of the devil? Would God punish the church for allowing this? But if Malcolm did not perform the magic, what would become of the taro crop? Traditional religion and Christianity were now in conflict. However, the greatest cause of anxiety, both for people within and outside of the church, was not the clash of theological systems but the disunity over how to handle the conflict. How could the issue be resolved in a way that satisfied both the church leadership and the village's leaders?

A number of solutions were suggested: Perhaps Malcolm could perform the ritual in the daytime, drink his kava, and then come to church at night. Maybe then he would enjoy the favor of both the ancestors and of God. Discussions went on for months; and finally, leaders from the Presbyterian session were summoned to a meeting with the "big men" in order to reach an agreement. In the end, it was decided that the church would pray to God to bless Malcolm as he performed the magical ritual, but the church would also formally discipline him for one year. He would need to step down as leading elder.

DANIEL: A "KASTOM-RELINQUISHER"

Just a half mile from Malcolm's village, Daniel leads a small Seventh Day Adventist (SDA) congregation. His church members are forbidden to eat pork, an important commodity in Melanesia. They cannot drink kava or attend kastom rituals because, in Daniel's words, "The Bible does not say that we should drink kava or attend kastom rituals." Daniel's father was a powerful sorcerer—a "taboo man." He could summon hurricanes and was responsible for the banana crop. During the taboo season, members of Daniel's clan cannot eat banana, because it is their totem. Daniel, however, believes he can eat banana anytime. He pointed out, "Such taboos and totems are not in the Bible."

Additionally, according to kastom, Daniel should have married his cross-cousin (i.e., his mother's brother's daughter or his father's sister's daughter), because Tannese have a cross-cousin kinship system. Instead he married an SDA woman from another island. His father disowned him for this, and began putting his efforts into actively instructing his other boys in kastom. Eventually, after a number of gifts to his father, Daniel was allowed to return to his father's village. Unfortunately, however, conflict over Christianity and kastom remains a regular reality in their clan.

ATTAINING AN EMIC UNDERSTANDING OF
ECCLESIASTICAL APPROACHES TOWARD ANIMISM

As the examples above show, the dynamics of kastom and Christianity on Tanna are being worked out by various denominations in different ways. And it is not just a question of doctrine. The church's response to kastom affects every aspect of social life, including marriage partners, involvement in ceremonies, exchanges and alliances, political power, healing practices, education, and economics.

Some churches, like Malcolm's, enthusiastically endorse the traditional religion. Others, like Daniel's, lean toward separatism—to the point of social isolation from family members who are not part of the same denomination. Some churches on Tanna, however, appear to have avoided either extreme. They are neither transplants of a Western denomination, nor are they syncretistic. In short, some indigenous churches have successfully captured and contextualized the essential message of the gospel. These are the contextualized churches.

In a homogeneous tribal setting like Tanna, how could such divergent ecclesiastical models for dealing with kastom come into existence? Why are some Tannese compelled to withdraw completely from anything resembling kastom upon conversion, while others enthusiastically maintain their tribal religion after identifying with the church? How do some churches on Tanna effectively contextualize the gospel while avoiding syncretism, and what makes those churches attractive to their members?

The theory and theology of contextualization has been well addressed in the past thirty years (D. Flemming 1980, Hiebert 1984; Kraft 1978; Moreau 2006). D. Flemming (2005) has outlined a model of contextualization in the New Testament. Brown's (2006) model specifically addresses contextualization without syncretism (albeit in the Muslim, rather than animistic, context). Contextualization within the animistic context has also been recently treated, relying particularly on anthropological data and theory (Friesen 1996; Halverson 1998; Harris and Parrinder 1960; Nida 1959). Hayward (1997), Burnett (1988), and Van Rheenen (1991) have developed comprehensive plans for contextualization in animistic contexts. Such plans involve more than communication (truth encounters); they also involve confronting the practitioners of witchcraft, sorcery, divination, and shamanism (power encounters). Further, contextualization models have been developed specifically for Melanesia (Tippett 1967, 1975; Whiteman 1983, 1997).

Much of the work on contextualization has been aimed at developing missiological theory and models to help missionaries develop a customized approach in their specific field. Far less research, though, has been done to grasp an emic understanding of ecclesiastical responses to animism. Why are indigenous communities drawn to one church model over the other? If syncretistic, Western, and contextualized church models can all be found within a given homogeneous setting such as Tanna Island, it would be helpful to understand the factors contributing to each ecclesiastical approach. What shared experiences and values, and what distinguishing features, were at work in the establishment of the churches that are sympathetic toward kastom and those that are not? On Tanna, and in the Melanesian context as a whole, little research has been done on the factors leading to the establishment of syncretistic and nonsyncretistic churches, and no theoretical models have been developed to predict what key elements may need to be in place to create a church in Melanesia that remains culturally relevant while transforming the islanders' worldview.

This book is a study of how islanders' values, experiences, and attitudes contribute to their variegated approaches toward animism and Christianity on Tanna. I examine how cultural components such as cosmology, cargoism, totemism, myth, ritual, kinship, and mission history have affected islanders' integration of gospel and culture. I interviewed a number of Tannese to find out what brought them to their current attitude toward kastom and Christianity, and have noted that there are four ecclesiastical approaches toward kastom and Christianity on Tanna: Mixers, Transplanters, Contextualizers, and Separators. In the last chapter I explore the practical and theological outcomes of each of these four ecclesiastical approaches. Ultimately, I suggest ways that churches can move people out of syncretism and into a well-contextualized Christian faith and practice.

PART 1

BIBLICAL AND ANTHROPOLOGICAL MODELS OF ANIMISM

E VEN though animism is one of the world's oldest religious phenomena, it is still widely practiced on every continent. Why are people animists? What is the origin of animism? What needs does it meet? This is a study of why some churchgoers retain kastom (animistic practices and beliefs) while others relinquish kastom. In order to understand that, we need to understand why people are animists in the first place. Why do people practice magic, shamanism, divination, and totemism?

When I began my translation work on Tanna Island, I attempted to obtain a vernacular equivalent for the pidgin English word kastom. One man suggested the phrase *to rapəh nirkəkien.* That is, "You couldn't do without it." Kastom is the *sine qua non* of life on Tanna. In fact, I later learned that the best vernacular equivalent for kastom is *nareiyen* (life). Animistic religious practices are responsible for all the good things for life in Tanna.

But what is kastom? Over the past two hundred years, missionaries and anthropologists have described traditional religion variously as (1) a set of disjointed superstitions; (2) false religion inspired by the devil; (3) God's general revelation, like the tribal version of the Old Testament; or more recently (4) a sociopolitical movement of national identity meant to subvert oppressive Western influence.

Sadly, throughout the history of the Christian missionary endeavor, many missionaries simply labeled animistic practices as "savage" or uncivilized, and they assumed that traditional religion could be readily replaced by Christianity. Many missionaries have been unfamiliar with the function of animism, not realizing that it is so intricately tied to worldview that it cannot be quickly surrendered. Seeing this gap in prefield missionary training, Alan Tippett (1968) issued a call for missionaries to study theories of "primitive religion." Modern schools of world mission took that call seriously. In an endeavor to understand the people they are trying to reach, recent missiologists have interacted with anthropological theories of animism.

A simple definition of animism is the belief that the material world is populated by spirits. One college student in Vanuatu summed up his worldview by saying, "we believe there is a spiritual cause behind everything physical in the world, including the existence of rivers, rock formations, trees, animals, crops, people and sickness." Typically, the definition of animism is expanded to include the manipulation of inanimate objects, usually through sympathetic magic, for a desired end (whether good or evil). As a result of the present research, I have arrived at the conclusion that animism does not as much boil down to a belief that fetishes inherently have power, but that the psyche is connected to the physical world. That is, regardless of whether they professes a genuine faith in Christ and the Bible, animists maintain that people's emotions and beliefs will result in physical consequences such as sicknesses (either in themselves or others), rainfall, drought, earthquakes, and abundant or scant crops from the farms.

Here, in Part 1, I give an overview of various historical understandings of animism in general. (Then, in Part 2, I give a detailed ethnography of kastom on Tanna and antici-pate the challenges it would pose for biblical Christianity.) I attempt not only to describe animism, but also to utilize both biblical and secular anthropological theories in order to explain its psychological and sociological functions. I also suggest briefly how these con-ceptualizations inevitably affect missiology—for each missionary who has encountered traditional religion has responded to it based on one of the following conceptualizations of what animism is.

CHAPTER 1

Folk Religion for the Bible and Early Church Fathers

THE Bible contains more than 1,400 years of ethnographic observations related to animistic practices both in Canaan and in the surrounding regions. Ancient Israelites could hardly be considered animistic, but the prophets recorded numerous animistic-looking behaviors of the Israelites, including astrology, sacrifice of children, idolatry, and prayers to lower gods. Often, these animistic-ish practices were borrowed from the Assyrians and Babylonians as a safety net by Israelites who were less devoted to Yahweh. Likewise, the Egyptians were not animists proper, for they had a pantheon and well-developed priestly system, but their practice of magic and veneration of images, in modern terms, would be considered vestiges of animism.

The Bible regularly proscribes such animistic practices, and describes them to a small degree. However, the prophetic books usually expect the readers to understand implicitly the types of practices that are condemned. The purpose of Scripture was not to give an ethnography of neighboring religions; rather, it was meant to help the people of God determine how they would respond to them.

Further, the Scriptures do little theorizing about what social or psychological function animistic practices and beliefs served. Certainly the project of studying the origin and social or psychological function of religion is a recent one. However, a systematic study of the biblical descriptions of foreign religions suggests that they are considered to be corruptions of the true worship of Yahweh. McDermott argues, "There is a line of teaching in both biblical Testaments that non-Jewish and non-Christian religions were inspired by divine powers that were created good but then went bad . . . Hence the religions were born in deception and malice" (2007, 163). Wilhelm Schmidt (1931) painstakingly delineated his theory of "original monotheism," arguing that the earliest cultures exclusively worshiped God and did not perform magic (cf. Corduan 1998, 33). Missionaries who adopted this approach have seen animism not primarily as a social or psychological phenomenon, nor as a political movement, but as worship gone awry. Hence, their descriptions of tribal religions are rife with descriptions like "consummate degradation" (see early missionary descriptions of kastom in Chapter 10).

OTHER RELIGIONS IN THE OLD TESTAMENT

While the Bible regularly condemns animistic practices, it does not contain a univocal response to competing religions. McDermott contends that there are instead four archetypical responses to them, ranging from "neighborly pluralism" to "competitive pluralism" to "vehement missionary exclusivism" to "cosmic war" (2007, 61–64). In some passages, there is evidence of religious tolerance, but Yahweh is certainly supreme: he is "God among gods" and "Lord among lords." Such titles intimate that God was in competition for worship among other deities. In later passages, the call is more exclusivistic: "Worship God alone." By the time of prophetic literature and the Babylonian exile, the ethos was "there are no other gods" and "all other gods are idols" (ibid., 58–59).

McDermott's point is that the Bible does not dismiss outright the religions of foreign nations; there are numerous examples of God entering into relationships of self-revelation and fatherly chastisement with other nations. The Old Testament prophets understood it to be God's plan to make himself known to all nations in order that they would glorify him (Piper 2010, 39–46.). To this end, God's handiwork could be seen in the lives of foreigners. "[God] declares that through his chastisements the following peoples will discover that he alone is God: the Ammonites, Moabites, Philistines, residents of Tyre and Sidon, and the Egyptians (Ezek 8:22,23; 25:5,11,16,17; 26:4–6; 29:6,8,16; 30:19,26; 32:15)" (McDermott 2007, 29–30). Other Gentiles in the Old Testament who had some relationship with God, either as instruments of his will, prophetic voices, or receptors of chastisement, were: Balaam, Rahab, King Huram of Tyre, Abel, Enoch, Noah, Job, Abimelech, Jethro, Ruth, Naaman, and the Queen of Sheeba (ibid., 32). Elsewhere, Don Richardson has spoken of the "Melchizedek factor"—somehow this foreigner gained enough knowledge of *Elohim* to become a priest (Gen 14:18–24) (cf. ibid., 31; Richardson 1981, 13).

Therefore, we can see that the Old Testament's response to animistic-ish religions ranges from severe condemnation to hope. Missionaries who have emphasized God's influence in all nations and religions are likely to refer to traditional religion as a type of general revelation—a local version of an Old Testament. However, those who emphasize the corruption of folk religions will prohibit it; not recognizing it as a part of God's revelation.

OTHER RELIGIONS IN THE NEW TESTAMENT

The New Testament also reflects a multivocal attitude toward the world's religions and allows for an amount of God's revelation through them. Jesus commended the faith of the Syrophoenician woman (Mark 7:24–30) and of the centurion: "In all of Israel I've never found anyone with this much faith!" (Matt 8:10; Luke 7:9). How did these foreigners come to have faith? God, in his sovereignty, must work in the hearts of those outside the covenant of Israel. Other Gentiles who had a measure of estimable faith were Cornelius (Acts 10:34,35), the healed leper who returned to give praise to God (Luke 17:18), and the good Samaritan (Luke 10:25–37) (McDermott 2007, 40). Jesus did not merely write off foreigners as lost causes; they too may have commendable faith.

Paul, too, believed that God's revelation was directed toward the Gentiles as well as the Jews. For Paul, the Gentiles were the polytheists of Greece and North Africa. Romans 1:18–2:1 and Acts 17:16–31 indicate that Paul believed that God had revealed himself generally to all nations. Paul found some kernel of truth in the Greek poets Epimenides and Aratus, quoting them in his sermon in Athens (Acts 17:28). Of course Paul also believed that the false doctrines and forbidden practices of pagan religions were a result of demonic involvement. There is a cosmic warfare between light and dark, and the world's religions are evidence of demonic tampering with people's minds and culture. "A Pauline approach can say that while the religions originated in rebellion and deception, their origins are supernatural, not natural; they teach some truth about God; and they are used by God to advance His own plan of redemption" (ibid., 83). Again, missionaries who have approached animism with this lens have tried to find vestiges of truth in it.

FOLK RELIGION AND THE EARLY CHURCH FATHERS

The various biblical motifs of God's interaction with foreign religions are also present in the work of the early church fathers. Justin Martyr and Origen held a radically exclusivistic stance; Iranaeus and Clement emphasized God's general revelation in other religions (McDermott 2007).

Justin Martyr believed that

> evil demons, effecting apparitions of themselves ... showed such fearful sights to men, that those who did not use their reason in judging of the actions that were done, were struck with terror; and being carried away by fear, and not knowing that these were demons, they called them gods. (ibid., 90)

This is a radically different explanation of the origin of religion than the psychological and social evolutionary schemes that would later be suggested by modern anthropologists (discussed below). Martyr's view is representative not only of his time, but of Judeo-Christian thought for subsequent centuries. Missionaries have typically diabolized local deities as they encountered them in the mission field.

On the other hand, Irenaeus stressed the sovereignty of God, seeing him as the great pedagogue who revealed himself in stages to humanity. The world's religions were part of God's progressive revelation first general, and ultimately specific (through Jesus Christ). God, being omniscient, was not taken off guard by foreign religions; he maintained a relationship with nations outside of the covenant community, and his Spirit was not too distant to be felt by some "godly pagans" in those cultures (ibid., 104).

Like Irenaeus, Clement believed that all people had some access to general revelation. God entered into covenants (albeit not salvific ones) with various nations. God prepared the hearts and minds of the pagan Greeks by giving them some notion of the *logos*. Clement and Irenaeus both taught that when Christ was in Hades (1 Pet 3:18,19) he made himself known to those who whose hearts were prepared to receive him (ibid., 111, 124).

Origen believed that the world's religious systems were the result of demonic powers. His theology involved a number of relevant concepts in regards to religious diversity and the origins of religion. It began with the Fall, when Satan and a percentage of demons rebelled. Since then, they have waged war against God and humans. Although God is sovereign, he allows humans the choice to accept the truth or follow a lie. The tension between providence and freedom is a historical teaching of Judeo-Christianity; however, Origen had come to some rather unorthodox conclusions by today's measure. Essentially, he said that God evaluates all people based on their own merits (in previous lives, perhaps) and distributes them amidst the world's corrupt religions as a punishment for wrongdoing. This pattern began in Old Testament days, when God sent the Israelites into exile as punishment. Likewise, Israel was the locus of God's blessing not because of his grace, but because of its meritorious track record. But the scattering among foreign nations was not just a punishment. In Origen's mind, it was also a plan for protecting them against the full-fledged demon worship he believed was inherent in foreign religions (ibid., 147).

There was, then, the same multivocal response to foreign religions in the patristic age as there was throughout Scripture, and as continues today. The church fathers evidenced a continuum of interpretations of foreign religions, ranging from providence and general revelation on the one end, to demonic inspiration on the other. Indeed, the same spectrum of responses toward animism has been evidenced by missionaries on Tanna Island, as I show in Part 2.

CHAPTER 2

Folk Religion and Modern Anthropology

MODERN theories of animism diverge significantly from historical Judeo-Christian thought on the subject. Judeo-Christian theology envisions folk religions as degradations of the true worship of God. Secular anthropology envisions their origins the other way around, portraying animism as the "primitive" religion and monotheism as a late development. My goal is not to discover the origin of animism or monotheism here, since that is a question of little missiological significance, and is impossible to determine anyway. Instead, I am looking at Schmidt's "original monotheism" and various secular models of "primitive religion" because all of these theories provide insights regarding the function of animistic religions today. The psychological, social, cultural, or religious critiques of animism, each on their own, is not a holistic enough picture of the phenomenon. We need a "systems view" which takes into account each of these theoretical frameworks (Hiebert, Shaw, & Tienou, 1999, 35ff). Further, missiological theory and practice in Melanesia has been influenced by these anthropological models, so it is important to understand each of them.

Evans-Prichard (1965) recounts two major developments in the modern thought on the subject: (1) the psychological explanation; and later (2) the social explanation. These two major positions can be further atomized into seven modern explanations of the phenomenon of folk religions. Significantly, none is akin to the degradation theory or "original monotheism" found in the Bible and the early church fathers. That is, no modern theory has held that the monotheism of Adam and Noah morphed into polytheism and fetishism. The "degradation theory" was largely absent because a survey of particularized ethnographic data appeared to suggest that the world's primitive religions do not have vestiges of monotheism. In order to remedy this lack of data, and to lend credence to the degradation theory, Richardson (1981) presented data on particular tribal religions that do seem to have a vestige of monotheism. Most modern anthropologists were not privy to that data, or they rejected it as untenable. Instead, secular anthropology's legacy from the past century and a half is the formation of the following seven theories about folk religion:

1. The animistic theory (folk religion is based on a belief of the soul)

2. The nature-myth theory (folk religion is about reverence for nature)

3. The magico-religious theory (folk religion is about reverence for land, conservation of food staples, and homage toward totems or gods)

4. The social theory (animists practically deify society because it endures eternally)

5. The psychological theory (folk religion is displacement of libidinous desires)

6. The economic theory (folk religion is about survival, harvest cycles, and status)

7. The structuralist theory (folk religion is a result of structural determinants in the human mind)

ANIMISTIC MODEL (SPIRITS)

For Tylor, folk religion was an identification of humans with nature through the device of the soul (Howells 1948, 185). Beginning with the concept of the soul, the world's religious thinkers were able to imagine all sorts of spirits, including God.

> It seems as though the conception of a human soul, when once attained to by man, served as a type or model on which he framed not only his ideas of spiritual beings in general, from the tiniest elf that sports in the long grass up to the heavenly Creator and Ruler of the world, the Great Spirit. (Tylor 1891, 110)

Tylor posited that primitive peoples were initially incapable of conceptualizing a supreme being; "savage" culture was too limited to come up with such a grandiose cosmology (cf. title of Tylor 1892). Therefore, he theorized, what the missionaries termed the "Great Spirit" (in North American religions) was an erroneous projection of Christian ethnographers onto indigenous religions (Tylor 1891, 248). Primitive religion must have something less esoteric than God or a Great Spirit at its foundation. Tylor believed that this foundation was the notion of the soul.

James Frazer's (1854–1941) notes on primitive religion showed a nearly universal belief that the soul can leave the human body. As long as the soul was deposited in an external object for safe keeping, the individual would live; but if it was harmed, the person would soon die as well. Anxiety over the safety of the soul, then, is the basis of much religious activity, according to Frazer. "It remains to show that the idea is not a mere figment devised to adorn a tale, but is a real article of primitive faith, which has given rise to a corresponding set of customs" (Frazer, 1922, 679).

Herbert Spencer's (1860–1929) scheme also had to do with the soul. He theorized that primitive people saw natural phenomena come and go: the seasons change, the sun metaphorically lives and dies every day, people sleep and awaken. There is a dualism in the world. This duality, which primitive people observed in every aspect of life, led them to conceptualize their own duality. People must have a double—a soul. It was a short jump from the concept of the soul to the concept of ghosts (Evans-Pritchard 1965, 28). Dead ancestors were ghosts, and some were eventually revered as gods. However, not all ancestors made the jump from ghosts to gods. Important men who died were especially revered.

For Spencer, this explained the emergence of ancestor worship and belief in deities in the ubiquity of religion (Howells 1948, 171).

Hodder Westropp's (1820–1885) was an evolutionary scheme like Tylor's and Spencer's. But Westropp's first stage focused instead on what he termed "pre-fetichism" (cf. Marett's "pre-animism" discussed later), which led to fetishism and eventually to worship of the fetishes, and later to a stage where people "grow out of fetichism") and into polytheism, and eventually monotheism (Westropp, 1880, 309). Ignorant of modern explanations for natural phenomena, primitive people personify, or animate, natural objects; they feel a need to propitiate them. This model was based on a belief in unilineal evolution of culture: The theory that all cultures instinctively pass through a phase early on when they began having vague ideas about spirits and ghosts before they progress to more "civilized" religious ideas.

Tylor, Spencer, and Westropp's theories are representative of European understanding of tribal religions in the late nineteenth century. During the great missionary expansion in the first half of the nineteenth century, European missionaries encountered the ghosts and taboo men of traditional religions, and considered such religious concepts to be "degraded," "uncivilized," or primitive.

NATURE-MYTH MODEL

Max Müller's model, which has been called the nature-myth scheme, also characterized primitive religion as an ontological fallacy. Tribal people personify natural phenomena such as the sun, moon, stars, and rivers, and eventually turn these phenomena into gods. Müller's data was based on extant linguistic connections between natural phenomena and religious ideas such as names of deities:

> [Müller's] thesis was that the infinite, once the idea had arisen, could only be thought of in metaphor and symbol, which could only be taken from what seemed majestic in the known world, such as the heavenly bodies, or rather their attributes. But these attributes then lost their original metaphorical sense and achieved autonomy by becoming personified as deities in their own right. The nomina became numina. So religions, of this sort at any rate, might be described as a "disease of language." (Evans-Pritchard 1965, 21)

Whereas Tylor and Spencer's schemes focused on cultures where ancestors were revered, leading to eventual polytheism, Müller's scheme drew on data from cultures where nature was revered. Müller's model may well have described tribal religious expression in India (his primary field of interest); however, nature is not venerated in Melanesia—at least not in the sense that Müller describes nature-veneration. Neither missionaries nor anthropologists in Melanesia have found Müller's theory to be a fitting description of kastom.

MAGICO-RELIGIOUS MODEL

For Codrington, primitive religion appeared to be about the accumulation of *mana*, the Melanesian concept of supernatural power. He described *mana* as follows:

> *Mana* is a power or influence, not physical, and in a way supernatural; but it shows itself in physical force, or in any kind of power or excellence which a man possesses. This *mana* is not fixed in anything, and can be conveyed in almost anything; but spirits, whether disembodied souls or supernatural beings, have it and can impart it; and it essentially belongs to personal beings to originate it, though it may act through the medium of water, or a stone, or a bone. (Codrington 1891, 119)

The basis of primitive religion, in this model, is the pursuit of *mana*. Some magico-religious societies began to see certain ghosts or spirits as reservoirs of *mana*. This was the beginning of elevation of fetishes to the status of deities (Howells 1948, 25–33).

Robert Marett's (1866–1943) explanation followed Codrington's *mana* model. He wrote witty aphorisms about animism such as "thin partitions often divide the spell from prayer" (Lowie 1948, 140), and "savage religion is something not so much thought out as danced out" (Evans-Pritchard 1965, 33). Religion, in Marett's scheme, is about emotion and action, not a coherent systematic theology (Marett 1900, 164).

The *mana* model from Codrington and Marett also served as an evolutionary scheme, moving from magic to polytheism and finally to monotheism; but in this scenario the first cause of religion was not the soul, nor the nature-myth model, rather it was the notion of power attained through magic. The most primitive form of folk religion is an emotion of awe (ibid., 170) especially due to the horror of the corpse (ibid., 178). Marett calls this feeling of awe variously "supernaturalism" (ibid., 168), "animatism" (ibid., 171), and "pre-animism." In pre-animism, people believe fetishes have magical power, but they do not animate these fetishes by conceptualizing them as spirits (cf. Tylor 1891). Calling on the rain, Marett said, does not equal animism, but calling on the spirits for rain is "full-fledged animism" (1900, 172).

Frazer, too, saw magic as the basis of animistic religion. He proposed that the magical worldview of primitive peoples could be explained in terms of two laws: the "law of sympathetic magic" and the "law of contagion" (1922, 11–44).

Both of these laws are summarized by a larger ontological "mistake" that "things act on each other at a distance through a secret sympathy, the impulse being transmitted from one to the other by means of what we may conceive as a kind of invisible ether." Therefore, many magical practices in folk religions are referred to as "sympathetic magic."[1] The law of imitative (Frazer preferred the term homeopathic magic) means that objects which share

---

[1] Islanders have pointed out to me that not all magic in Vanuatu falls into the category of sympathetic magic. For instance, there is a belief that one can place a white chicken in a basket and dunk the basket in the Lapankauta river. After waiting a few hours, the chicken will be replaced by a greenstone pendant. This magic does not rely on the law of imitation or contagion, but it is still magical.

similar properties are cosmically connected. "Like produces like...or an effect resembles its cause" (ibid). A stone shaped like a banana must have similar properties to a banana. The law of contagion requires that personal "leavings" such as a man's nail clippings, hair, excrement, or food rubbish remain connected to him. If the "leavings" are deliberately harmed (especially heated by fire), harm must necessarily befall the person to whom they originally belonged.

It may seem like Frazer is speaking tongue-in-cheek to call these "laws" as if they are laws of nature. However, Frazer is not being sarcastic or condescending. People from animistic backgrounds do not consider their magical behavior as *magic*. They perceive that when they perform sorcery or make rain that they are operating within the laws of nature. When I teach on magic in Melanesia, the audience usually objects, "But that's not magic! That procedure really works!"

A few decades after Frazer's theory was formed, Malinowski collected extensive data on the Trobriand Islanders, and arrived at a conclusion similar to Codrington and Marett's. Primitive religion, at least in the Pacific, is about an impersonal magical force. "The garden magician utters magic by mouth; the magical virtue enters the soil" (Malinowski 1935, 64). It was unclear whether islanders believed their garden was growing because of their hard work or because of their magic (ibid., 77); but gardening was done on two levels: the mechanical and the magical or symbolic. The point of the magic was to achieve prosperity—the antithesis of hunger. It means the absence of disease, dangerous influences, and disaster (ibid., 200, 224).

Of the anthropological theories that were available to missionaries in Melanesia in the early twentieth century, the *mana* motif was the most apt depiction of kastom. Indeed, to this day, Codrington's *mana* theory remains a starting point for ethnographers throughout Melanesia.

PSYCHOLOGICAL MODEL (FREUD)

For Freud, animism was not about the soul, nor magic, but about "[man's] practical need to control the world around him" (Freud 1950, 78). Primitive religion must be about gaining control over nature, including people's natural desires. Taboos, then, are a repression of libidinous desires. Incest is taboo because men apparently want to sleep with their sisters. After all, there would be no need for making something taboo if people did not exhibit interest in that behavior. As Codrington noted, and later Freud, when a man encounters his sister on a trail in Vanuatu, the woman must turn her back to him. Ni-Vanuatu see this is as a sign of respect; Freud sees it as sublimation of incest—a repression of a libidinous desire. There is "no doubt" that these kastom rules are "universally regarded as protective measures against incest" (ibid., 13; cf. Nida 1954, 34).

Taboos are also displacements, according to Freud. What looks like respectful behavior between sibs as they pass on a jungle trail is actually about repression of incestuous desires. Totems, then, are displacements par excellence. Totems represent ancestors, and clan members are forbidden to eat (or touch, or cut) them, because touching the taboo food or stone totem is tantamount to killing the ancestor. (In fact, in the kava ritual in

Tanna, touching masticated kava is equated with committing incest.) Freud saw totem-ic taboos as a displacement of men's desire either to kill their parents or commit incest with them. The taboo is necessary precisely because people have these libidinous desires (Freud 1950, 98).

For Freud, taboos are also related to *mana* because they involve an impersonal reg-ulatory power (ibid., 20; cf. Nida 1959, 25). But where does the notion of *mana*—and souls—come from? Freud's explanation was humankind's narcissistic notion of the om-nipotence of thoughts. Primitive people are guilty of the same ontological misconcep-tion that children exhibit; namely, that thoughts can be fulfilled simply by wishing them. But practitioners of folk religions, unlike children, also have the motor response to act on their wishes. Magic, then, is the combination of a childish belief in the "omnipotence of thoughts" plus a motor response (Freud 1950, 82–89). As magic developed into full-fledged religion, people "handed over" the locus of the omnipotence of thoughts from themselves to the gods (ibid., 93). Thus Freud's model was an evolutionary scheme from animism to theism.

Of the early theories of tribal religion, Freud's theory was the least accessible to mis-sionaries who encountered kastom in Melanesia. However, Freud's pejorative tone—likening practitioners of tribal religion to children—was certainly perpetuated in the days of colonialism. The three models that I will discuss in the next sections (i.e., social, economic, and structural models) were not formed until well after Melanesia had been colonized and the church was on its way to independence. Therefore, while these models are essential for contemporary missiologists to understand as they grapple with tribal reli-gions, they were not incorporated into missiological theory in the first half of the twentieth century.

SOCIAL MODEL (TOTEMISM)

Many folk religions involve some sort of totemism, and anthropologists have attempted to uncover the emergence and role of totems for tribal societies. Malinowski's magic motif theorized that local crops were revered, therefore the stones they represented were essen-tially deified. However, Durkheim saw crop totems as symbolic of societal roles; they were revered because of their societal function rather than because of their magical power to produce crops. "If the symbol of the god and symbol of the society [totem] are one and the same, are not society and god one and the same?" (Durkheim 1915, 154). In this view, magic cannot be the basis of religion because religion is by definition a social activity, but magic is private. Magic has "no lasting bonds that make members of a moral bond like the one formed by worshipers of the same god" (ibid., 43).

Therefore, for Durkheim, society is the basis of tribal religion, because society alone outlasts human generations; in fact, it is eternal. Humankind has found in society a syn-ergistic power that is exceeded by nothing else. Primitive religion is a reification of the society, beginning at the clan level. It begins as a village cult, centered on its totem. Evans-Pritchard summarized Durkheim, "For Freud, God is father; for Durkheim, God is soci-ety" (1965, 63).

Evans-Pritchard agreed with Durkheim, maintaining that psychological explanations for primitive religions are untenable because: (1) people learn religion when they are young, long before they attach psychological meanings to ritual or myth; and (2) even prescientific people know that just wishing for something does not make it happen. Religion, then, must serve some other purpose. Since religion is (1) transmitted, (2) a closed system, and (3) obligatory, it must be fundamentally social (ibid., 54). This social explanation given by Durkheim (and further developed by Levi-Strauss) did not relegate folk religion to mere ontological misconceptions. It was, instead, an affirmation of society. If the soul was the metonym for religion in Tylor's scheme, and magic in Codrington's, for Durkheim and Levi-Strauss it is the totem.

ECONOMIC MODEL (HOPKINS AND RADIN)

Hopkins (1918) disagreed with Durkheim's concept of totemism as the basis of folk religion. Totemism is not a homogeneous phenomenon, and too many of the world's religions have no vestige of totemism, such as Semitic religions, folk religions in South America, and certain African religions (ibid., 151). But Hopkins also disagreed with Frazer's theory that totems are about food exchange. Frazer understood taboos as an early form of sacrifice: a clan of a certain totem would refrain from eating the food of their totem so that there would be a sufficient supply of this food for the other clans in the tribe. Hopkins held this to be untenable.

In totemic systems (such as Tanna), clans must fast from their totemic crop for several months each year while they undergo ritual cleansing for the benefit of the entire tribe's harvest. Hopkins could not imagine that "savages" would be benevolent enough to come up with a system that involves this sort of self-sacrifice for the good of others (ibid.). He believed, instead, that tribal religion has more to do with preoccupation over seasonal changes than with totems (ibid., 157). The diet of tribal peoples is limited at times to a dozen or fewer nutritious items. As the seasons change, these items change in their availability. Whereas in Durkheim's theory primitive humans reified society because it was greater than themselves and seemed to be eternal, in Hopkins' theory animists revered the reliable, almost eternal, staple foods such as taro and yams. Of course this scenario only speaks to beneficial crop totems. Unusual or poisonous totems (also found throughout Melanesia) must have an alternate etiology. Perhaps there are hygienic or safety reasons that led animists to revere these items. Hopkins' theory, then, relegates the basis of animism to an ontological misconception, where the impetus for primitive religion is economics.

Paul Radin (1883–1959) also focuses on the role of economics in primitive religions. He sees economics as the foundation of the doctrine of ghosts, spirits, totems, magic, and ritual. Primitive religion is about humankind's fight for survival. Since survival relates to finding sufficient food supplies, religion is essentially an economic endeavor. Primitive people fear normal cycles such as harvests and the sunrise more than crises like birth or death (Radin, 1957, 22).

Radin further developed his economic motif by paying special attention to the role of the "religious thinker" in primitive religions. His thesis was that, even in primitive societies, people fall on a spectrum from devout on one end to weakly religious at the other. Many are simply laymen, with little inclination toward religious thought. Others, the priest-thinkers, are religious formulators (ibid., 11). Their job is twofold: (1) to secure their position (an economic concern), and (2) to increase the authority of the elders (a societal concern) (ibid., 18–24). Radin conceptualized animism as an economic arrangement where the chiefs maintain social order by threatening to work in league with the shaman to make social deviants sick. Subsequently, health could be restored by paying the shaman for his services of healing. In this scenario, the shamans essentially extort the laymen, and the common people fear the shamans, which keeps them in line. For Radin, animism is more about fear of economic ruin than fear of spirits (ibid., 44).

STRUCTURAL MODEL (LEVI-STRAUSS)

Whereas early anthropologists used the totemism of tribal religions to highlight the differences between simple primitive societies and complex modern ones, Levi-Strauss concludes that totemism in fact serves the opposite function: it shows how all human minds are alike in their need to distinguish between types of people and between classes. He was most concerned with how totems reveal innate cognitive structures (1963b, 33) or how totems fit into a hierarchal structure (ibid., 65). Levi-Strauss also observed an animistic tendency in modern Western societies, as evidenced in pop culture and linguistics. As Goldenweiser pointed out, modern societies anthropomorphize animals (cf. Mickey Mouse), have mascots for sports teams, and speak of humans in animalistic terms—e.g., "What a louse!" or "What a snake!" (Sapiro 1991, 605). Structuralists like Levi-Strauss do not employ the evolutionary schemes of early secular anthropology; instead they focus on themes that are evidenced in all religious systems. These universals can enlighten us about the structure of the human mind.

THE POSTMODERN MODEL (SUBVERSIVE DISCOURSE)

Just as early anthropological theories of primitive religion reflected the ethos of colonialism, the most recent developments in the anthropology of folk religions reflect the postmodern ethos. Studying folk religions at face value was the first step in postmodernism toward vindicating them as legitimate worldviews of marginalized peoples. It is no longer acceptable in postmodern scholarship to frame tribal religions as if they are based on epistemological or ontological misconceptions and superstitions. Instead, current anthropologists give voice to indigenous people groups who have long been the silenced subjects of colonial oppression. This is not to say that contemporary anthropologists have ceased looking at animism through the psychological, economic, social, and structural frameworks. The voices of the nineteenth- and twentieth-century anthropologists still resound. But folk religions are now given a voice to speak for themselves in their particular situation, rather than being forced to fit into the evolutionary schemes of early anthropology.

In his essays on Aboriginal religion, Stanner (1966) takes issue with the early evolutionary schemes, not because of the futility of attempting to reconstruct the origin of religion, but because the psychological, social, economic (and even structuralist) theories failed to recognize that religion—in and of itself—is meaningful to its adherents. Religion is *religious* in nature. Is it not arbitrary to assign social or psychological meanings to the deep structure of a religion? Is that not imposing modern criteria on primitive religion? Does this not strip animists of the part of their worldview that is most significant to them? Tribal peoples do not conceptualize their own belief in spirits and magic as a psychological, economic, or social phenomenon. To them, totems are simply their ancestors; and it is pejorative, and even myopic, for Western anthropologists to redefine totemism in foreign terms such as Durkheim's social scheme or Levi-Strauss' structural framework (ibid., 47–49, 131).

Postmodern anthropologists see modern conceptualizations of primitive religion as too general to be helpful. Evans-Pritchard (1965) gave a harsh critique of the animism of Tylor and Levy-Bruhl, and the magico-religious theory of Marett and Codrington. He referred to early theories of religion as "erroneous," saying that "no theoretical statement would pass muster today" (ibid., 5). These early theorists were guilty of "absurd reconstructions, unsupportable hypotheses and conjectures, wild speculations, suppositions, assumptions, inappropriate analogies, misunderstandings, misinterpretations and . . . nonsense" (ibid.). Today, they are considered irrelevant or wrong: "No one accepts Frazer's theory of stages today" (ibid., 28).

Harvey (2006) has recently taken issue with modern anthropological theories for presenting animism as if it were based on epistemological and ontological misconceptions—the products of naive, primitive minds. In the view of early anthropologists, animism was simply an ontological mistake; it confused the animate with the inanimate. In the new (postmodern) view, animism is not a mistake; instead, it is a subversive worldview, protesting the empiricism of the Western epistemology. Animism, today, is not about belief in talking animals and magical stones, but about subverting "the oppositional and divisive binarism and destabilizing the hierarchy of science over magic" (Garuba in Harvey 2006, 26). Postmodern anthropologists have redefined animism as a celebration of primitivism in light of a complex and impersonal world.

In this way Harvey has demystified animists, making them seem less esoteric. Animism is not merely a superstitious belief in souls, it is a perfectly tenable belief in personhood—even in the personhood of animals, trees, stones, and artifacts. "A fuller dialogue with animist discourse would further open the possibility . . . that life and personhood may not be solely human traits" (ibid., 24). Animism is a "style of worldview that recognizes the personhood of many beings with whom humans share this world" (ibid., 205). It is talking to trees rather than cutting them down (ibid., 21). Postmodern anthropologists describe animists as having a personal relationship with birds, fish, local rivers, and thunder. Unlike the modern worldview, animism's concept of personhood is not a binary category (i.e., something is either a person or it is not); rather, it is a continuum. There are degrees of personhood (ibid., 106).

Harvey contends, then, that Marett and Codrington were wrong to define *mana* (or *wakan*, or *manamanitou*) in terms of a magico-religious—as opposed to scientific—epistemology. Rather, animism is about social relationships, including the maintenance of relationships with dead ancestors (ibid., 129). Animistic praxis is no longer defined as a

superstitious way of ensuring health, happiness, or cargo, but as a way of defining relationships (even relationships with the environment) to make better hawks, better people, and
live the "good life" (ibid., 172–73). "Life is a process of becoming increasingly human, of
learning what it means to be a human person, and how best to achieve and enact such lessons. A similar point might be made about tree persons, animals persons, bird persons and
rock persons" (ibid., 175). In this scenario, shamanism is about restoring social relationships, because "ill-health is often understood as a result of inadequate interaction with other persons . . . Ill-health results from inadequate relationships and knowledge" (ibid., 149).

Postmoderns describe animism as subversive discourse, a rejection of binary categories, and an emphasis on relationship rather than power. These are unarguably postmodern
values, but whether they can accurately be described as values in the folk religions of today
is questionable.

MISSIOLOGICAL CONSEQUENCES OF
ANTHROPOLOGICAL THEORIES ABOUT ANIMISM

Both testaments and the church fathers saw foreign religions as degradations of Yahweh
worship. Modern anthropologists developed an entirely different framework for understanding folk religions, focusing on the psychological and sociological function of these
religions. Additionally, postmodern anthropologists see folk religions as a program of rei-
fying personhood. How can theology be synthesized with modern and postmodern anthropological insights?

First, we need to summarize what Christian theology has to say about folk religion.
The following biblical concepts have guided the church's approach toward folk religion
and continue to frame evangelical missiology:

1. God's plan is for all nations to know him, and he has revealed himself throughout history—to some extent—to peoples outside of
   Israel (and the church). All peoples and religions are under his
   providence. God appoints the times and places where people will
   live, and he chooses how he will reveal himself to them.

2. God is the source of truth and light. To the extent that other religions reflect the truth, they are of God.

3. Foreign religions are degradations of true worship. God allows
   people freedom to chose or reject him. God has, at times, "given
   people over" to their human-made religions as chastisement.

4. To the extent that the world's religions are in error, they are of Satan, the father of lies.

5. Animistic practices such as witchcraft, sorcery, divination, idolatry, and clairvoyance, are forbidden in Scripture.

Historically, missionaries have presented the gospel as a corrective measure for doctrine and practice. Missionaries assumed that the light will shine in the darkness, people

will come to know God fully, and they will leave their animistic ways; non-Christians would recognize the shortcomings of their folk religions and come to true faith.

This historical-missiological view toward animism seems rather straightforward. What can modern (and postmodern) anthropological theories add to this discussion? Coming from a worldview of materialism (the material world is all there is), secular anthropologists seem to contribute little to the missiological questions of providence, freedom, revelation, orthodoxy, or conversion. Further, evolutionary schemes and Freudian psychoanalysis can be at odds with evangelical thought. Secular anthropological theory, however, is helpful for missiologists in working out the nuances of the particular folk religions in which they work. The anthropological models discussed above should encourage missionaries who work among practitioners of folk religions to understand the social, psychological, and economic ramifications of the particular traditional religions they encounter. Table 1 lists numerous questions for missionaries to pursue as they analyze the traditional religion in their context. Such questions are the makings of a worldview analysis and are, in fact, the substance of Part 2, "Kastom on Tanna."

Table 1: Questions raised by various anthropological models of animism

| ANIMISTIC (Soul and spirits model) | 1. **Cosmology**: What are the named deities? Is there a distinction between "devils" and "dead men?" Is that distinction fuzzy? Is there a hierarchy of spirit beings? How do people enter the spirit world? Through kava? Singing? In dreams? Can musical instruments summon or shoo away spirits? Which ones? What else shoos away or summons spirits? Certain leaves, ceremonial bathing?
 2. **Souls and spirits**: What is the view of the soul? Is there a concept of dualism? Are spirits either totally bad or totally good? Or are they conceptualized as more or less like humans without bodies? What evidence is there of a belief that the soul can leave the body, or that the soul is bound to some external object?
 3. *Mana*: How is power accumulated? Through rituals? Through magic? Through good behavior? Is power located in material objects or in spirits? |
| ONTOLOGY (Nature-myth model) | 1. **Epistemology**: How are things known? What sorts of things are known by trial and error (scientific)? What things are known through religious transmission (myths, etc.)? Do informants mind when two truths contradict themselves (in mythology? in the Bible? when told a story about some- |

thing in recent history?) How is the truthfulness of something evaluated? (That is, what is the plausibility structure
for evaluating truth: because someone said so? Because it
was on a computer? Because the myths say so?) How do they
"know" about the origin of the universe, about the taboos,
about everything kastom teaches?

2. **Myths**: What types of stories are told? What heroes can appear in which myth cycles? How is knowledge copyrighted?
When are myths told? Which myths are tied to geographic
areas? How does magic show up in myth? Are myths told the
same way each time? How many myths can a single person
tell? Compare at least two variants of a myth cycle and show
the differences. Compare discourse features and a plot out-
line of at least two myths (from different myth cycles). Find
commonalities in discourse features or plot outlines. What
cultural values are reinforced in the myths? What social or-
ganizational structures are reinforced in the myths? What are
the major themes in myths? (Hint: In Melanesia, they tend
to be heroes outwitting ogres, or tricksters causing calamity,
and a broken world which gets restored—the source of cargoism. This, as opposed to the "Indo-European myth" which
is found in the West, about good always triumphing over
bad, or two people falling in love). One function of myth is
to bridge dyadic categories (death/life, clean/unclean) by
speaking to in between categories, like spirits (which are neither dead nor alive). What betwixt and between categories
are evident in the myths you've collected?

MAGICO-
RELIGIOUS
model

1. **Magic**: How is magic used? Chart the various types of magic,
who uses them, how often, whether it is secret or not. Where
are the charms located? Who has gotten rid of charms/to-
tems? When, why? Are there memorized incantations involved in magical rituals? Is there a stigma associated with
magic today?

2. **Sacrifice**: How is it practiced? What ritual is done for reconciliation? Before a birth? At a funeral? To "release" a sickness? What do they believe is happening through sacrifice?

3. **Causation**: Document actual sickness case studies, and the
cause determined for these sicknesses. Also document the

healing methods employed. What explanation is there for an "incurable" disease? Do some sicknesses have more than one cause? Are causes of specific cases of illness conflicting and subjective, or is there a consensus for causality?

4. **Dance**: How often? How many types? How long does each dance last? How many dances are held in a single dancing event? How old are the songs? Are they repeated year after year? Who writes the songs? How does the author become inspired to write songs? How are the dances learned? How long do practices take? What's the purpose of dancing? Are there different purposes for each of the dances? Transcribe at least one traditional song. Or better, compare two. What are the discourse features of the songs?

SOCIAL
model

1. **Society**: How is society elevated to the status of a god?
2. **Marriage**: Arranged or not? Bride price or not? Exogamous or endogamous? Do a genogram of a middle-aged person, back two generations and forward one or two generations. Note in the genogram (1) proper names, (2) how that person is called by "ego." How far back can people trace their lineage, before ancestors are simply called "ancestors?" How is divorce done? What makes someone a lousy spouse? A great spouse? Document cases of infidelity, and emic ways of talking about infidelity. (In what circumstances is it condoned? What is the spectrum of acceptance?) What do married people fight about?
3. **Roles**: What's the role of uncle/aunt? Older brother/sister? Younger brother/sister? Grandparent?
4. **Time**: Record how informants talk about history. How far back does their collective conscience remember dates? Are they time or event oriented? When is the best time to do various events, like: fish, drink, pray, go gardening, wash, rest? Why? Do they have names for different time periods/ generations?
5. **Group discipline**: Document cases of shaming. How is kastom or sorcery involved in issuing discipline? How do people describe teenagers? What makes children lousy or exemplary?

6. **Group decision making**: Note how group decisions are made in various domains (gardening, market) and social settings (church, women's groups). Compare group decision making synchronically (across domains and social settings). Can an individual decide how he votes? What religion he'll be? Where he'll live? How he'll celebrate a holiday?

7. **Leadership**: Are there leadership ranks? How do "big men" disagree? Cite actual examples. Who is the ideal follower? What are leadership qualifications? How does a leader give a speech?

8. **Land**: Map your village. How many houses? Who claims to have been there the longest? What land disputes are there? What is the shared land? Collect stories of land disputes. How does adoption affect land disputes? What Western names are given for land—what's the history of those names? How was church land allocated?

9. **Leadership**: How is leadership succession done? How is a leader legitimated? What are the symbols of leadership? What makes a great follower?

10. **Is this a patron-client society?** What is the role of the rich person? Is he expected to share his resources?

11. **Grid-group**. Read Lingenfelter (1998) and determine whether your culture is high or low grid, and high or low group. Is it Authoritarian, Egalitarian, Anarchic, or Hierarchal (or a bunch of hermits).

12. **Change**. How is reciprocity seen in the changing society (politics, government leaders, the church)?

13. **Purpose**: How are social structures (alliances) reinforced through reciprocity? Is sorcery involved in issuing discipline?

ECONOMIC
model

1. **Religious thinker:** What is the role of the "religious thinker" (*vis-à-vis* Hopkins and Radin)? Does he have an economic motive? What are the dynamics of the relationship between the shamans and chiefs? Who can heal? Describe in detail how herbal medicines are prepared (this borders on material anthropology, described in a later section). Some herbal medicines are rubbed, others are spit, others are diluted in water and drunk. Are there other methods of preparation? Try to make a chart of sicknesses, and show what methods of preparation are employed and what remedies are given. What is the role of the shaman? Document actual cases where a shaman, clairvoyant, or diviner was consulted. How did people respond to his diagnosis? What is determined to be efficacious? How are healing practices taught? Is this information copyrighted? What pay is given to a healer? What is the consequence for a shaman that doesn't heal the sickness? Is the pay less for an inefficacious shaman? Are certain shamans considered more efficacious than others?

2. **Givers and gifts:** Who gives gifts to whom? What kind of gifts? What is the market value of the gifts at a certain event? What are the gift-giving occasions? What are the common and diverging elements in each of these occasions? How are gift-giving occasions arranged? How often? What are all the gift-giving events that happen in a certain region over a given time? How long after the prestation (giving of gifts) must the gifts be reciprocated?

TABOOS
(social and
psychological
models)

1. **Totems:** People think they are descended from what? Do different clans trace their ancestry to different totems (animals, crops)? Is marriage selection (exogamous or endogamous) affected by clan totems?

2. **What are the taboos?** Is there a taxonomy of taboos? What are the taboos displacements of? Taboo foods? Taboo places (e.g., bodies of water, trees)? Taboo actions? Taboo words (e.g., saying an uncle's name or saying certain body parts)? What are the menstrual taboos, pregnancy taboos, and post-partum taboos? Do people really follow them? What if they don't? Are there menstrual taboos about gardening? Are there special houses for pregnant or post-partum women?

3. **Totem and taboo**: What is the relationship between totems and taboos? What is the emic explanation for why certain things are profane and others sacred?

4. **Breaking taboos**: What are consequences of breaking taboos? How do taboos reinforce social rules and cultural values?

STRUCTURAL
model (symbols)

1. **Dyadic categories in myth**: What are the dominant ones? (Hint: people organize their world into dyads: hot/cold, sacred/profane, clean/dirty, male/female, true/false, rich/poor, pretty/ugly, cooked/raw, rich/poor, generous/stingy. Some of these dyads will be more salient in your field than others. Rich/poor, generous/stingy).

2. **Rites of passage**: What are they? How long do they last? How are rites of passage mentioned in the myths? Describe the three stages of the rite of passage: Preparation, Separation, Aggregation. Make a chart of rites of passage, noting the frequency, duration, location, participants, ostensible purpose, and assumed deeper purpose.

3. **Rites of intensification** (regular rituals, church, etc): What are they?

4. **Common signs**: What are the various gestures? How do you signal: come, sit, stop, not possible. What are the meanings of facial expressions? How are foreign signs being adopted (holding hands, certain clothes)? How is wealth signified? How far is the "personal space" of people in your field? Can people eat in front of others? How is eye contact practiced during conversation?

5. **Functional substitutes**: How have traditional rituals been replaced by Christian rituals? Which traditional rituals/myths are counter to the gospel? How do traditional rituals meet a societal need, and how can the contradictory ones be changed to be Christian, but continue to meet the society's need?

6. **Religious signs:** What symbols are used in church?

POSTMODERN   1. **Subversion**: How does tribal religion form group identity
             and help rural people cope with the drastically changing
             world around them?
          2. **Changing worldview**: How is the worldview changing?
             How do people feel about the generational changes in
             worldview (don't forget to use actual interview data, rather
             than guessing). How do they describe the "heathen" days?
             Are both Western and magico-religious explanations simul-
             taneously held for illness causation? Give examples. What
             does "adequate healthcare" mean in your area? To the lo-
             cals? To the health care providers?

ETHICS

          1. **What acts are considered right and wrong**? Present infor-
             mants with ethical dilemmas to see how ethical processing
             is done. Is there a hierarchy of ethics? What does sin mean?
             Why is sin bad?
          2. **Consequence**: What are the consequences for bad behav-
             ior? Is there an afterlife? Does it involve punishment for evil-
             doers? Is it valuable to be pure for purity's sake, or only to
             achieve prosperity/*mana*?

PART 2

Kastom On Tanna

THE English speaker may inadvertently equate the pidgin English word kastom with "customs"—foods, dress, language, music style, holidays, etc. While it is important for missionaries to understand such *customs*, in this book when I say kastom, I am limiting the topic to the traditional religions of Vanuatu, which are particularized forms of animism. Cross-cultural workers (and ni-Vanuatu as well) find it difficult at times to distinguish between *customs* and kastom. Is music religious or cultural? Are the exchange ceremonies and other holidays religious in nature? It is difficult to determine the religiousness of animism because it is not as systematically laid down as the so-called world religions such as Islam, Christianity, or Hinduism. There are no Ten Commandments, eightfold paths, or Four Spiritual Laws in kastom. Instead, if we must study myth to understand kastom epistemology and cosmology, we must look to shamanism and taboos to understand the logical process; we must analyze ritual and magic to grasp the kastom value set and ethics.

As the previous chapter indicates, animism is not only tied up with religious ideas like cosmology and magic, but is also linked to economics, psychology, and cognitive structures. It even serves political purposes. This chapter gives specific examples of how the generalities about animism that were discussed in Part 1 are played out in Tanna Island's version of animism. I will look at the following seven domains that are essential to kastom on Tanna: (1) transmission of knowledge (especially myth), (2) cosmology (ghosts and spirits), (3) *mana* (magic and power), (4) healing, (5) taboo and ethics, (6) cargoism (millenarianism and salvation), and (7) ritual and exchange. My overall thesis is that kastom is more than a set of superstitions and rituals; it is a fully developed worldview. If missionaries wish to transform the worldview of people from animistic backgrounds, they first need to attain as thorough an understanding of the particular form of kastom as possible.

CHAPTER 3

Kastom and Knowledge

HUMANS gain knowledge in different ways depending on the domain. For example, mechanical skills are often learned through trial and error. This is a basic form of the scientific method. While the animistic worldview is not as thoroughly scientific as post-Enlightenment worldviews, mechanical or scientific knowledge is part of any culture. For instance, Tannese learn how to construct houses, build fires, fish, and speak, through experimental learning. That is, they learn through trial and error.

However, scientific knowledge is only part of the knowledge that is transmitted in traditional cultures. Unlike scientific knowledge, magico-religious conceptualizations and praxis are not learned through trial and error; they are primarily transmitted through myth. Mythical knowledge differs significantly from the notion of divine revelation in theistic systems of the so-called world religions. Whereas knowledge is achieved in theistic systems through divinely inspired texts such as the Bible, Upanishads, or Qur'an, in magico-religious systems the "texts"—that is, the myths—are not conceptualized as divinely inspired. This is because divine inspiration and absolute authority of texts are concepts that belong to religious systems that have personal and transcendent beings who could transmit that knowledge. Such beings do not figure in prominently in magico-religious systems. For these systems, the religious texts—namely, orally transmitted myths—are dynamic value sets that reflect the worldview. Further, the canon is not closed in these systems. Taboo men can be inspired in a dynamic process of prophesying, mythmaking, and sacred music composition.

In other words, religious knowledge is typically transmitted through static propositions and divinely inspired texts in theistic systems, but in magico-religious systems knowledge (about, e.g., cosmology, soteriology, and ethics) is taught through dynamic oral narratives. The Tannese term for "oral narrative" (*kwanage*) is complex, having at least five nuances: (1) stories about imminent deities, (2) geographic etiologies, (3) etiologies of living things, (4) didactic stories, and (5) funny stories. Each nuance is indicative of the different type of knowledge that is being conveyed. For example, the stories about imminent deities offer explanations for the source of suffering and evil. Geographic etiologies reinforce taboos about sacred places.

TANNESE MYTHICAL CORPUS

At first glance, it seems like myth-telling on Tanna is simply a trivial pastime—a recreation that doesn't affect daily life. In fact, during my tenure on Tanna I rarely observed someone making reference to the mythology during conversation. I recorded more than a dozen myths (two of which are related here), but only came across those myths because I deliberately elicited them. It turns out that myth-telling is not a regular public activity. Does this mean that myth has little effect on the lives of Tannese? Is myth an incidental part of culture, or is it at the fore? What do stories of men-eating ogres and devilish women have to do with life today?

It would be a mistake for missionaries in animistic societies to write off myth-telling as merely a pastime. Instead, missionaries should devote as much effort to understanding myth as they do to understanding the other aspects of traditional culture. True, the social functions of other aspects of traditional religion, such as shamanism or magical garden rituals, are readily apparent: they create opportunities for reciprocity, and they ensure prosperity. The function of myth, on the other hand, is elusive. That should be all the more challenge to the missionary to comprehend it!

It turns out that anthropologists have not come to agreement on the function of myth. Functionalists argue that myth reinforces social norms, obligations, and relationships. Those influenced by Freud argue that myth serves as a catharsis: tensions are solved in ways that are not socially appropriate in "real life." Idealists argue that myth is a picture of the "way things should be." Structuralists influenced by Levi-Strauss see myth as a resolution of binary oppositions such as life and death, men and women, hot and cold. More recently, myth has been described as a mechanism for giving agency to silenced voices. They are a way of making sense of the changing world (Bonnemaison 1994; Harvey 2006).

Each of these frameworks is alluring; they each have merit when it comes to describing the function of myth on Tanna. Here I argue that the primary role of myth is to transmit kastom. In addition to introducing the characters of kastom cosmology, myths reinforce rituals, symbols, and social obligations. They even serve to redefine the world today.

The Tannese Mythical Pantheon

There are around twenty named supernatural beings in Tannese cosmology; however, characters from one myth cycle almost never appear in other myth cycles. Instead, the mythical corpus is a set of disconnected myths. This segmentation is due in part to the multiple settlings of the island. When the Melanesians settled Tanna 3,500 years ago, they brought their own mythical corpus of stone-gods who appeared out of the ground and became food (either crops or animals). Islanders gradually added myths to explain local topography. Most large stones, bays, caves, and the volcanos are connected to etiological myths. Around a thousand years ago, Polynesians shared cultural knowledge and artifacts with the islands in southern Vanuatu (Spriggs 1986). They brought versions of the Maui cycle to the Tannese mythical corpus.

Each Tannese myth is an isolated unit. For example, although the Polynesian demigod Maui is known throughout the island (as Matiktik or Matiktiki), he does not traditionally appear in the Melanesian myths of, for example, Karpapeng, Nasaper, Nura, Sapai, and Mouga. Even purely indigenous mythical characters are limited to their own myth cycles.

The deities Sapai and Mouga, from a volcano myth cycle, may not appear in the myth of Nura and Nevaru, a stone off the coast of West Tanna. Likewise, Karpapeng and Nasaper, of the inland mountain range, do not appear in myths about coastal topography. Therefore, there is no metanarrative in the mythological corpus. Myths may appear to contradict in chronology, metaphysics, or ontology. Missionaries would be tempted to point out these deficiencies in an attempt to poke holes in the worldview. But it would be to no avail, because such contradictions do not present a problem for the Tannese. They do not view the myths as an integrated body of knowledge; instead, each myth transmits a specific piece of knowledge about a certain place or deity.

Below I have categorized the Tannese myth cycles based on the type of *kwanage* (oral texts) and the protagonists in each type (see Table 2).[2] The last row of the table is a compilation of independent animal myths that do not have proper names. Space does not permit an elaborate discussion of their myth cycles; instead, I have provided the full text of two myths—one autochthonous, the other a Polynesian import. I will parse the myths into "mythemes" in order to show a typical plotline for Tannese myths. This will also allow me to unpack a number of the symbols in these myths and to show how they are tied to kastom ritual. Lastly, I also look at the contemporary interpretations of these myths. This should give a broad picture of how kastom knowledge is acquired and transmitted through myth.

Table 2: Five types of *kwanage* in the Tannese mythical corpus

SOCIAL	CHARACTERS	THEMES
IMMINENT DEITIES	**Matiktik** 1. Matiktik and Kwelenak cycle 2. Matiktik and Taransamus cycle	1. Hero defeats the ogre, etiology of Futuna 2. Etiology of a stone in West Tanna resembling a round, fenced-in area
	Semusemu, aka Siku, or Semsem. (Optional: boys named Kaniapu and Kamiapeng; alternate boy characters are Kasasao and Kanapnin and Naleya)	Ogre, twin heroes, origin of the *imarəm*, explanation of the diaspora; creation restored, circumcision ritual reinforced; etiology of a stone resembling a breastfeeding mother
	Karpapeng (Optional characters: Kalpapen, Nasaper, Prince Philip, John Frum)	Ogre; etiology of mountains

SOCIAL	CHARACTERS	THEMES
IMMINENT DEITIES	**Karwas**	Dwarf responsible for causing sickness; eats people at night
	Tagarua (Optional character: Seimata)	Mythical beast causing sickness; reinforces kava ritual; also etiology of coconuts, rivers, and the diaspora
PHENOMENOLOGICAL MYTHS	**Yakwier** and family (boys named Kasasao and Kamarinu, or Nuras and Batras, or Koyometa and Numurkuen)	Etiology of Lapangkauta River and the coconut, the origin of foods, diaspora, and more recently, explanation of foreign cargo and the world's races
	Kaoman (first boy) and his pigeon wife **Nowaitalap**	Origin of foods; etiology of stone in North Tanna, reinforces *nier* (exchange ceremony); reinforces
	Mwig, Sapai, Mauga	Etiology of volcano
	Nura and Nivaru (alternately, Nowanorek and Nowanaon)	Etiology of stone southwest of Imrao or, alternately, at Loweian
	Torikya and **Napua**	Etiology of a hole in a stone near Waisisi Bay
	Woman who sheds her skin	Millenarian hope; also etiology of a stone in South Tanna
ETIOLOGIES OF LIVING THINGS	**Mirirıg, Nuauo, Nivesu** (also the myth cycle of kava and her husband coconut, or kava and coconuts are brothers)	Etiology of kava; explanation of why kava and coconuts and banyans are found in the sacred dancing place
	Shark, lizard, Tiputim (lizard responsible for echo), **Mimitoga**; **rat** and **eagle** story	Etiology of animals: why they live in their current habitat, why they are feared, why the rat steals food, etc.

SOCIAL	CHARACTERS	THEMES
LIVING THINGS	**Namke**, dies because he alone mixes kava and is given no *nohunu*	Etiology of the *nohunu* ritual; reinforcing of the communal kava mixing
DIDACTIC STORIES	Bat in a basket; sea cucumber and the dog; grandmother who sheds skin; boy who cannot get rid of a pig; man who holds a butterfly in his hand; etc.	Lessons about listening to parents, kicking bad habits, respect for elders and life, planning ahead, etc.
FUNNY STORIES	**Ramato**	Various

Maui Cycle

The Maui/Matiktik myth explains the origin of Futuna Island, a truncated cone-shaped island thirty-five miles southeast of Tanna. The version recorded here was spoken by Nisa in the Vaha language of Isaka village, Southeast Tanna:[3]

> Now I'll tell a story about Matiktik and his wife. Matiktik and his wife, her name is Kwalenakw. The two of them live over there at that mountain which is called Melen. Melen has a former name, but I don't know its name.[4] The two of them lived there for a while. Once, his wife became pregnant. And once, at night, his wife said, "Matiktik, let's go to the ocean, and you catch a fish for me."
>
> They go down to the ocean and walk along the coral. As they were walking along the coral, Matiktik speared a fish and gave it [to his wife], so she put it in the basket. They went on and on, and a *yarmhə* (ghost, spirit) was sitting ashore and saw what was going on—that Kwelenakw was putting fish inside her basket. And she [the *yarmhə*] coveted the fish. So she followed the two of them.
>
> They all went and went and the two of them are near the edge of a spot where it is very deep and are walking on the reef—scavenging on the

---

[3] I have attempted as literal a translation as possible, but have supplied a variation in English synonyms to facilitate ease of reading.

[4] This is probably named after MacMillan, early missionary to Tanna. An early French map has the name of the mountain Ughin (God).

coral. And immediately, that woman-*yarmhə* swallows a shell which made her pregnant. And then she went near to that other woman and pushed her so she falls down to the ocean.

And as she is swimming, the *yarmhə* follows Matiktik. When Matiktik sees her, he thinks she is his wife. They go on, and he catches fish and gives them to her; she swallows them. They go on; they ascend to the village. And he sleeps with her. The next day, they keep living together, etc., etc. Matiktik asked [her], "When will your beloved child be born?" But she said, "Well, [about the time of] cutting leaves."

At that time, his real wife, Kwelenakw, is swimming and swimming and swimming. Her arms and legs have gotten tired. And she sang a song:

Hwei tuampo Preinap. Tuampo Preinap. Trasak yan narepan.
The ground, the ground has broken off and come here. Look!
Ye nepek ireinia. Na reskapek yeni maspao i pa reinyo.
Na reskapek yeni maspao i pa reinyo. Tanei po. Tanei po.[5]

And she said, "If I were a taboo woman, I could stand on a rock and rest." And her leg was about to tremble. But immediately one thing [happened], her foot stubbed a stone. She stands up on top the stone there, and breathes and breathes and breathes. That stone arose and arose and arose and arose and arose and arose. It became land. That's that land there, Futuna.

After that, the woman lived there. And lived and lived and lived there. Two children were born. They were twins.[6] Then the three of them lived and lived and lived, but the older one said to her, "Mother, we speak unto a mother, but where is the father?"

But their mother became angry and said, "Hey, your father is naught." And they lived and lived and lived; the two boys grew up. They went and went and went and became grown, and then they went to go catch fish. They took their canoe and went out in the ocean and went fishing.

The elder said again, "Mom, where's dad?" But she said to him, "Precious child, your father hated you two. But that over there is his mountain." And she pointed here to this mountain. She pointed to this mountain "Melen." He lives there. The boy said, "Mother, suppose the two of us go sometime and visit him?"

But then they lived and lived and lived, and she said to him, "It's fine if

---

[5] The words which are unintelligible to the Tannese are left untranslated here. *Tuampo* probably comes from the Tannese for "she has become tired"; and the name Preinap may be from the Tannese word "prostitute" or "young woman" (Lindstrom, pers. comm., 2010).

[6] Nako in Atenes calls the twins "Noti" and "Moti."

you two want to go and visit your father. But go, and don't take [him] back here."

Then they got the canoe and pushed it into the water. And one sat in front, one in back. And they paddled and paddled and paddled. And went and went and went, and came near to Mt. Melen, down from it, by the ocean.

The man [Matiktik] stood above [on the mountain] to see down below, that thing—the canoe—coming straight for his coastline. He stood firmly and took his spear and descended.

But their mother had said to them, "If you two go, and if you see a man coming with long, braided hair down to his shoulders, then that's him." He took his spear and ran, and descended towards them. Immediately, the two of them ran carrying sand like this, and saw their dad carrying a spear and running, coming from above.

He came and stood up his spear, and said to the two of them, "You two figured you'd come here to do what? Where have you come from?" But they said, "Nothing. We've just come here for [no purpose]." "No, tell [me]. Men don't just come to my homeland randomly. You've come here to do what?" But the older one said, "Don't talk to him. Let's get our canoe inland." They planned to take their canoe inland, and saw it was heavy.

Then immediately he walked up to the two of them and scolded them saying, "What have you two come here for?" They said, "Nothing. We've come to see our father."

He asked, "Who's your father?" They said, "Our father's name is Matiktik."

Just then, their father was surprised, saying, "Where have you two just come from?" They said, "Our father and our mother went searching for shells on the coral reef, and a *yarmhɔ* came and pushed her over [into the ocean]. And she swam until she reached an island; and she lives there. We've come from there, and have now come here. Our father is Matiktik."

Their father cried and cried, and knew that he'd been living with a *yarmhɔ*. Then the three of them went up and went over there, and said to the *yarmhɔ*, "Grate that yam into a tuber pudding for us to eat." She grated and grated and grated the yam. Immediately she said, "Matiktik, where will we get meat to put in this?" But he simply said, "Hey, grate it all, and then I'll show you the thing that I'll put in it." She grated and grated, and finished, and cooked it.

She cooked and cooked until it was done. Immediately he came to her neck, and came and pushed and grabbed her and shoved her into the tuber pudding. And the three of them covered her. And covered her/it and carried it and threw it into the fire. The fire burned it. The shells burst out of her belly and came out. Then they went down and went to the ocean, and took their father and went over to Futuna, and slept in a cave. They slept and slept in that cave, and another time they took him and went to the village.

This is all of the story of Matiktik and Kwelenakw.

Yakwier Cycle

The Matiktik myth was clearly a Polynesian import, being based on the Polynesian fisherman hero who pulled up Hawaii and New Zealand. The Yakwier myth[7] below is a Melanesian theme of two brothers; it also provides an etiology for various crops and sacred places:

I'll tell a story, the story about Yakwier. It begins, basically, with some women who go to harvest wild yams. And so a young girl figures that she'll accompany them. Her fathers/uncles had forbidden her from following them, lest while accompanying them on their way, she'd end up following Yakwier's trail.

And so she follows them, and figures she'll accompany them. And she follows them as they are going and sees a wild yam that has bulged up through the mound. At that point she lifted up her knife to stick [the yam]. But it said to her, "Don't stab me!" It stood up and became like a man, and was saying to her, "Where have you come from?" But she said, "Uh, I've come from my village." He asked her, "Where are you going?" "I'm [going out] to dig up yams." And that fellow said to that girl, "Go on then, let's go to my home."

Then the woman gets up and follows him. They go and arrive at a village. And they live there together. And live, and live together, until they have two children: twin boys. And they all live and live: that woman and her husband and the two kids. The man says to his wife, "Hey. Let's go to your home and check up on your father and mother." And the woman agrees to it. So they make a good meal, planning to carry it and go [to the village].

While they're on their way, the man says to his wife, "I know that we'll go there, and those people will kill me because I've stolen you. But if we go and they say they'll kill me, carry me and come [back] and hide me here—in our home village. But if they kill me, the three of you should go to the *imaram* (sacred dancing place) and see that I've piled up banyan leaves, and I'll be sleeping on them. Then carry me [back]."

---

[7] Narrated to me by Tom Makua in 2005 in Yanemilen village.

So they went to the village and saw the mother and father of that lady. And they stay there, and stay. And people say to that man, "Let's go to the *imarəm* and drink kava." But that woman and her two boys are still in the village.

The [others] go to the *imarəm* and make their kava drink. He went and heaved up banyan leaves. And as he piled up banyan leaves, they made his kava drink and squeezed *nukun* (poison) into it, and squeezed in some *navuru* bark. They squeezed it into his kava drink, and he lifted up his kava to drink, and took his food, and sat on those banyan leaves and ate. And after he'd eaten, he died. He was lying there on those banyan leaves that he'd heaved up. Then they're sitting and sitting in the village, and the two boys thought of [the father].

At that point, the men got up and [returned to the village]. And people asked, "Where's the father of these two boys?" But the men simply lied and said, "Uh, he's drunk, and still in the *imarəm*."

The three already knew that their father had died. And then they sat there and sat there and sat there until morning, knowing that their father had died. And they cried and cried and cried. Then that woman said to the men of her home, "Let's take the father of these two fellows and go to our [exclusive] home." And they all agreed to it.

So they took the father of those two boys and went to their home. But their father had said to them that they should take him and bury [hide] him, and that they should weed [the gravesite], and [if so] they'd see something would pop out of that spot.

So then, they took him and buried him. And they weeded the gravesite. And after they'd weeded the mound, they returned and returned. Then his one eye burst forth with ocean water, and the other burst forth with a coconut [tree]. And the coconut stood and stood and bore fruit. And the coconuts became dry and fell from the tree.

Then they took that coconut and cut it, and milked their food with it. And the boys bathed in the coconut, and washed in that ocean water. They washed and washed, and their bodies were in top shape. Their food was good and in top shape.

But when other people washed in their own water, they were still dirty. And people saw that these two boys were in top shape and their food was good. So people wondered and wondered about this.

But once, before their mother went into the bush to defecate, she said to the two boys, "If you're here, and you see some people come, don't point out this coconut and ocean water. Leave it just for the two of you." They agreed to that, and she went away. They were there and saw some children coming. [The children] said to them, "Hey, your bodies are tops, and your food is tops. What makes you so great?"

But those two boys went on as they were. And at one point, the older boy told. He told, saying, "We wash with coconut." And people asked about that. And he said that they washed in that ocean water. And one said, "Let me show you." And they went, and [the elder] showed. And after he showed the spot, they went and took the coconut, and broke it open, and scraped it out, and heaved up the pulp, and they bathed in it. They bathed in it, and went and bathed in that ocean.

They bathed and bathed, and the ocean filled up. As the water swelled, the children there took off, and only the two boys stayed. They stayed and saw their mother appear before them. She said, "Hey! What made the ocean swell up?"

But the younger said, "My older brother showed!" And their mother said to him, "Hey. I forbade you from showing, and you showed."

The two of them caused the ocean to burst forth. They burst forth the ocean, and cried, and cried out, and went and took *niavia* branches, and tried to make a dam with them. But the current burst through and carried off the branches. They sang a song about it. The song goes like this:

O Ground, you've come!
Father, ooh. Father, ooh.
It's me, it's me. Father Father, ooh, ooh.

They took *nases* branches and built a dam with them. But the current burst through the *nases*. And they sang the song:

O Ground, you've come!
Father, ooh. Father, ooh.
It's me, it's me. Father Father, ooh, ooh.

And they cried out. And took *nepkapek* branches and came and tried to dam the water. But the current burst through and carried the branches off.

O Ground, you've come!
Father, ooh. Father, ooh.
It's me, it's me. Father Father, ooh, ooh.

They took earth to dam the water. The current carried off the earth. Then they were floating on top of the ocean water. The water carried the two of them, and they went and went.

Now the older one, they say he is the French. And the younger, he is the English. That now is my short myth.

ANALYSIS OF TANNESE MYTHS

At first, missionaries may just see these myths as merely individual stories of ogres and tricksters. But they are much more than that. Below I employ a structuralist, functionalist, and postmodern framework to argue that while myths are not a regular part of public discourse on Tanna, they are central to the task of transmitting kastom knowledge.

Structural Analysis

A comparison of Tannese myths suggests that there are smaller units of discourse that may regularly appear in the mythical corpus, such as instructions, social obligations, and tricks or betrayals. I call these smaller discourse units "mythemes." I have listed the mythemes present in these two myths below (see Table 3). These mythemes demonstrate how kastom knowledge is transmitted through myth. For example, the animation of nature is a mytheme that reinforces magical knowledge. Mythemes about patrilocality reinforce social obligations.

Both myths employ the mytheme of separation and reunion. There is a pregnancy; then, of course, birth. There is a trick or betrayal; and at the denouement, the trick is avenged or reversed. Homeostasis is achieved. Finally, both end with an inclusio such as, "That's my myth about So-and-So."

Certain mythemes appear in both myths, but in a different order. Nature is animated in both, but in the Matiktik cycle, the yam becomes a man immediately; in the Yakwier cycle, the man becomes a coconut near the end.

The songs that show up in so many myths are an alternate genre for transmitting knowledge. The actual meaning of the songs in myth is often obscured; because myth-songs use "ancient language" which is no longer intelligible. However, myth tellers do not seem to be bothered by the fact that they do not understand the songs. Perhaps myth-songs are meant to transmit emotion rather than propositional meaning.

Table 3: Gross constituent units in two Tannese myths

	MATIKTIK CYCLE	*YAKWIER* CYCLE
Setting	"Matiktik and his wife . . ."	"Some women go to harvest yams . . ."
Origin	• Pregnancy and birth of twins • Origin of an island	• Pregnancy and birth of twins • Origin of coconuts and a river
Social Obligations	Returning the father to the mother	• Obeying instructions given by male family members • Choosing the right mate according to endogamy norms

	MATIKTIK CYCLE	*YAKWIER* CYCLE
Social Obligations	Returning the father to the mother	• Protecting the father • Providing kava for father
Deixis	• Going fishing • Treading water	• Going to the hometown • Caught in flood
Trick/ betrayal	Attempted murder of wife	Murder
A wish/ foreshadow	"If I were a holy person this land would come up."	"They're going to kill me."
Nature animated	Yam becomes person	Man becomes coconut
Instructions	• "Look for a man like this . . ." • "Don't take him back." • "Grate some yams."	"Tend my grave."
Separation	• "Who is our father?" • Wife separated from husband, boys separated from father, later from mother	• "Where is your father?" • Boys later separated from mother
Instructions in retrospect	(She'd said, "If you see a man . . .")	(He'd said, "Weed my grave.")
Dominant symbols	• Ocean • Tuber pudding	• Banyan • Kava
Song in myth	Preinap's song	Song to the dead father
Homeostasis, reversal of the trick	• Family reunited • Demon killed	• Failed attempt to restore homeostasis • Disappearance of younger brother
Ritual in myth		• Ritual bathing in coconuts, used in male and female puberty rites • Kava ritual reinforced

In addition to the gross constituent units, there are a number of binary oppositions present in these two myths (see Table 4). These dyadic categories give us a window into the values and structure of Tannese society. Many of these oppositions are further discussed below.

Table 4: Dyadic categories in the Tannese myth cycle

Showing	Hiding
Clean	Dirty
Older	Younger
Forbidding	Agreeing
Dams	Floods
Village	*Imarəm*
Patrilocality	Matrilocality
Living in a cave/mountain	Living in a village
Pregnant	Faking pregnancy
Inland	Coastal

Myth Teaches Social Obligations

All myths, even though they appear to have different plots (and all rituals, even though they appear at different times in a life cycle), have the same fundamental function regarding, inter alia, norms for sex and aggression. Myth is often about the breach of norms (Levi-Strauss 1963a). It is a way of knowing about (or teaching about) abnormalities, and the disaster that will ensue when the rules are broken. The Matiktik and Yakwier myths both involve a breach of social norms and the ensuing disaster.

The social breach in the Matiktik myth is subtle. A father and mother have been separated. This causes great anxiety; they must be reunited. However, the father dies in the Yakwier myth, as a redemptive figure and as an Oedipal father. He is redemptive because from his death issued coconuts, which make tuber pudding so tasty, and the sacred river, which not only serves to (ceremonially?) cleanse but to provide the precious resources of eel, crayfish, and magical rain stones.

Yakwier is also an Oedipus figure. The boys knew in advance that their father would die—he told them in plain language that he would be murdered at the *imarəm*. Yet they let him go unaccompanied. It was wholly unnecessary for the boys to remain in the village with their mother, and it would be entirely uncommon for boys to do so today. At kava time, the men send out a messenger boy to round up all the boys who are still playing in the village and bring them back to the kava ground. Tannese boys play a necessary part in the kava preparation, since only circumcised virgin boys may wring out the kava pulp. These two boys were in the wrong place at the wrong time.

In fact, the Yakwier myth is the antithesis of how the kava ritual should be performed. Not only are the boys in the wrong place, the men of the village severely breach Melanesian norms of trust and norms for hospitality. Strangers who visit a new *imarəm* should be treated with honor, given the first shell of kava, and the best portion of the *nohunu* (food eaten with kava). They should be protected and cared for. Here, the villagers betray Yakwier. Myth teaches values such as honor, protection, and hospitality, and shows the ensuing disaster when those norms are breached.

But whose fault was it that Yakwier was killed? Was it the boys' for not accompanying their father to the *imarəm*? Or was it the wife's fault? She was, after all, the original sinner in this story. Her fathers/uncles told her not to leave the village, lest she be led astray by a noneligible marriage partner. The Tannese have a cross-cousin kinship system, and it was the girl's role to have her fathers/uncles arrange a marriage partner for her. One can only imagine that, if she had listened to them, there would have been no death of Yakwier. Here, the myth is reinforcing family structure and obligations.

The woman's disobedience caused death, which turned into a blessing. The boys' disobedience caused a flood that, while it may have been a momentary crisis, also turned into a blessing. It made coconuts accessible to all people, and revealed the source of *nauta* (material goods/cargo). In Southeast Tanna, islanders locate the Yakwier myth in Lapangkauta River. *Lapangkauta*, loosely translated, meant something in the old language like "the source of material goods/cargo." Yakwier's river housed the magical stones for making rain and hurricanes, and these stones are available to magicians today because the twins made them known. A material benefit of the flood was that, as the freshwater connected to the ocean, eels and crayfish were able to swim upstream, providing meat for inland villages. Myth here highlights what is important, such as magic and prosperity.

Myth Restores the Status Quo

The Matiktik myth restores homeostasis, especially the solidarity of the clan. Matiktik is tricked, separated from his family, and remains essentially barren. But in the end he goes home, albeit not to his own home, but to the village of his wife. His family is restored to him.

The Yakwier myth restores homeostasis more subtly. The father dies and is not replaced; the flood forever changes the topography of Tanna. But the disaster that resulted from the boys' breach of their mother's instructions was reversed. The floodwaters brought forth magical stones and a channel between the ocean and inland villages.

The ending of the Yakwier myth, however, seems to be eclipsed. One boy is washed out to sea, but what happens to him? The story needs an ending. Tannese regularly supply interpretive summaries at the conclusion. The story "ends better" with an explanation of why white people have cargo, or how men dispersed from Tanna and ended up in France (specifically Paris) or America.

Myth Explains Origins

For Levi-Strauss, it is a universal that myths have humans originating from the ground

(1963a, 212). The Yakwier myth is a perfect example. The yam-man was hidden in the ground until the woman discovered him. Yakwier the yam was more than a man, but he was also a coconut and a river, and the progenitor of all *nauta* (material goods). Interestingly, in the Matiktik myth, the ground originates from a woman. She is taboo, being the wife of a heroic god, and simply wishing for a place to stand is efficacious.

Myth also explains the origin of the totemic classes. Yams are an important totem on Tanna, but in this myth they are elevated as the source all other totems.[8] In one sense, though, the yam is a metonym for all totems, because the myth is simply showing that men/gods/stones/crops emerged from the ground in the mythical age.

Myth Explains the World Today

While some myths are very old, the modern telling helps make sense of the world. They use magico-religious thinking to explain migration throughout Vanuatu, modern events, the influx of tourism, and the production of manufactured goods.

The inhabitants of Futuna are more Polynesian in skin color, language, and culture. Tannese say that Matiktik is rightfully one of their *kughen* (god or gods); they are aware that the myth is the result of foreign (that is, Polynesian) influence. Maui/Matiktik plays only a small role in Tannese folklore. Tannese use the Matiktik myth recorded here to explain why he is not one of Tanna's own *kughen*. Long ago he went to Futuna. Tannese are aware of him, and he sometimes visits, but Tanna is no longer his home.

Since European contact, the Yakwier myth has been recontextualized to integrate cargo, kastom, and the church. A sign in front of a Presbyterian church in Southwest Tanna has the picture of a sailing boat, and in its hull are twelve *kivar* (magical stones) from the taboo river Lapangkauta. The church has been reified as the true Lapangkauta River that brings the key to rain, crops, health. In short, the church brings cargo.

While the Yakwier myth has accretions in its concluding commentary about France and England, it would be a mistake to consider the entire myth a recent one. Versions of the coconut or river springing out of a man's eyes can be found throughout Vanuatu (see Gardissat 2005), suggesting that the myth is centuries old—if not millennia—dating back to the days of proto-Oceanic. However, as Tabani (2009) argued, most post–European-contact myth cycles are "rejuvenated" with contemporary symbols and ideals. This syncretistic nature of myth can be quite complex at times. Myths about John Frum,[9] for instance, have a black (or white) man who speaks a Tanna language but is a foreigner; he wears Western clothes and comes from America but is responsible for saving kastom (ibid., 6).

Since myth-telling is such a flexible process, the iteration of any given myth cycle changes depending on current exegesis. One informant says that the two brothers in the Yakwier cycle are France and England. Others have said that they were named Peaceful (the younger) and Stormy (the elder). In another version, Karpapeng or Karapanuman's two sons are Nuras, who went to America, and Batras, who stayed behind (Lindstrom 1979, 42). Perhaps the two brothers were originally the two moieties on Tanna: Koyometa

---

[8] It is curious that this myth, declaring the yam to be the primordial totem, was told to me by the guardian of the taro stone.
[9] Numerous spellings are used for John Frum, so I have used this spelling for consistency.

and Numurkuen (Bonnemaison 1994, 152–56).

Recent versions interpret Peaceful to be the Tannese boy who stayed on the island while Stormy is washed out to sea. His skin gets whiter and whiter until he reaches America. There he said, "*Yakam-arka*," meaning in one dialect, "I am afraid." That is where the name "America" came from—the root of the word "fear." We see here the epistemological value of myth. Myth is being used to this day to reevaluate the world. America is a stormy, fearful place; Tanna is peaceful.

Tricksters, Ogres, and Taboo People

In Polynesia the Maui cycles are replete with tricksters and pranksters (Keller and Kuautonga 2007, 100). Usually it is Maui himself who is the trickster, taking advantage of his younger brothers. In the South Vanuatu versions, Maui is tricked by the woman *yarmhɔ*; but with the help of his two boys, he eventually outsmarts the *yarmhɔ*. In another Matiktik cycle, Matiktik outwits his nemesis Taransamus.

Ogres are found in a number of Tannese myths. They threaten to depopulate the island entirely by eating everyone. In the Semsem cycle, only one woman is left to repopulate the island. In the Matiktik-Taransamus cycle, Matiktik defeats the ogre. Keller and Kuautonga suggest that the motif of ogres who completely destroy the populace of an island is a remnant of the anxiety islanders feel when their traditional lifestyle is threatened (ibid., 98). In the Futuna cycle (an outlier of Tanna), Matiktik's enemy has chased the inhabitants around the island, disrupting their traditional settlement patterns. "Resettlement resulting in the proper placement of people in villages around the island circumference is the overt object of the narrative" (ibid., 105).

Taboo people are also part of the mythical corpus. Matiktik's wife's comment, "If I were a holy woman," is curious. The taboo man is a mediating third person between mortals and supernatural beings. Taboo men are common on Tanna (Lange 2005, 247), but there are no instances of taboo women. Taboo woman, as Durkheim might have said, is an oxymoron in Melanesia. Oxymoron is a useful device in oral performance, though. Whereas a taboo man would be commonplace, the taboo woman is a fresh image.

Myth and Symbols

Myths condense dominant symbols in a culture, and a study of myth can reveal what those symbols are. The shells coming out of the belly of the *yarmhɔ* in the Matiktik myth is an interesting detail. Capell (1938, 78) noted that in Aniwa, people descended into the afterworld (*ipai*) and eventually sank even lower, to the ocean, becoming shells. Shells are a symbol of life, but not earthly life. Shells are alive, but not to the same extent as human beings.

The banyan is the dominant symbol in the Yakwier cycle. Yakwier's arrangement of banyan leaves in the *imarɔm* appears to be nothing more than a prop to distract him while his in-laws prepare his poisonous kava. However, the banyan tree condenses a number of symbols, much like the mudyi tree for the Ndemu (V. Turner 1967, 30–31, 61). Banyans symbolize authority, inspiration, exchange, dance, and community. Centuries ago, when the *imarəm* were laid out, they were placed in banyan groves, or banyans were planted at the perimeter of the *imarəm*.

Banyans are associated with exchange and magic. During the *nier* (exchange ritual), prestations are hung from banyans. Certain magical banyans involve supernatural phenomena. One banyan in Yanemilen village is said to cause "pins and needles" when a person walks past it. Others are known to be sacred places of inspiration. Taboo men chew kava and sit under certain banyans to receive supernatural inspiration for songs that will be sung in the pig exchange ritual called the *nokiar* (Bonnemaison 1994).

Death and Resurrection in Myth

Death is a theme in most of the myths in the Tannese mythical corpus. Dying at sea is a major unsettling theme on Tanna. Virtually everyone in Tanna knows someone who has died while fishing from a canoe or diving for crabs. One pastor set out on a canoe from Aniwa and drowned en route; his story shook everyone for months. It inspired songs and created a bond among mourners. In both myths recorded here, drowning is threatened but redeemed. Good comes out of something otherwise dreadful to the Tannese: An island is born out of Kwelenakw's near-drowning. In the Yakwier cycle, all of Tanna's wealth is brought out to sea and distributed throughout the world.

The mythical corpus is has an element of hope in resurrection. Both of the ogres Semsem and Taransamus incarcerate and devour the inhabitants of the island; however, in both stories a hero comes to the rescue. When Semsem[10] was slain, all of the people on whom he had feasted came back to life and repopulated the island.

Myth and Retribution

Retribution (in Tanna the word is *tain*) is fundamental to Melanesian religious systems (Trompf, 1994) and is a theme that regularly shows up in the mythical corpus. In the Matiktik myth, the conniving devil who pretended to be Matiktik's wife eventually gets her just desserts: the boys bake her into tuber pudding. In fact, this act of cannibalism is quintessential Melanesian payback. Retribution in the Yakwier myth is a bit less subtle. The boy, "Stormy" who disobeyed his mother's instructions was washed out to sea. Here we see nature animated as a punitive force. As we will see later on the discussion of disaster causation and Tannese ideas of salvation, people from animistic backgrounds require the universe to be balanced; this is a deeply ingrained sense of justice. Acts of kindness must be reciprocated, and sins must be punished—if not by humans then by spirits or nature. Retribution appears again in our study of sickness (Chapter 6). In Chapter 12, I address ways for the church to contextualize the theology of retribution.

Myth Reinforces Ritual

The Maui cycle is a Polynesian import, therefore it would be rather surprising if it reflected

---

[10]   In both stories a hero comes to the rescue.

the structure of local ritual (it may, however, reflect rituals still practiced in Polynesia). The Yakwier myth, however, has some striking links to the *nakur* (circumcision rite). The circumcision rite is held every three or four years, allowing families to accumulate enough pigs, chickens, kava, and cows for the cross-cousin exchanges. Chickens and kava are presented every other day for a number of months, making it the most costly of Tanna's rituals. Boys are not entirely circumcised; a small portion, the *yakmun*, is left, in a procedure that Humphreys called circumcision-incision (1926, 76; cf. *Rivers* 1926, 62). Traditionally, the foreskin was wrapped in a taro leaf and buried. A coconut was planted at the site, and adult men could point out the very trees that were planted above their foreskins.

Coconuts growing from body parts is not the only link that connects the Yakwier myth to circumcision. A more salient symbol is the bathing in coconut milk and subsequent washing in the river. Just like the two boys in the myth, Peaceful and Stormy (or France/England, Batras/Nuras, or Koyometa/Numrukuen), newly circumcised boys are bathed in coconut milk every other morning and evening for months. After they are smeared in coconut milk by their sponsor, older boys blow conch shells, and all the males march in procession to the river (or ocean, for coastal villages) to bathe. The conch shells ward off the females; they cannot see the boys until they officially come out of hiding at the large exchange/feast. Initiates are separated from their mothers (as were the boys in the Yakwier myth, when she went to defecate) and sleep in the *imarəm* until the circumcision wound is completely healed.

The Semsem-Matiktik cycle is an etiology of the circumcision ritual. Semsem eats every inhabitant of Tanna, but tosses one baby girl into the ocean because she is too diseased to be eaten. There she[11] copulates with a vine and gives birth to twins, Kaniapeng and Kosasao. She circumcises them and places them in a cave in South Tanna, where she breastfeeds them through a hole in the cave wall. After this, the boys grew big and strong enough to defeat the ogre Semsem. Therefore Tannese boys learn that even their mythical heroes had to hide in a special circumcision house before they can become strong men.

ASPECTS OF KASTOM KNOWLEDGE

I have so far shown how myth is a way of knowing. It conveys knowledge through instrumental and dominant symbols, and gives etiologies. It reinforces societal norms and shows the disaster that will ensue when the norms are broken. It serves as a proof text for magical knowledge and local cosmologies. Myth even anticipates aspects of ritual.

In addition to the value for transmitting knowledge through myth, there are other epistemological considerations about kastom knowledge. Namely, it is ecocentric, relative, and has a different view of time than the modern conceptualization. I discuss each of these aspects of kastom knowledge below.

Kastom Knowledge Is Ecocentric

By the "ecocentric" nature of kastom knowledge, I mean that knowledge about spirits, sto-

---

[11] Humphreys has the mother's name as Nepkalam (1926, 95).

ries, and magic is inextricably tied to the local geography. Resources such as inheritance and access to gardens, identity and names, power, and magico-healing herbs are all tied to kastom places (cf. M. Patterson 2002). World religions such as Christianity and Islam may locate their religious center thousands of miles away, but kastom does not venture more than a few miles.

Kastom teaches that the world began on Tanna, the sacred foods are on Tanna, and the spirits and ghosts dwell on Tanna and are controlled by magical stones that are located on the island. The site of taboo afterworld places differs from village to village, but they are all agreed to be situated somewhere on Tanna. Authority is also located on Tanna; a leader's title is not only inherited but depends on the land he owns. Indeed, it is a thoroughly ecocentric religious system. And how could it be otherwise? Until Captain Cook arrived, the Tannese world was no larger than the five southern islands of Vanuatu. Tannese epistemology and ontology is the product of a "homogeneous and closed culture" (Brunton 1989, 148). That is, there has been little opportunity for outside influence and knowledge to affect kastom.

KASTOM KNOWLEDGE IS RELATIVE

Each village or clan has its own myth cycle to tell; at times myth cycles contradict. Westerners would imagine this to be a cause of cognitive dissonance for the Tannese. In fact, the variants do not seem to prove logical inconsistency; they only reinforce the notion that myths are locally "copyrighted" (Lindstrom 1990a) and that the knowledge they transmit is relative.

Traditional myth-tellers compose as they perform (Finnegan 1996, 890). This may raise the question for a Westerner, "Do Tannese see the stories as *true*?" That is, after all, an essential part of Western epistemology. Since such variegated versions of the myths exist, it is difficult to tell whether Tannese generally accept these myths as historically accurate, or true in some general or symbolic sense. In Chapter 11, I report results of interviews with Tannese, some who evaluate myths in terms of their plausibility, and some who do not. The abstract categories of *nafrakisien* (truth) and *neikuэyen* (falsehood) do exist in Tannese, but when *kwanage* (stories) are evaluated as true, it is usually in the sense that they are true-to-life. That is, they make a good point. In all aspects of public discourse on Tanna, one's authority to speak (legitimized by his tie to the *imarэm* at which the discourse takes place) is more important that the factuality of his discourse (Lindstrom 1990b, 50ff.).

KASTOM VIEW OF TIME IN MYTH

Tannese myths begin with origins. The land somehow appeared, and stones began populating the land with men and crops. This mythical time of stones/men/crops/gods is called the *rao nepro*, which we would call the "golden ages" of mythical past. In those days, the lines between people, spirits, magical stones, and totems (foods, animals, etc.) were blurred.

The second *rao* (canoe or generation) was the prehistory of humans—the time of cavemen. People did not cook their food or make houses; they ate wild foods like black palm, and they lived in dens or caves. This generation is called the *kaprɔrao* (dispersion) because it was the time when people dispersed throughout the land. The third generation is a time of fighting and land disputes. It is named for two brothers who fought: Koyometa and Nímrukuhen. This generation coincides with Western contact, when missionaries witnessed cannibalism and intraisland fighting. Cannibalism and tribal warfare have ceased, but the fallen nature of that generation is said to be pervasive today. The fourth generation is present day.[12]

---

[12] I know one chief who further atomized these generations into about a dozen different time periods.

CHAPTER 4

Cosmology (Ghosts and Spirits)

A SECOND foundational domain of kastom is cosmology: the hierarchy of gods, spirits, humans, animals, and plants. Kastom cosmology involves two worlds: the seen and the *naripai* (spirit world). Ghosts and spirits transcend the unseen world and occasionally haunt inhabitants of the earth. But transcendence goes both ways. Taboo men can also transcend and go into the other world. The colloquialism employed to describe a journey into the spirit world is *nivənien ye nikar nai* (going around the side of a tree).

While I have said there are two worlds in Tannese cosmology, it would be a category error to describe Tannese cosmology as multitiered the way Christianity is (e.g., God, angels, people, animals, demons). Tannese have three terms for supernatural beings, but as Hiebert suggested of folk worldviews, the boundaries between the terms are "fuzzy" (2008, 33–36). Here I use the English terms "ghosts" and "spirits" regarding supernatural beings throughout Melanesia. A tentative distinction between the two terms would be based on linguistic grounds: *yarhmə* (ghost or ghosts; literally, "one who is dead") are deceased people—especially recently deceased people; while *nanmin* (spirits) and *kughen* (eternals) have never been people. I will expand on these terms and explain the interaction they have with humans.

The *kughen* are spirits with personal names such as those found in the mythology: Matiktik, Taransamus, Karwas, and Karpapeng. Knowledge about these demigods is transmitted through the myths. The part that these personal demigods play in the daily experience of kastom is vague. Capell connects the *kughen* with Codrington's *mana*. *Kughen* "created the people and set them in their land and gave them their customs. He provides them food and gave them their stones, but he is not the center of mythology or worship. The Tannese are deists rather than theists" (1938, 77). Tannese believe in the existence of eternal beings, but do not worship them. They relate more easily to a mechanistic power (*mana*) than to a personal God.

The impersonal (unnamed) spirits, on the other hand, are a daily part of kastom because nonpersonal spirits or totemic spirits are feared and controlled. *Yarhmə* literally means "one who is dead," but in pidgin English the equivalent "devil" is more descriptive. These beings are mischievous spirits, but not necessarily ghosts of recently deceased people. It is not clear how much of an ontological distinction is made between *yarhmə* and *kughen*.

Nanmin is polysemous, or "fuzzy." It can mean "spirit," "dew," "shade," at times "powerful" (*nanmin aikin*, "it has spirit"), and at times "fake" (ror *namin*, "it makes spirit"). When "spirit" is connoted by *nanmin*, the meaning is "dead people." Therefore, the nanmín, like the *kughen*, may have personal names. There are times (e.g., if a man is murdered, or commits suicide, or when his body is defaced) when a *nanmín* does not go to the sacred place but roams about haunting people. If one enters the sacred place or sees a *nanmín* roaming in some other area, it is believed he will get sick or die.

Campbell described the supernatural beings on Tanna:

> Their gods are all evil, and their religion consists mainly in endeavors
> to propitiate them. They have gods of the sea and of the land, geologi-
> cal and botanical gods; but the most dreaded beings of all, perhaps,
> are their human gods, viz., the disease-makers. (1873, 168)

By "their gods," Campbell was probably referring to the *kughen* or *yarhmɔ*; by "human gods" he probably meant the *tupunas* and shamans. Like Capell, Campbell observed that the more tangible magicians are more a part of the religious experience of the Tannese than the esoteric deities.

Lustration, which Campbell mentioned above, involves sacrifice of a chicken or a pig to take away sickness. It would be a misappropriation of categories to interpret sacrifice as an offering to a specific *yarhmɔ*, *kughen*, or *nanmín*, as Campbell implied, or as an act of satisfaction for atonement of sins. These concepts are theistic in nature; however, as I argue in the next chapter, kastom is coercive, not theistic. Sacrifices are performed with little fanfare and no liturgy, and to no spirit or ghost in particular. To perform the sacrifice, the animal is simply brought to the *imarɔm* and dealt blows to the head. Later the meat is divided up and eaten. Sacrifice "without the mediation of God or Saint, is felt to have power" (Leuba, 1909, 108). As Yerkes noted of animistic systems, sacrifice is "*by* somebody, *of* something, and *for* something, but never *to* anybody" (in Van Rheenen 1991, 292).

Kastom utilizes a number of symbolic props for summoning or shooing spirits in their cosmological system. Means of summoning them include playing the bamboo flute, wearing the *nísei* (scented armlet), and dancing. Spirits are sent off by blowing the conch shell, by using certain leaves, or by ceremonial washing and shamanistic spitting.

Amazingly, little has been written on Tanna cosmology. Since cosmology is central to the Christian worldview, missionaries should make it a primary focus of their study.

CHAPTER 5

Magic and "Goodness"

MYTH, ghosts, and spirits are obviously integral to kastom. However, most elements in the traditional religious life of the Tannese center on a quest for goodness, which is achieved not through spirits, but through some cosmic, positive force, like what Codrington meant by *mana*. *Mana vis-à-vis* Codrington is "an explanation for whatever is powerful" (Howells 1948, 25–26). Keesing (1984) and Tomlinson (2006) have argued that *mana* is better understood as a verb rather than a noun. They suggest that *mana* is best translated "to be efficacious, or to make effective." This gloss allows for a positive and negative side to *mana*, and ensures that one's wishes for ill or good will come about.

It is problematic to the ethnographer that no word for *mana*, or even magic, is in the Tannese lexicon. Instead, the following terms approximate the discourse of *mana* on Tanna:

1. *Nanmin aikin* (literally, "the spirit is there"): That is in contrast to "the spirit is naught," which means something is ineffective. When something "has spirit," it is powerful. Things that "have spirit" include magical stones, prayers, or true speeches.
2. *Nagheen* (literally, [its] power): This lexeme is an inalienable possessive. One cannot speak of power in general, but of something's power. One could speak of a river's *nagheen*, or of a god's *nagheen*.
3. *Nisaninien* (strength): This word works much like *nagheen*, but is the nominal form of "to be strong" and does not need to have a possessor. In other words, one may simply wish to have more *nisaninien*.

Therefore, while there is no word in the language for "magic" or *mana*, there is a lexical apparatus for the discourse of *mana* or "magic." Tannese speak about the effectiveness of a ritual, such as kava, circumcision, or the *kajia*, in bringing about "goodness" (health, peace, abundant crops). "Goodness" may not technically be an equivalent for *mana*, but it is the desired result of Codrington's *mana*.

How do Tannese get *mana* to achieve goodness? Or, to use the verbal construction, how do Tannese make their rituals effective? The common way is through magic. Frazer's concepts of sympathetic magic (things that are alike are the same), and the law of contagion (things that were once in contact continue to be connected), adequately describe much magical thinking on Tanna. The rain stone can serve as an illustration of sympathetic magical thinking on Tanna: Rain stones are doused with water, and water is like rain. If a rain stone is like the earth, and the water used to douse it is like rain, then the rain will douse the earth.

The practice of sorcery (or black magic) is evidence of Frazer's law of contagion on Tanna. One man, named Kota, went to the capital city to work. While he was there, he committed adultery with another man's wife. Before long, Kota found himself paralyzed from the legs down. He and his clan conjectured that the enraged husband had taken Kota's shoes during the night to perform sorcery on them, causing the paralysis.[13] Sorcery is considered efficacious because of the (albeit uniterated) law of contagion.

From an emic standpoint, Tannese do not recognize magic as an ontological category. They are not operating in the epistemological sphere of the Enlightenment in which the Western ethnographer is entrenched. Magic is an obvious etic category for outsiders who study kastom because "the principles of science make the limits of magic a little clearer for us" (Howells 1948, 48). To Tannese, magic is just doing things effectively. The difference can be illustrated with an anecdote: Tannese have asked me to use the computer to find where a missing child is, or whether a disaster will happen if tourists are allowed to hike up Lapangkauta River to the waterfall. At first, I found such requests to be confusing, because a computer is not a crystal ball. However, for the Tannese, boundaries between the technological and magical are not distinguished. Computers are effective for gaining all sorts of knowledge, why would they not be effective in ascertaining possible consequences of future actions?

MAGICAL BEHAVIORS IN KASTOM

To summarize magical thinking on Tanna, there is no lexeme for "magic" or *mana*; Tannese speak instead about "having spirit, strength, or power." Their desired end of magic is "goodness." And their thinking well follows Frazer's laws of sympathetic magic and contagion. What remains for this discussion on magic and power, then, is to describe what kastom magic involves.

In Tanna's version of kastom, magical behavior involves shamanism (herbal medicines and cutting), sacrifice, divination, sympathetic garden magic, sympathetic magic for natural phenomena, sorcery (revenge), and homage to ancestors. Table 5 shows various types of magical behavior in kastom, their location, actors, and desired ends.

All the magical behaviors in kastom are an attempt to bring about some type of "goodness." However, magic is only one way of effecting "goodness." Other ways of obtaining "goodness" include maintaining peaceful relationships and observing taboos. More recently, observing church rules and praying are also ways of securing "goodness." This is the only magical realm that invites the participation of women.

To summarize the domain of supernatural power, animists believe in and attempt to control eternal spirits, who are perhaps benevolent and evil at the same time. Melanesian animism leans toward the coercive end of the continuum, exhibiting a tendency to focus

---

[13] About a year later, Kota was miraculously and completely healed of his paralysis.

on achieving power or manipulating impersonal beings. Speaking of kastom on Tanna, Capell noted, "It is the complete superiority of magic over religion (to use Rivers' distinction) that this religion is particularly characterized" (1938, 78). Kastom is predominantly magic-focused, not worship-focused. To apply Hiebert's model, kastom operates almost exclusively in the mechanistic domain of the "excluded middle" (1982, 43).

Table 5: Types of magical behavior in kastom

KIND OF MAGIC AND PURPOSE	ACTOR	LOCATION	METHOD
Herbal healing (from sickness, infertility, dementia/demonization, or preparation for birthing)	Virtually all men, but especially the Karwas *tupunas*	Village	Herbal medicine (topical or drunk), spitting, cutting
Sacrifice for healing	Any man	*Imarəm*	Fatal blow to the head of a pig or chicken
Divination, future-telling	*Kleva* (diviner)	Village	*Kava*, dreaming
Health and fertility of pigs	Virtually all men	Pig pen	Herbs
Crops	Specific *tupunas*	Gardens	"Paddling" a hidden canoe
Natural phenomena, e.g., sunshine, waves, earthquakes (good or evil)	Specific *tupunas*	Rivers, taboo houses	Washing a *kivir*, putting leaves in a sacred river
Revenge	Taboo men	Taboo house	*Netik*: victim's rubbish in a fire, cursing of the ground
Homage	Every man	*Imarəm*	*Tamafa* libation
Protection against sickness	Everyone	Church	Prayer, observing church rules

But why the quest for power that Codrington called *mana*? Some anthropologists studying the psychology of religion have suggested that the concept of *mana* is meant *inter alia* to abate fears about the present and future, to emphasize cultural values, *vis-à-vis* Radcliff-Brown (Howells 1948, 70), or to explain accidents (ibid., 44). However, I suggest, after having done missionary fieldwork on Tanna for nine years, that the heart of the desire for *mana* is what Tannese call *nihuəyen* (goodness). That is, they observe taboos, perform magical rituals and sacrifices, engage in exchange festivals, and observe garden rituals because they believe it will bring them such "goodnesses" as prosperity, health, peace, happiness, and life. Figure 1 shows the various ways within kastom that people attempt to gain power or manipulate impersonal beings for the desired end: goodness.

Figure 1: Ways of attaining power or manipulating impersonal beings in kastom.

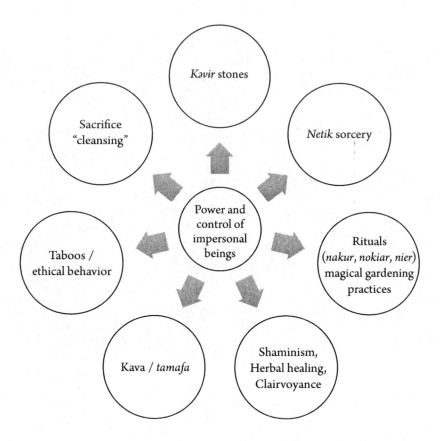

PRAXIS: MAGICAL STONES, TOTEMS, AND BLACK MAGIC

Most magical behaviors are covert, and Tannese are elusive when asked about them. However, pioneer missionary William Watt recorded a rather detailed description of a rain-stone ritual. It is worth quoting at length, because his description can be extended to other instances of sympathetic magic in kastom.

> When rain is wanted the rain-maker takes a canoe, puts it somewhere in the bush, and fills it with water; fresh water, it must not be salt. He proceeds inland to some known pool, accompanied by several others, who, though ordinary men, want rain, and help him. Each makes a cocoa-nut leaf basket, into which he puts leaves of certain trees and plants (I am not aware that any of them are from fruit trees), such as stone palms, etc., and a small banana plant. When they think they have enough, taking a few leaves, or a branch of kava, they go direct to the aforesaid pool, where the rain-maker commences his incantations. Taking a basket of leaves, he calls on his departed father and friends and asks them to join him and his party in making rain, and then places the basket in the pool. He does the same with each basket, until he has placed them all in the water. He then rolls a large stone over them to keep them down. This done, he places the twig of kava on a ledge of earth or stone near. He calls on his departed relatives to note the fact of his having brought kava for them to drink, and enjoins them to see that even now the clouds may darken the sky, and that by the time they reach home the first drops may be falling. The whole party then starts for home. On the way the rain-maker suddenly breaks from the party, and following a bypath, gathering certain leaves as he proceeds, he carries them to the place where he had previously put the canoe full of water. On reaching it he puts in the leaves he has gathered and the sacred stones, only reserving one or two. With a prayer to his departed relatives he returns to the village. That day he must not eat anything that has been cooked in an oven; only such things as have been roasted on an open fire; nor may he bathe in or even touch the sea. (A. Watt 1896, 178–79)

In addition to the stones for natural phenomena, each clan on Tanna has a totem; every clan is said to have descended from a certain crop or animal (taro, banana, pig). Members refer to their clan's totem as their *kaha* (ancestor). One can inquire of another person's totem by asking, "What is your ancestor?" In the *rao nipro* (mythical golden ages), crops blurred the lines between stones and people. Today, clans' totems are represented by *kivir* (totemic stones) that at times resemble vaguely the shape of the crop. For example, a kava stone may be thin and elongated like a kava root; the volcano stones are round. Many (but not all) *kivir* are kept in small canoes that are hidden in gardens. To perform magic on the stone, the *tupunas* (magician, or guardian of the stone) bathes ritually, fasts from food, coitus, and at times, talking, in order to "paddle" the magical stone over a period of weeks or months. That is, he washes the stone in the replica of the canoe with water and special leaves. By making the banana stone smooth, for example, the *tupunas* is ensuring that the banana will be free from disease.

A rain stone (from Aneityum) with the complementing leaves that cause rain.

Totems in Melanesia are inherited and involve taboos. Members of the taro clan cannot boil or cut taro during the taboo months, for this would be regarded as eating one's ancestors. The taboos are called *natuakəmien* (fasts). Typically in totemic societies, clans are also known to have the distinguishing characteristics of their totems. For instance, the lion clan may be bold and the snake clan tricky. If this type of totemic identification is present in Tanna, it is uncommon or subtle. Humphreys (1926) believed this was a feature of Tanna's totems until the era of missionaries, but he may be projecting foreign concepts of totems onto Tanna.

Kivir are dangerous; in fact, one man suggested to me that the word means "dangerous thing." If one breaks the laws regarding *kivir*, he may become sick or die. However, if one follows the laws, the *kivir* are beneficial; they ensure a good crop. Early missionaries ascertained that the reason Tannese "hated the worship of Jehovah" (F. Paton 1903; J. Paton 1889; A. Watt 1896) was their fear that if they ceased to "work their stones," their gardens might not grow. Or worse—there would be drought, hurricane, sickness, or some other disaster.

Kivir are not idols in the usual meaning of the term, because they are not worshiped. While the *tupunas* does not pray to the *nanmin* (spirit) of his stone (e.g., taro, banana, kava), he does attempt to appease or control the spirits in general. In fact, using Bronwen Douglas' (1989) distinction, it is probably accurate to say that on Tanna spirits can be controlled while ghosts are autonomous.

A man shows his breadfruit totemic stone, hidden in a canoe in a garden.

Typically, totemism is thought of as a way of demarcating eligible marriage partners. Clans must marry outside of their totem. However, while this is common in Tanna, it is not always the case. Table 6 shows that out of nine couples, seven married outside of their clan's totem, while two did not. That is not to imply that there is no social function of totemism on Tanna. The totems still create a division of magical labor, and an avenue for exchange.

Table 6: Exogamy and clan totems

HUSBAND	TOTEM	WIFE	TOTEM
Jakob	Yam	Kep	Taro
Makua	Taro	Rosi	Yam
Napiko	Banana	Esta	Taro
Purengok	Banana	Arlis	Taro
Yema Prah	Taro	Dorkas	Yam
Kai	Yam	Mena	Yam
Saen	Kava	Lilian	Yam
Jonri	Banana	Noano	Taro
Rebeka	Banana	Naursen	Banana

To this point I have only discussed magical practices that are considered beneficial, and therefore acceptable, which include *kivi nitə* (sacrifice—literally, "pulling blood") and *kivir* (totemic stones). Disease-making is universally considered objectionable. The dark side of magical powers, black magic, is called *netik*.[14] The phenomenon of *netik* has been widely reported (Adams 1984; F. Paton 1903; J. Paton 1889; A. Watt 1896), and islanders believe the practice continues today. The prevalence of sickness and death only serves to confirm this suspicion.

To perform *netik*, hair or other leavings may be taken from a victim for the purpose of placing a curse. One method involves heating a magical stone that represents human beings along with the victim's leavings. As long as the stone is on the fire, the victim will be ill. If the stone stays in the fire long enough, the victim will die. Another method is less immediate. The victim's exuvia or "leavings" are buried along with taro, or are placed in a hole in a tree. As the leavings disintegrate, the victim falls ill. One mother and son were continually suffering from diarrhea. The pastor discovered that a sorcerer had placed the "human" stone along with some cloth that belonged to the woman and coconut husk (which is used like toilet paper in Vanuatu). The pastor explained to me, "The husk sorcery made it so that the body part that pushes feces out was ruined, so they had chronic diarrhea. Once I exposed the sorcery they got better." The pastor explained that if a woman's bra is wrapped along with the sorcery stone, the woman will develop a sickness "that looks like breast cancer."

Accusations of *netik*, then, are a regular part of life on Tanna. Whenever someone is ill, *netik* is suspected. Discerning (or divining) the guilty sorcerer occupies a good deal of discourse in the men's meeting place, the *imarəm*. Early missionaries reported that accusations about *netik* regularly instigated intervillage warfare. *Netik*, according to the early missionaries, was the bane of Tannese kastom. Since the efficacy of black magic is recognized throughout Vanuatu, it has been declared an illegitimate use of kastom and therefore illegal (D'Arcy 2003).

Like many aspects of Melanesian life, *netik* is a social phenomena; it may also be performed against an entire community. Occasionally the wind will shift directions and the volcano will send ash toward the northwest (which can kill the crops); villagers have become irate and have accused southern villages of causing the shift. The same is true when mudslides affect only one portion of the island (usually the southern portion), or in times of drought (especially on the western side).

It is unarguably a positive thing that *netik* is discouraged, but *netik* may serve as a form of social control (Tonkinson 1982, 311). When people act out, island leadership can threaten to use *netik* as punishment. One Tannese man called *netik* "our jail" (Brunton 1989, 142). The social benefits of *netik* may explain why Tannese are unwilling to relinquish it—it has served well for thousands of years as a deterrent and as a form of punishment.

---

[14] In Southwest Tanna it is actually called *narak*, but here I have used the lexeme that is most commonly found in the literature.

A "person" stone wrapped along with coconut husk and a victim's cloth.

CHALLENGES TO THE CHRISTIAN CHURCH

Church leadership on Tanna readily accepts that bad magical behavior should be discouraged, such as sorcery (and perhaps even love magic). That they would discourage such negative magic reifies it as a credible phenomenon. Elders and pastors discourage sorcery specifically because they maintain a belief in what Frazer called the "law of imitative magic" and the "law of contagion." Is a belief in this sort of "sympathetic magic" in line with biblical teaching or not? Should church leaders discourage "bad magic" or should they discourage the belief in such types of magic all together? As Part 3 shows, even if we determined that a belief in sympathetic magic is unbiblical, we would have a difficult time convincing Melanesian church-goers that the laws of imitation and contagion are misguided.

CHAPTER 6

Healing "Badness"[15]

THE corollary to the magical quest for "goodness" is the shamanistic method for undoing "badness." The practice of healing sickness and undoing natural disasters is at the nexus of epistemology, cosmology, ethics, and praxis in kastom. Therefore I discuss it at length here. But first I relate a story that instigated my investigation of kastom and badness.

A woman named Mary lives in the village where we worked for eight years on Tanna. She had complications during delivery, and her girl, Anna, was born breech. Perhaps because of the breech delivery, the girl suffered with cerebral palsy. She never developed a strong cry, she couldn't eat, and at the age of two she had limited ambulatory function. Much later, I asked villagers about the cause of her disease. Immediately, a shaman of the village offered an explanation: When Mary became pregnant, another woman named Sarok had said to her, "If you have a girl, she will be my namesake." After this, Sarok and her husband fought, and he slit her throat, killing her. After seeing what he'd done, he climbed a banyan tree and hurled himself to his death. The shaman explained, "Just like Sarok's throat was slit, Mary's baby's throat could not function. She couldn't eat or cry. Sarok's jealousy and untimely death are the cause of Mary's child's misfortune."

The shaman's explanation was baffling to me. How could one woman's jealousy and untimely death be responsible for another woman's breech delivery and daughter's cerebral palsy? Clearly, Tannese have a different plausibility structure for explaining the causation of misfortune. I began a lengthy study of the causes that islanders attributed to the various misfortunes that befell them, and eventually categorized them into six main categories:

1. "bad insides"
2. breaking of taboos
3. spirits
4. mechanical causes
5. intentional causes
6. testing from God

---

[15] Nehrbass, K. (2011). Dealing with Disaster: Critical contextualization of misfortune in an animistic setting. *Missiology*, 39(4), 459–471.

Westerners have radically different explanations for misfortune causation; namely accidents, germs, the weather, heredity, or the laws of nature. These are not salient causes for misfortune on Tanna. Since so much of Tannese village life centers on achieving "goodness" and avoiding misfortune, it is necessary to comprehend these six emic categories of misfortune causation. I will discuss each of these below.

CAUSED BY "BAD INSIDES"

When a young boy with an infection in his leg died (a day after his family refused him antibiotics), people suggested that his adoptive father and true father had "bad insides" about the adoption, thus causing the misfortune. "Bad insides" can mean jealousy, anger, doubt, fear, depression, or any negative emotion. Such emotions are the de facto explanation for sickness and tragedy on Tanna. I have heard "bad insides" suggested as the cause for, inter alia, scabies, broken bones, stroke, stomachaches, and, as in a case I mentioned above, cerebral palsy.

Westerners concede that fear or anger can adversely affect one's health, but the parallel stops there. How can negative emotions cause mudslides, earthquakes, or broken bones? The connection seems quite evident to people from animistic backgrounds. D'Souza demonstrated that premodern cultures believe that moral failures inevitably have consequences in the moral world (2007, 256–57). On Tanna, "bad insides" are considered responsible for misfortune because of the fundamental concept in animism that a person's will is efficacious. Recall Frazer's law of sympathetic magic. If the magician responsible for the banana stone sincerely wishes for his banana crop to grow, it must come about. I submit that Melanesians do not perceive the stones themselves to have magical powers, as Codrington proposed a century ago. Instead, they perceive that the will of the individual is powerful. If the banana magician performs his ritual on the taboo stone with "bad insides," it will not be efficacious. Instead, his "bad insides" will have an adverse effect.

When disaster strikes, the connection between "bad insides" and the natural world becomes evident. Tannese engage in lengthy public discussions about the cause. They urge one another, "Tell what is in your insides!" Or they ask, "What is ruining your thinking?" In kastom, people must be sure to keep their "insides" good.

CAUSED BY BREAKING TABOOS

Many misfortunes are seen as the result of breaking taboos; however, it is inaccurate to describe the resulting misfortune as a punishment given by a supernatural being for breaking the taboo. Instead, there is a mechanistic force, a rule of the universe, perhaps the loss of *mana*, which may not actively cause misfortune, but inevitably leads to it. There are three subcategories of taboo breaking: taboo places, menstrual taboos, and garden taboos.

The taboo places in Tanna's jungle include the place of the gecko, the lizard, various winds, rain, and the home of certain *kughen*. People can pass through these taboo places inadvertently or even intentionally to perform magic (i.e., to make rain or wind), as long as their "insides are good." But if they attempt to perform magic with "bad insides," the result will be severe headaches, asthma, or death.

Many Tannese men are responsible for performing sympathetic magic on their clan's totemic crop. If the ritual is performed incorrectly, if the *tupunas* has not bathed ritually or fasted, or has engaged in intercourse, or if he has "bad insides," the ancestral spirits will cause serious illness, death, or widespread calamity, and the magic will not work.

Breaking menstruation taboos also causes different (less serious) illnesses. For example, if a man eats food prepared by a woman who is menstruating, it can cause diarrhea, stomachache, weight loss, and fatigue. If a menstruating woman touches a man's hair, he will lose the hair. Tannese also believe that intercourse with a pregnant woman can cause miscarriage.

CAUSED BY SPIRITS

Some disasters are caused by spirits, not for retribution, but merely out of maliciousness. Unprovoked evil spirits cause *korior* or *katamnemen* (seizures), *kapaap* (tumors), and birth defects. They take on the physical form of birds or lizards and bring sickness on people. One girl was born with a severely deformed head and lived for only a number of days. Some suspected the mother of deliberately causing miscarriage (see the section on intentional causes below), but others said it was an evil spirit that caused the birth defect.

Evil spirits also come to people in dreams resulting in illness. The evil spirit Nakua causes men to commit adultery with other women in their dreams, resulting in spiritual progeny who haunt the living and must be exterminated. The spirits lure people in their dreams, and become an obsession to them so that they cannot think about their living relatives, or even about taking care of themselves. Karmi contracted tuberculosis, but the shaman said, "His deceased wife is preparing his meals in his dreams, causing him to resent his living relatives who are actually meeting his daily needs." He gave Karmi an herbal drink to ward off the deceased wife so that he would no longer resent his relatives and would then become healthy.

Other evil spirits take the blood of their victims while they sleep. When they awake, they feel fatigue, and have "no blood." We are often at a loss for what medicine to give people who come to our door asking for "medicine for the blood" when they "have no blood." The shamans know exactly what this means, and have special leaves that will return a victim's blood.

NATURAL OR MECHANISTIC CAUSES

Many Tannese are aware of mechanistic causes of sickness, including microorganisms. They recognize that if they eat rotten food they may get a stomachache or diarrhea. They also recognize the part that natural forces play in trauma. If a child throws a rock down from a cliff onto somebody below, the stone can cause severe trauma. One man chopped off a tree limb that landed on his granddaughter, crushing her skull; the mechanical cause of this trauma was the first cause to be mentioned, but it was not considered an exclusive cause. (Family discord was also cited.) Other mechanistic causes of sickness involve logical associations: being in the rain will cause a runny nose, and playing in the sun will cause fever. At times, the nexus is less obvious: eating cold foods at night can cause runny nose and fever, and being out in a breeze can cause conjunctivitis.

Additionally, many Tannese recognize the efficacy of Western medicines. One man told me, "I had a fever and vomiting for months, and we killed numerous chickens and pigs to get rid of the sickness, but to no avail. When I went to the hospital, they gave me medicine for malaria, and I got better."

CAUSED INTENTIONALLY

While much misfortune is a result of breaking mechanistic moral laws or taboos (or for having "bad insides"), some misfortunes are believed to be caused intentionally. Most Tannese have a knowledge of poison or sorcery. The terms *kwanpanahr*, *narak*, and *tapwahin* (poison or sorcery) are interrelated and their distinctions are fuzzy, suggesting that poisoning is more magical and less physical. We have observed four victims of paralysis (all who recovered within a year), and the cause in each case was said to be poison or sorcery.

Self-inflicted misfortune usually involves attempts to induce abortion or sterility. Many Tannese maintain that women can cause abortion by drinking hot water, or by masticating roots of a casuarina (*Casuarina equisetifolia*) tree.

TESTING FROM GOD

Many Tannese Christians emphatically believe that a person who is free from sin and enemies should suffer no misfortune—except, perhaps, testing from God. The church planter in the village where we work told me proudly, "Since we started the church, the village has been free from sickness." This was a remarkable claim, considering that we had operated a regular ambulance service from that village to the hospital ever since we arrived two years earlier. The point is, provided that they are obeying the church rules and the village taboos, Tannese Christians can see no other likely explanation for misfortune except that God is testing their faith, as God tested the faith of Abraham and Job.

SUMMARY OF "BADNESSES"

Westerners, being more dichotomous and crisis-oriented (Lingenfelter & Mayers 1986), see misfortune as more or less subject to predictable natural laws. The flu virus is contagious and will cause the flu, resulting in certain predictable symptoms. Bacteria in old meat will cause severe gastrointestinal symptoms. Too much rain will cause a mudslide. Trauma causes broken bones. However, the Tannese evaluate misfortune causation more on a case-by-case basis than by a set of natural laws. If someone has a headache and scabies, both symptoms may be results of the same infraction: perhaps "bad insides" or breaking a garden taboo. Further, Tannese, being more holistic than dichotomistic, do not rule out any possible cause for misfortune within their plausibility structure: a person's sickness may be caused by sorcery, but it may be testing from God, and it may be the result of someone's sin. Therefore, shamanistic practices inevitably involve divination to determine who caused the sickness.

A "bone doctor" uses shamanistic lancing and "leaf medicine."

PRAXIS: SHAMANS AND SICKNESS

At the practical level, shamanistic healing in kastom involves spitting, mixing leaves and spit, and lancing. Since this is a public ritual (as opposed to the *kivir* ritual, which is performed in a garden), there is a degree of pageantry in the preparation stage. The shaman takes time in the bush to gather the right leaves for herbal treatment, or to smash the right piece of glass to use for lancing. The preparation is a ritual in its own right. After lancing, the shaman spits on the fresh wounds and packs them with leaves.

The healing ritual of an elderly woman, Arlis, serves as a good example of how the entire village gets involved in the pageantry of healing. Arlis fell unconscious where her hamlet borders the jungle. Half a dozen men began tossing her unconscious body up into the air. They were supporting her under each armpit and "bouncing" (that is the vernacular word for what they were doing) her about three feet above their own head level. Then they would drop her—knees and feet hitting the ground—while still supporting her armpits. After a few minutes, I asked if they would stop the bouncing long enough for my wife, a registered nurse, to check her pulse. Her pulse seemed fine. She was breathing and began grunting. They continued bouncing her for a few minutes and dragged her closer to the middle of the hamlet.

Several men had prepared herbal medicines. They squeezed leaves into cups of water and tried to force them down her unconscious mouth. One herbal medicine they gave her is nicknamed "punishment" since it is meant to release the punishment of infractions such as anger or trespassing on another's garden. Another herb is nicknamed "dream," and is meant to undo the effects of a demon-inspired dream. Another herb given to her was called "Karwas" after the so-named spirit who causes sickness. Other men had chewed leaves and spit them into her nostrils. Some spit on her without leaves. My wife went to check her lungs but got caught in the line of fire of someone's "medicinal spitting." Later, we noticed bits of chewed and spit leaves in the nooks and crannies of her stethoscope.

"Mama, wake up!" People were pinching her all over, especially on her arms and head. "Mama, don't sleep!" They were slapping her face gently, if there can be a gentle slap.

After about half an hour, she seemed to be recovering. "Mama, do you see me?" "Yes." "What's my name?" "Kilion." "Good. She can see. She can talk." "Mama, what are you worried about? Let go of it. Speak it. Let go of it. Let go of your worry." (Remember that worry is one of the most common causes attributed to illness.) "Her two boys left her, to go to Vila. Now she's left doing the hard work taking care of her grandchildren. This is making her worry. It's their fault she's sick." Someone tried calling her boys on the mobile phone. The crowd grew larger as Arlis' daughters arrived from their nearby villages, where they live with their newlywed husbands.

Someone gave Arlis a spoonful of mashed manioc. She vomited, revealing that she had eaten *kwanagen* (boiled manioc wrapped in spinach) and rice. "Oh, a thing [spirit] did this. Now she's vomiting out the thing's [spirit's] handiwork." Actually, nobody expressly mentioned the word "spirit"; it was implied. They said, "A thing did this to her." "She's vomiting something." But what they implied was an evil spirit.

Arlis was constantly going in and out of consciousness. When conscious, she complained, "My head is crazy. Don't slap my head. Oh, my head hurts. My head is crazy. I'm exhausted!" She kept trying to induce vomiting, but that seemed counterproductive to those who were feeding her manioc. "Don't vomit." "I want to stick my hand in my throat and vomit." "Don't stick your hand in your throat," her husband told her. They restrained her hands to keep her from inducing vomiting.

She seemed to be reviving, so they dragged her into a lean-to. Immediately upon being set down, her eyes rolled back and she stopped breathing. Breathing, to the Tannese, is a thing; it is like an organ. Breathing belongs up in the chest, behind the sternum. But sometimes the breathing moves around or drops down. Arlis' breathing dropped to her abdomen, so it needed to be squeezed back up into the chest. Two men firmly squeezed her abdomen upward, to force the breathing back into place. Some men squeezed leaves directly in their closed fists and let the liquid drip off their thumbs into her mouth to put her breathing back where it belongs. There is a sticky type of phlegm, *nargha*, which can accidentally pull the breathing into the throat; the squeezed leaves are intended to push the breathing back down.

Another half dozen men started bouncing her again. There were three at each armpit, but one man found he had the best leverage by grabbing her bare breasts and thrusting her upward along with the other men. Others poured jugs of water on her head and body. One woman had an idea: "Blow her ear!" A few people obliged by blowing into her ear.

While they were bouncing her, a young boy scrambled up the cliff with a young kava cluster. I knew where he was heading—to the *imarəm*, where a pig was screaming to be unfastened. I followed the boy, the kava, and the noise of the screaming pig. There were four men in the *imarəm*, and one woman with a baby. Saen, a distant relative who would call Arlis "auntie" clubbed the pig to death with three blows. Without saying a word, he left the pig and returned to Arlis' hamlet. One man explained, "It's Arlis and Tom's pig. It's her insides (volition). She's not speaking, so the pig will 'speak' for her. It'll tell what is worrying her so. It will speak on her behalf."

Sensing the action in the *imarəm* was complete, I returned to the hamlet. They were still bouncing Arlis, but she gained consciousness after about ten minutes. There was more herbal medicine, more pouring of water, more feeding manioc. She complained of terrible pain in her head and abdomen. At this point, family members began considering taking her to the hospital. Her husband said, "I depend on Western medicine. We've done all we can do here. We killed the pig, brought the kava, gave the leaf medicine. Everything the village can do has been done. So, let's take her to the hospital."

I took Arlis to the hospital where she lived for only two more weeks. Her death provoked more discussions about whose "bad insides" were the cause. I relate more about her death in a subsequent section on the death ritual.

PRAXIS: GROUP DISCUSSIONS AND EXCHANGE

Because misfortune is tied to moral failures, anger, anxieties—in sort, it is tied to the ups and downs of village life—the undoing of "badness" is a village affair. On a practical level, it creates opportunities for the village to mete out old conflicts, and provides opportunities for exchange of material goods.

Tragedies call up disagreements about land use and observations of taboos that were latent—at times for years. Therefore disagreements are seldom solved; they are revisited at every major tragedy.

> The normal hostilities that emerge between people living together in close relationships are forced underground, further building up stress in the society. At some point this hidden anger bursts out when someone accuses someone else of being a witch and causing all the problems. (Hiebert, Shaw, and Tienou 1999, 151)

Tribal discussions of misfortune, then, are a group catharsis; they serve as a platform for solving conflict. And, as Radin suggested, there is an economic factor. Sufferers of misfortune must offer a small gift to the shaman for herbal medicine. And if the potion is proved to be efficacious, another offering is brought (usually kava). Missionaries need to recognize that healing in animistic cultures is vastly more complicated than curing diseases or treating symptoms.

CHAPTER 7

Ethics and Taboos

MANY of the world's cultures distinguish between the sacred and the profane. In kastom, that distinction is not an ethical separation between the good and the bad; rather, it is more accurately a bifurcation between *imorhakə* (taboo) and *apnapig* (commonplace). Taboo items are powerful and dangerous (not holy or good), and commonplace items are mundane or impotent. Just because kastom does not distinguish between sacred and profane does not mean that traditional religion does have an ethical system—contrary to colonial-era prejudicial ethnographic reports. Kastom ethical discourse is not as salient as the discourse of taboos; nonetheless it exists. Below I discuss taboos and ethics because both are evaluative domains in kastom.

RETRIBUTION

Islanders do not expect the punishment of bad behavior to be postponed until the afterlife. Instead, all "badnesses" (whether outward actions or internal negative emotions) are avenged immediately, either by human beings who act violently, use sorcery, or impose fines; or else they are avenged by more mechanistic forces which cause sickness, disaster, and death. The impetus for behaving morally, then, is not purity for purity's sake or to please God, rather to avoid retribution—the inevitable consequences of moral failings (see the previous section on health).

With little emphasis on purity for purity's sake (cf. the eighteenth-century Pietists) or on the consequences of behavior in the afterlife (cf. nineteenth-century evangelists), behavior is controlled either punitively or manipulatively in kastom. Punitive behavioral management involves fines of chickens, kava, and pigs. Manipulation, on the other hand, involves gossip, threats of black magic, and, *ex post facto* accusations that one's bad behavior caused sickness or disaster. Tribal discussions about the most recent "badnesses" and the moral failings that led to them enable the group to castigate those who break the rules.

But what of the afterlife? While there is no eternal retribution for evildoers and no eternal reward for the good, Tannese religion does have a doctrine of the afterlife. All souls (good or bad) eventually go to the taboo places, which are usually one or two miles inland from the villages. It is said that at night one can hear the spirits there, making conversation and drinking kava, and can hear their pots and pans clanking as they prepare food.

KASTOM TABOOS

Foreign ethnographers have noted correctly that what is acceptable or unacceptable in Melanesian religion is not based on the character of a holy God; rather, "straight behavior" is that which does not bring retribution while "taboo" behavior does. That kastom ethics are not based on the decrees or character of a holy God led early missionaries to the erroneous conclusion that primitive religion has no ethics. However, kastom has a complex taxonomy of taboos, some of which are clearly immoral or "bad behavior" in Westerner's minds, and some of which a Westerner would find surprising or confusing in a list of right and wrong.

Taboo objects can be either good or bad; they produce good results when the taboo is observed, and bad ones when the taboo is broken. The following categories are taboo in kastom:

1. Foods, at certain times, e.g., when a *tupunas* (magician) is doing magic for that particular food

2. The man who performs sympathetic magic

3. *Kivir* (magical stones)

4. Reproductive body parts

5. Members of the opposite sex with whom it would be considered incestuous to copulate

6. The resting places of the spirits

7. Certain trees (e.g., nafa) used for firewood related to sunshine-magic

8. Certain bodies of water, such as Lapangkauta River

9. Sins (e.g., stealing, adultery, lying, anger, hatred, gossip, slander)

At a deeper level, taboos are symbols of something else, and can be interpreted like all other symbols. Certain items are taboo to reinforce societal structure (taboo men). The taboo places are off-limits to reinforce a healthy fear of spirits and ghosts. Other places (e.g., Lapangkauta River) are off-limits as perpetual reminders of their importance to islanders' health and welfare.

Because of this highly nuanced conceptualization of "taboo," missionaries in Melanesia have found it difficult to get across the idea of "holiness." A "taboo/holy" God is seen as dangerous and off-limits. Because the biblical conceptualization of holy/profane does not correspond to the Melanesian taboo/commonplace ideal, the churches need to work through these differences.

KASTOM ETHICS

If taboos are not inherently bad or sinful, how does ethics fit into kastom? Early ethnographers believed that "primitive religions" did not have an ethical system. Nida's characterization of animism as a valueless system is typical of early twentieth-century portrayals. "The animist's religion is essentially non-ethical. To him, religion is primarily a technique for procuring the best advantage in the power struggle in the spirit world" (1959, 52). "There is no fundamental moral basis in animism" (ibid., 57). Elsewhere Nida has said:

> It is implicit with us that a religious man should be a good man, but for most of the predominantly animistic religions of the world there is no essential connection. Such a religion is primarily a technique for dealing with supernatural phenomena, and it makes few or no moral demands on anyone . . . a genuine sense of guilt (as we understand the word) is by no means as widespread in the world as we would imagine. (1954, 41–42)

Similarly, John Inglis, an early missionary to South Vanuatu, gave a rather harsh interpretation of the ethical ramifications of kastom:

> Their deities, like themselves, were all selfish and malignant; they breathed no spirit of benevolence, and the rewards and punishments of the future state were connected more with ritual observances than with moral character. Their religion contained no principle that could lead to a holy life; they certainly thought that their gods were like themselves, and that they approved of their sins. It would have been morally impossible on Aneityum for any man to have conceived of such a character, morally and religiously, as that of the man Christ Jesus. To have done so would have been a miracle as great as that of His resurrection. (Inglis 1887, 32)

European visitors and early missionaries reported numerous instances of warfare, cannibalism, and widow-strangling (cf. W. Watt 1895). Inglis had formed the opinion that the ni-Vanuatu were not only heathen but savages. Kastom, "their religion" as Inglis put it, was to blame for their apparent savagery.

Alas, Inglis and Nida have not given a fair representation of kastom's ethics. Indeed, kastom is a tight ethical system since (1) it has a rather unanimously agreed upon set of standards, (2) it has mechanisms for making moral choices, and (3) there are ramifications for breaking the rules. However, Inglis accurately recognized a tendency in kastom to emphasize ritual obedience over personal reform. People follow the rules for fear of negative consequences, or to gain positive results, rather than seeking purity simply for purity's sake. Moral laws are impersonal—mechanistic—therefore, breaking the laws results in judicial guilt that must be atoned some way. However, since the moral law is impersonal and "fuzzy," all members of the society may suffer tragedy as the result of an individual's infraction. In that sense, breaking the law is a sin against society, bringing shame on the offender (Hiebert, Shaw, and Tienou 1999, 215).

Kastom employs both mechanistic and organic metaphors in regards to ethics. It emphasizes elements of the "straight life" such as peace, unity, calm, gentleness, and generosity. To live in hostility, or to have "bad insides," invokes a mechanistic retribution: sickness or disaster. Stealing, murder, and selfishness are considered wrong because they hurt relationships, and they require public reconciliation. The list of nine categories of taboos above suggests that Tannese have social mores regarding sexual immorality, respect for deceased ancestors, respect of the elders (at least of magicians), and respect of the environment. What is notably missing in the list of taboos is murder, stealing and taking from another clan's garden. Tannese don't usually refer to these behaviors as "taboo" but they certainly see such behaviors as wrong and requiring retribution. For example, it is "not straight" to enter another person's garden, to take food from it, or even to let domesticated animals enter it. The first line of defense for the garden (undoubtedly the most prized possession for the Tannese) is magic or threats of retribution from the spirits (or ghosts). Men cast prophylactic spells in their gardens to castigate intruders.

Like Westerners, Tannese may justify murder or stealing from gardens under certain circumstances, such as when they are carrying out revenge. In that case, they would not consider the behavior to be a moral failing.

In summary, kastom ethics is complicated and "fuzzy." Behavior is evaluated by its ultimate effect on the clan. If a behavior will bring badness on the clan, it is "unsatisfactory;" if it will have positive consequences, it is "satisfactory." Retribution in this life is the consequence of both bad behavior and bad thoughts.

CHAPTER 8

Cargoism

AROUND the time of the Second World War, syncretistic movements sprung up throughout the Pacific. Prophets began proclaiming the eminent arrival of ships loaded with European goods which would be distributed freely. Some promised that America would be joined to their island by a highway. A new age would be ushered in where the old would shed their skin, school and work would be unnecessary, and everyone would have as much "cargo" as he or she wanted. Followers, even some in highland villages, constructed wharfs and wrote down orders of trucks, generators, and other coveted items. The popular explanation for these "cargo cults" was that Melanesians saw the jeeps, airplanes, and personal items of the allied soldiers, and not understanding Western economies and manufacturing processes, imagined that such goods were obtained through magical rituals.

Since they have been greatly influenced by European contact, cargo cults are not kastom-proper. However, cargo cults are linked with kastom, especially since they are born out of traditional religious worldview, and they endorse a return from Christianity to animistic practices. They are typically syncretistic, since many of these movements consider Jesus Christ, the Bible, and the church to be part of the process by which cargo must be obtained. The (albeit faulty) syllogism would go like this: Westerners go to church and pray to Jesus, Westerners have cargo, therefore Jesus (the Bible, the church) is a way to obtain this cargo.

This popular explanation for cargo cults is simplistic and only partially true at best. Undoubtedly, cargo cults are a result of Western contact. However, there is evidence that at least some of these nativistic movements began before the influx of Europeans and their goods during WWII. And anthropologists suggest that these movements are not as much about obtaining cargo as they are about millenarian hopes, resistance to colonialism, and disillusionment with Christianity.

This popular explanation for cargo cults is simplistic and only partially true at best. Undoubtedly, cargo cults are a result of Western contact. However, there is evidence that at least some of these nativistic movements began before the influx of Europeans and their goods during WWII. And anthropologists suggest that these movements are not as much about obtaining cargo as they are about millenarian hopes, resistance to colonialism, and disillusionment with Christianity.

The phenomenon of cargo cults has been well studied; there is a substantial body of popular and scholarly literature on Tanna's prominent cargo cult, the John Frum cargo cult (Crowley and Crowley 1996; R. J. Gregory 1984; Guiart 1956; Rice 1974; Trompf 1990). Space does not permit me to relate in depth the historical and cultural factors that led to the rise of Tanna's cargo cults. However, a few brief comments can be made about cargoism, Christianity, and kastom.

First, cargo cults are a product of the Melanesian worldview, which has a predisposition toward millenarianism. The concrete symbolism, use of rituals, millenarian tendency, and charismatic prophets of the cargo cults resemble more closely the deeply ingrained worldview of Melanesians than Christianity does, making cargo cults more accessible and palatable to them. Bieniek and Trompf (2000) have suggested that the basis of cargoism is not so much the cargo itself, but the ushering in of the millennial age. Cargo cults promise more tangible and immediate benefits than traditional Christianity offers. The Christian gospel of forgiveness by substitutionary atonement that the early missionaries proclaimed was too abstract—almost irrelevant—compared to the concrete this-worldliness of cargo cults. Salvation, for the Melanesians, is about health and wealth.

> It is a concrete, this-worldly salvation for which Melanesians hope. Salvation means freedom from want and sickness, relief from the pressures of work and time, a state of wholeness and health, a regaining of one's prestige and self-respect, an ordering of relationships so that proper balances obtain in the social structures. (Strelan 1977, 81)

By the Second World War, some Melanesians had become disillusioned with evangelical Christianity, since it did not seem to promise a prosperous life on earth.

However, cargo cults are also born out of a disillusionment with traditional religion. They are an innovative response meant to mitigate the apparent deficiencies of kastom, which taught that local communities are the nexus of creation and prosperity. If magical fetishes ensure good crops and health, why do foreign nations devoid of fetishes have so much cargo? Kastom could not explain Western cargo, so kastom needed to be altered. Cargo cults are an answer to this enigma.

For Tippett, cargo cults (which he called "nativistic movements") are not as much about millenarianism or cargo, but resistive responses to the severe culture clash between colonial powers and traditional societies. The degree of resistance varies and can be plotted on a number of axes, including passive or aggressive, revivalistic or perpetuative, organized or revolutionary, rejective or accommodative (1987, 270). Tippett described various nativistic movements as "anti-Government," "anti-Mission," "counter-conversion," or "defectors." They usually herald instead a return to kastom (ibid., 272). The antimission or antigovernment attitude can usually be traced to a belief that something has been lost at culture contact. Tippett asks, "Had the white colonial administrators and missionaries robbed [Melanesia] of her birthright: her cultural heritage, authority, wealth and religious power?" (ibid., 274). That is, they can be considered more political than religious (Bonnemaison 1991, 72). Along these lines, Lindstrom calls them "homegrown oppositional discourse" (1990b, 40).

In the heyday of cargo cults (ca. 1940s), Tannese threw their British currency into the sea in protest of the Western economy (Bonnemaison 1994, 221). A number of villages banned their children from going to church, school, or the hospitals. Crowley and Crowley reported, "They are against the long-ruling government of Vanuatu's prime minister, Rev. Walter Lini . . . against missions and conversion; against the use of money; and in favor of a return to the customary culture and ritual *kava*" (1996, 160). At this point, anything European was considered off-limits. By the 1970s, the John Frum cargo cult began to associate closely with a movement for national independence for Vanuatu (Trompf 1994, 256).

JOHN FRUM CARGO CULT

Vanuatu was colonized by both the British and the French in 1909. Resident commissioners were stationed on Tanna to establish law and order. As the island slowly developed, more ships began to call on the island; expatriates began frequenting the island and even taking up residence. Some tried to run businesses or copra plantations.

Tannese became increasingly exposed to Europeans, but did not fully comprehend capitalism. (To this day, there is misinformation about how money is printed and the role of the government. Even the people I work with on a regular basis still assume that the US government hands out money to its citizens, while Vanuatu's "bad government" refuses to print money and give it to the people.) By the 1930s, Tannese were becoming suspicious of the colonists and missionaries. Europeans seemed to have unlimited wealth, but were apparently unwilling to distribute this wealth to the natives, or to show them how to obtain it themselves.

Somewhere between 1939 and 1941, villagers in Greenpoint began speaking about a spirit-human prophet named John Frum. John required his followers to stop going

Men in the John Frum movement paint USA on their chests and carry mock rifles.

to church, to throw their money into the sea, to leave coastal mission stations, and to return to kastom. If they did so, things would go back to the way they were in the mythical golden ages.

Islanders give conflicting etiologies for John Frum. His surname either means "from" as in "John from America," or it comes from "broom" as in "John who will broom out all the European colonizers, finally establishing an independent nation." Some say John was a US soldier—either black or white—who spent some time on Tanna during the war and started spreading rumors or making false promises about cargo. However, the simultaneous arrival of these cargo cults in geographically distant islands makes that scenario seem unlikely. Were US soldiers all over the Pacific starting rumors? Also, Tannese memories of John Frum say he visited kava-drinking grounds and spoke the vernacular of Tanna. (Having devoted nearly a decade to learning the languages of Tanna, I find it highly improbable that a visiting US soldier mastered it enough to found a religious movement.) Further descriptions of John Frum have him arriving out of thin air at dusk on an illuminated broomstick and magically throwing his voice. Folk explanations of his lineage are vague (he is from Tanna, he is from America, he is Jesus Christ, he is the god Karpapeng). John Frum looks more like a modern legend than a historical figure.

SUMMARY OF CARGOISM

In summary, while cargo cults are not kastom proper, they are a modern outworking of kastom. And while only a small percentage of islanders directly affiliate with a given cargo movement, the ideology of cargoism is virtually islandwide. It is the product of kastom epistemology, which is mythological and magical rather than scientific. They are an application of millenarian kastom hopes for salvation or "goodness." Cargo cults are an appealing arena for living out kastom in the face of foreign governments and churches that threaten the values of kastom.

CHAPTER 9

Ritual and Exchange

W HEN people talk about kastom, they usually mean ritual, because it is more poignant than the more esoteric facets of kastom described above, such as epistemology, cosmology, or *mana*. Rituals are not just events people attend, like Westerners attend sports events or concerts. They create and reinforce relationships, and they help form a worldview. They also alleviate anxiety. Life is full of dangers: Gardening involves the potential of hurricane and drought; raising children is wrought with dangers such as illness and death; death means ghosts will be nearby. Ritual is meant to obviate those dangers (and the anxiety about those dangers) by warding off evil forces. Harvest rituals ensure good crops and the right amount of rain. Rites of passage ensure prosperity. Proper mourning rituals ensure the ghost will not be harmful.

Therefore, animistic ritual is more than exchange, fellowship, and celebration. It engenders a worldview of dangerous forces that must be manipulated to ensure fortune. This worldview creates problems for Christian theology and practice, and church planters of the various denominations on Tanna have had to ponder the meaning behind these rituals as they lay down church policy. In Chapter 11, I discuss the various ways churches on Tanna have dealt with kastom rituals. Some, seeing no contradiction with Christianity, have enthusiastically maintained these rituals as an important part of life; others have outright banned all kastom ritual; and others have substituted some or all of the rituals with Christian equivalents.

But we're getting ahead of ourselves. Before we look at church integration of ritual, we need to achieve a thorough understanding of what kastom rituals mean to the Tannese. In this section I will consider two major categories of ritual: intensifying rituals (involving exchanges) and rites of passage.

INTENSIFYING RITUALS

On Tanna, kava is a daily ritual for the men that reinforces values. Other intensifying rituals are held less often, such as the *kɔjiə* harvest ritual, the *nier* exchange ritual, and the *nokiar* pig exchange and dance. All of these rituals are discussed in the next few sections.

Kava Ritual

As Lebot and Lindstrom (1997) have recorded, kava is more than "the Pacific elixir" on Tanna. It is a daily reminder of the ideal society (cf. Brunton 1989). Virtually every ritual in kastom involves exchanging and drinking of kava. "Kava now stands for shared Vanuatu tradition—kastom—and that shared tradition bolsters sentiments of identity and unity" (Lindstrom 1991). Kava is the *sine qua non* of kastom ritual.

Colorful descriptions of the kava ritual are found in travel literature, and more analytical descriptions have been given by numerous ethnographers (M. Allen 1981; Brunton 1979; R. J. Gregory, Gregory, and Peck 1981; Lebot and Lindstrom 1997; Steel 1880). Such attention is paid to kava because it is a dominant metaphor of Melanesia. It condenses the great Melanesian values of exchange, *mana*, ancestors, and respect.

Kava is mixed in the *imarəm*, which has been variously defined as the sacred dancing place (Bonnemaison 1994), the kava drinking ground (Brunton 1989), or, using the pidgin term *nakamal*, the men's meeting place.[16] Men and boys meet in the *imarəm* every evening for the kava ritual. Females may enter the *imarəm* during regular time; but during kava time (Tannese men refer to this as "my time"), they may not enter because they may not see kava being prepared. At kava time, a fire is lit to signify to the women that it is now taboo to enter the *imarəm*.

Men gather an hour or so before sundown to begin cleaning kava roots. Villagers take turns providing the kava, but usually there is a work party or some other request for help, and the requestor supplies the kava. If a man regularly drinks kava but does not supply any, he will be mildly chastised. All males may chew the kava, but only virgin boys may handle the pulp, because married men may not prepare foods with their bare hands. The boys pour water over the pulp, filtering the drink through a coconut fiber into decades-old halved coconut shells that remain in the *imarəm*.

Kava was originally mixed in a canoe (*rao*), giving the nickname "canoe" to every kava drinking ground (and by extension, to every village). The practice of mixing kava in canoes has been largely abandoned for some reason. Since a communal kava bowl is not used, each heap lands on two prearranged *nivo* (*Hibiscus tiliaceus*) leaves (or some other large leaves). Then the kava is chewed by males of all ages and spit onto leaves, making softball-sized mounds. More descriptively, the "cud" is not expectorated, but "let out." The same verb for "letting out" is used in the vernacular to describe how a hen lays an egg, which is actually quite fitting, because that's what kava "spitting" looks like.

Once the kava is prepared, it is drunk from eldest to youngest—sometimes two at a time. Drinkers stand on the perimeter of the *imarəm* and face outward—toward the jungle. The shell of kava must be drunk entirely and quickly, leaving only the last drops for the drinker to shake out onto the ground as he shouts, "*K-spaa!*"—the way someone in a bar would grimace painfully after slamming down an emptied shot glass.

When the drinkers are downing their shells, everyone else in the *imarəm* is silent. As Asa Berger noted, even nothing can be a sign (1999, 159). In this case, the nothingness of silence signifies respect. A brief incantation follows, called *tamafa*, uttered to the ancestors or to the kava spirit (Lindstrom 2004, 21). Ethnographers have tried to explain to

---

[16] *Nakamal* is from proto-Oceanic *gamal* (men's meeting place).

whom the *tamafa* is directed, with various answers, including Matiktik, *kughen*, ancestors, the gods, and Jesus (Brunton 1989, 112). However, as with sacrifice, which I mentioned earlier, it is a misappropriation of categories to think of the *tamafa* as a prayer to a certain deity, since prayer is a theistic activity. *Tamafa* is coercitive—the power is in the act of *tamafa*. The *tamafa* is directed rather ambiguously to a deity or spirit. To "carry a *tamafa*," something is said like "that the gardens would grow!" or "that the newly circumcised boys would be healthy!" Thus, in addition to solidifying relationships and reinforcing status (age and role differences), the ritual is a coercitive act meant to increase *mana* or power.

After each kava-aged man (about twenty years and older) has drunk, all males share a light meal, prepared in advance by the women, called *nohunu*. Food is not eaten before the kava because it is said that food will impede the ability to get intoxicated.

In contrast to the kava ritual in other Melanesian nations (cf. Tomlinson 2009, 109), kava and discussion do not mix. In the hour or two before the kava is drunk, there are discussions and announcements. While the boys are chewing the kava, and the young men are cleaning the roots with coconut husks or knives, the elders stand and make brief speeches about pressing issues such as group gardening schedules, or reasons for current sicknesses or other disasters. However, within minutes after the *nohunu* is eaten, the boys silently walk home, and the men sit in absolute silence as the fire dies out. They sit a considerable distance from each other; if a brief discussion is absolutely necessary, it is done with hand signals and lip reading. This strict silence is observed for at least an hour, but may last late into the night if men drink more shells from the previously used pulp.

Tannese say the intoxicated men are "listening to their kava" and nothing should "startle their drunkenness." We have seen women severely beaten for allowing their children to make noise while the men are "listening to their kava." The meaning of "listening to kava" is enigmatic, or at least polysemous. It may either mean that they are feeling the effects of the intoxication, or that they are communicating with ancestors.

The kava ritual is replete with symbolism. Using a triadic model of semiology *vis-à-vis* Pierce, (sign, signifier, and signified), I list eleven signs in the kava ritual (see Table 7). Additionally, each sign can be alternately represented in the chart as an unstated imperative, directed at the signifier, and emphasizing the "signified" (that is, the meaning of the sign).

Kava embodies kastom, and the church's challenge of kava drinking is not merely a repudiation of intoxication; it threatens alliances, exchanges, community, sharing, connection with ancestors, and signs of respect. For this reason, kava is the most persistent point of conflict between kastom and Christianity in contemporary Melanesia.

Harvest Ritual

Annual exchange rituals called *kəjiə* (grating) are usually held during the first harvest, in April. *Kəjiə* are exchange rituals between clans. For example, a large offering of baked banana pudding would be given by the taro clan to the *tupunas* of the banana clan for his services of sympathetic magic. The banana clan would then reciprocate the gift with an offering at a later date of taro pudding to the taro *tupunas*. Noel enlightened me about the *kəjiə* in Yanemilen:

Ruben performs the [magic] on the [yam] stone. It sits [in his garden] and he [performs magic on] it. Then we cultivate yams and grate them, and he gives us [the firstfruits]. Then Kilion and Kai and Raga and Karmi and I grate and make a big tuber pudding with it, and when it's done, we give it to him in the *imarəm* and distribute the kava that goes with it. We make *laplap* (tuber pudding) with other foods— banana, or manioc, or whatever. The women make *laplap* with it—banana or manioc. Then we take it, and take also some kava [to the *imarəm*], and Ruben brings his [prestation], and we distribute the kava that watches us [points toward us]; the kava points toward him,

Table 7: Types of magical behavior in kastom

OBJECT (SIGNIFIER)	IMPERATIVE (SIGNIFIED)	SIGNIFICANCE	DIRECTED AT:
Imarəm	Meet here	Location of kastom	Everyone
Head of kava brought	Pitch in	Reciprocity	Adult males
Smoke	Don't come here now	Males serve in the "priestly" function	Females
Leaves	Spit here	Community	All males
Virgin boys prepare kava in a *nigis* (coconut fiber)	Don't touch prepared food	Sex is dirty	Married men
Water	Drink	Shared meals	Kava-age men
Oldest drinks first	Wait your turn	Social hierarchy, respect of elders	Younger men
Spitting the *tamafa*	Help me	Libation	Spirits/ancestors
Nohunu (shared meal)	Let's eat	Connection with women/village	All males
Dead fire	Leave me alone	Communication with ancestors	Intoxicated drinkers
Kwensiə (fire stick)	Don't talk to me	Respect	Everyone

for the yams, and we also give him kava. He gives us some, and we give him some, along with kava. He takes out what we have made, as his to eat. That is, he takes his tuber pudding and his kava to drink. That which we give him, he takes away. And we take away what he made. We swap. He gives us some, and we give him some.

The harvest rituals mark the end of a period where many foods are taboo. For example, seafood and freshwater fish are off-limits for the four to six months prior to the kɔjiɔ. Recently the government and aid organizations have recognized the benefit of these taboos, as they allow the sea life to be replenished. These organizations encourage ni-Vanuatu to continue practicing this aspect of kastom for the good of the environment and their future food supply.

However, many foods are off-limits only to the clan of that food totem for a taboo period. For example, family members of the taro tupunas can eat taro, but only roasted taro. They cannot cut, grate, or peel the taro, which would be necessary for boiling it or making it into tuber pudding. Cutting, grating, or peeling it would be tantamount to cutting their ancestors, an offense that would invoke retribution. (The sociological and economic benefits of this totemic exchange system were highlighted in Chapter 2.)

The harvest festival is meant to propitiate the ancestors—to apologize to them because throughout the remainder of the year mortals will be cutting and scraping and boiling them. Therefore, the kɔjiɔ is not simply a benign exchange ritual; it is a propitiation. For this reason, the church historically took issue with it. In 2009 the elders of a Presbyterian church prayed in the imarɔm during a kɔjiɔ ritual. This action precipitated months of bitter arguments over the ramifications of inviting the Christian God into the kastom rituals.

Cousin-exchange Ritual

The harvest ritual mentioned above is an annual reminder to Tannese that they should show gratitude to the tupunas for a good year of crops. The nier (exchange ritual is held far less frequently—perhaps once every other generation. It is called nier (cousin) because the exchange is made between cross-cousins. For example, some classificatory brothers will summon their classificatory mother's brother's family or their father's sister's family to attend an exchange of taro or yams.

To the outsider, the nier may seem like nothing more than an extravagant gift of crops given occasionally from one clan to another. But to attain a deeper understanding of the nier, one needs to take a look at what Marcel Mauss (1990) meant when he referred to the "potlatch,"[17] because the nier contains the important themes Mauss discussed: reciprocity; out-doing others; "free" gifts which are not free at all; and the "destruction of wealth."

Mauss contended that societies like those in Melanesia do not conceive of a "free gift" the way Westerners do. Consider the aid that World Vision, an American organiza-

---

[17] Mauss used the Native American term "potlatch" to refer to ceremonies where large gifts are given, and at times wealth is even destroyed. He notes that alms and sacrifice are both permutations of the "destruction of wealth" because both involve giving up something valuable with the hope that a deity will reciprocate with an even larger gift.

tion, provides to non-Western nations. The donors may remain anonymous, and many will never have a personal relationship with the recipients. The gifts come with "no strings attached" and certainly with no expectation of reciprocation. However, tribal societies see giving and receiving not as a way of meeting a need but as a way of establishing relationships. It is not that the cousins need the taro, which may in fact grow abundantly in their own garden; rather, they need the relationship with the cousins to be solidified. To Tannese, the whole point of gift-giving is to attach strings. Charity does not count as a gift, if inherent in the word gift is the notion of strengthening relationships.

The *nier* ritual does not make sense in a market economy where exchange is about meeting dietary needs; however, it is the quintessential gift-giving ceremony in Tanna. Westerners would see the large gift of taro, kava, and mats and wonder, *Doesn't the recipient grow the exact same crops and weave the same mats from the same coconuts and pandanus trees? Why give something to someone who already has exactly what you have?* True, in a market economy, there would be no reason. Because of this, we say that Melanesian gift-giving isn't at all like trading of goods.

The *nier* is also the Melanesian gift-giving ceremony par excellence because of what Mauss termed the "destruction of wealth." The prestation at the *nier* involves a mound of crops that is so substantial the receiving villages could not consume them all before they rot. Essentially, a portion of the crops, representing wealth, are destroyed rather than eaten. This indicates that the gift is partially about perpetuating a cycle of outdoing one's cousins with increasingly extravagant gifts.

Mauss theorized that "gift" is a magical item, because of Frazer's law of contagion (Chapter 2). Taros that were once in contact with a certain chief continue to be connected to him even after he has given them to his cousin. For a Westerner to give a gift of food is not dangerous, because once the food is given it no longer exerts influence over the giver. But animists are taking a risk to hand food to another, since it remains connected to them. Perhaps the recipient will perform sorcery on the taro, causing death in the gift-giver's clan. Gift-giving, then is dangerous[18] and shows trust. The *nier*, then, is not about taro, but about trust, alliances, and interdependence.

During the ritual, men arrange crop offerings in tall mounds or hang them from trees; then the crops are counted so that they may be reciprocated (or out-done) decades later by the receiving cousins. A permutation of the *nier* is the *niskir* (net or trap), where crops are displayed in a round cage for an exchange ceremony that will be reciprocated with different crops at a much later date.

In June 2007 the inland villages of Yanemilen and Yenapkasu held a *nier* along a kastom exchange road leading oceanward, through the villages in Yetap on to Kwotaperen. They spent several days stacking up six symbolic "boats" of taro about ten feet tall—approximately fifteen thousand taros. Then they summoned the coastal villages to come witness the display. Two days later, the oceanward villages arrived to build a platform of bamboo, on which they stacked yams. Makua explained, "The coastal villages are buying

---

[18] Mauss even noted that the word for gift in certain languages is connected to the word for poison. Among his examples was the Greek word *dosis*.

our taro with a pig and a cow. And we're buying their yams with a pig and a cow." In all, forty-two pigs from coastal villages were swapped with forty-two pigs of equal size from inland villages.

It is true that the *nier* is an exchange event, but it is an uneven exchange; the amount of yams offered to the host village does not compare to the amount of taros given. Therefore, the oceanward villages remain indebted to Yanamelin and Yenapkasu until, perhaps decades later, the "body of the *nier*" is held in their own village, where yams will be hung from trees and stacked, and the inland villages will bring a smaller prestation of taro.

As an exchange ritual, the *nier* does not appear to threaten Christian principles; however, it was suspended (not entirely abandoned) under the church's reign referred to as Tanna Law (see Chapter 10) because of its connection to the *tupunas* (crop magician). The *tupunas* of the host village inevitably uses the *nier* as an opportunity to remind everyone that he (and not God) is responsible for the abundance of crops. A story that has reached legendary status illustrates the tension between church and *imarəm* over the *nier*.

> They were holding a *nier* in Yelkenu, about the time of the fight [WWII]. And Daniel Keasi, an elder in a local church, told the people at the *nier* that it was God who provided the taro, not the *tupunas*. But Makua Senior was furious, because he was the *tupunas* and he said he provided the taro. So he figured, "Fine, nobody can eat taro then." So he took a musket. In those days they had muskets. And he shot the taros hanging up in the trees. They hung taros in the trees, because it was a *nier*. So he shot one, and hit the bull's-eye. Then he took the *kivìr* (magical taro stones) and hid them in Yenokuka so that nobody could have taro. But it didn't work. To this day, we have taro crops every year, even though he hid the taro stone.[19]

These sentiments are persistent. At a *niskìr* exchange ceremony I observed in 2005, the *tupunas* chastised Christians for ignoring the taboos related to his magical ritual. Then he dared them: "Anyone who dismisses the taboos must eat these crops." The crops were not yet ritually clean for eating, and the *tupunas* believed that eating them would result in death. Like Makua Senior, this magician was so angry about Christians disregarding his own powers that he wished them ill.

Modern discourse about discouraging the *nier* also focuses on more practical matters, such as its extravagance and supposed wastefulness of time and resources. Indeed, even enthusiastic kastom-retainers recognize that the gift of crops is so extravagant that a large portion go rotten.

The absence of a "free gift" in Melanesia may seem to cause problems for missionaries who are attempting to preach about God's free gift of salvation. However, I have come to the conclusion that the Melanesian idea of gift-giving better fits the biblical gift of salvation. Westerners may inadvertently project their idea of charity onto God's "free gift" of salvation. It is not as if salvation, while coming with "no strings attached" is an anonymous

---

[19] Told to me by Jakob Aiyo, Yanemilen village, July 2009.

An exorbitant prestation of 15,000 taros were given, along with kava, at the 2010 Nier ritual.

gift with no future exchanges. God didn't just say, "Here is salvation. Take it and have a nice life. I don't want any speeches or tokens of appreciation, and I certainly don't want you to ask anything else from me or to have some obligation to return to you in the future with more gifts." Instead, God's gifts to us were specifically to open the "road" (as Tannese would say) for a relationship with us. He intends for us to continue the reciprocation of trust and dependency the rest of our lives. In that way, while free, it is not free at all in the Melanesian sense.

Pig-exchange Ritual

The most documented ritual on Tanna is the *nokiar*—a pig-exchange ritual and dance held every few years (Bonnemaison 1994, 148). More than a hundred pigs were killed at the *nokiar* in Yanemakel in 2003, and given to the dancers. Two weeks after the *nokiar*, every dancer who received a pig reciprocated the gift with one of equal value. Two weeks later, the original givers offered gifts of pig parts—a leg, the ribs, or the rump. Two weeks after that, the dancers reciprocated with the same sort of gift. This made four exchange ceremonies in all, with the slaughter of nearly three hundred pigs. The pig is central to the *nokiar*; in the months leading up to the ceremony, men say, "I am dancing for a pig."

Folk explanations conclude that the historic purpose of the *nokiar* was to set aside a day for licentiousness. Three hundred and sixty-four days a year, a man must only sleep with his wife (or wives); but on this one day the chiefs allow "bad behavior" saying, "No problem, tomorrow, we will kill many pigs." Therefore, the pigs serve a dual purpose: they will serve as fines paid to offended husbands by men that sleep around (or perhaps just grope a little), and their blood will take away any punishment or "badness" resulting from the "bad behavior."

All the villages on a traditional exchange route take their turn dancing the dances of the *nokiar*. Two or three months prior to the actual date of the final culminating dance, various villages are invited to an initial "pig leg" ceremony, where they perform dances from previous *nokiar* rituals and exchange gifts of *topuga* (ceremonial kava). Afterwards, music composers drink kava and sit under energized trees to dream up the lyrics for the upcoming *nokiar* dances. The first village on the exchange route begins choreographing the dances. They practice every other day, at morning and in the afternoon, for about a month, with each practice taking about forty-five minutes. The *nokiar* mixes old and new songs. Some of the lyrics and moves in the dances persist decade after decade, marking it as an authentic *nokiar*. Many lyrics and dance moves are new, making the dance relevant.

Some members of the next village on the traditional trading route participate in the practice sessions so they can learn the dances and teach their own village. They, too, practice every other day, morning and night, for about a month. Then the "*nokiar* will come out" and go to the next major village on the route. In this way, the *nokiar* moves across the island. The 2003 *nokiar* moved from Green Point to Yanemakel—through five major villages, two language groups, and a distance of about eleven miles. The last village, Yanemakel, practiced the dance for the month prior to the actual date.

Dancers in the *nokiar* hold a prop called a *nasko*—a piece of soft wood carved to resemble a shepherd's staff, which is meant to represent an instrument for "pulling cargo." The pulling of cargo refers to the exchange of pigs at the end of the *nokiar*. I submit that the dancing with the *nasko* is imitative magic (see Chapter 2). If the dancers act out a ritual of pulling food toward the clan with a shepherd staff, the cargo must come.

On the actual night of the *nokiar*, as many as two thousand people gather to watch each village along the exchange route take their turn dancing the exact same series of songs that they have been rehearsing. Therefore, the *nokiar* is repeated over and over again

Gifts of taro, kava, mats, cloth, and tuber pudding are piled up during exchange rituals.

through the night. The songs and moves are the same, but the actors change.

The *nokiar* event is actually a series of four different dances, in the following order: *nokiar, nai, kosasiva,* and *napenapen.* After each village has taken turns dancing the *nokiar* through the night, at daylight villages that have prepared to dance the *nai* (wood) take the stage. The *nasko* of the *nokiar* are replaced with lengths of wild cane. Then villages that have prepared to dance the *kosasiva* (index finger) take the stage. And lastly, the women who have rehearsed the *napenapen* take the stage while security guards hold pointed sticks to stave off would-be gropers from going too far.

It is not difficult to imagine why the early missionaries prohibited the *nokiar* with its nuance of promiscuity. Nor is it particularly difficult to imagine that in the 1950s the cargo cults revived the ritual for the same reason.

SUMMARY OF INTENSIFYING RITUALS

In each of these exchange rituals, the prestation (cf. Mauss 1990) is an event in itself. It is drawn out and public, with intricate rules, including which way the leaves point. Gifts are laid down by the givers, then taken and put in another spot by the receivers, then divided into smaller parts for the members of the receiving clans. The exchange rituals are considered intensifying rituals because they serve as occasional reminders of alliances and totemic divisions. Table 8 shows how the four exchange rituals differ in preparation length, duration, motive, time held, inferred ultimate goal, relation between principals, and frequency.

Table 8: Aspects of intensifying rituals[20]

RITUAL	*KƏJIƏ* (harvest ceremony)	*NIER* (exchange of food among cousins)	*NOKIAR* (pig exchange)	*NɨPE* (common dances)
PREPARATION LENGTH[21]	Entire harvest, but especially April	After harvest	3–4 months	Several weeks
DURATION OF MAIN CEREMONY	7 hours	2 days	18+ hours	8 hours

---

[20] These categories are based on Stanner (1966, 49).

[21] Preparation time includes learning songs and announcing the date and venue, but excludes gardening and purchasing of items.

EXPRESSED MOTIVE	Thanksgiving to the *tupunas*	"Life and respect"	"Dance the *nokiar* for a pig," license for carousing	Happiness/fun
DAYLIGHT/ NIGHTTIME	Daylight	Daylight	Night until daylight	Daylight and nighttime
INFERRED ULTIMATE GOAL	Magic, propitiation	Alliances and exchanges	Alliances and exchanges	Unclear
RELATION BETWEEN PRINCIPALS	Totemic or clan lines	Cousins	Flexible: intervillage or intertribal exchange partners	Whole village: men and women
FREQUENCY	March/April every year	25+ years	2–5 years	Several a year, April–November?

RITES OF PASSAGE

In addition to the exchange rituals, there is a second major category of rituals on Tanna: rites of passage. The islanders experience kastom on a regular basis in the rituals of marriage, birth, circumcision of boys, a girl's first menses, a boy's first shaving, and death. Each of these life-cycle rituals creates an opportunity for exchange.

> Life cycle exchange has a simple dualistic structure. The family of the
> person concerned presents pigs, kava, mats, baskets, bark skirts, blan-
> kets, lengths of imported cotton cloth, *nifar*, cooked and raw taros,
> yams, and other staple foods to the family of one of his mother's
> brothers, or the family of one of his wife's brothers. Sometime later,
> the exchange will be reversed, and the same kinds and numbers of
> goods will be returned. (Lindstrom 1990b, 35)

As I show throughout this chapter, the exchange remains lopsided or uneven. Since there is no bride price in the technical sense, Tannese men spend the rest of their lives restoring balance to the wife's family, from whom a highly valuable commodity (namely a labor-producing woman) has been removed. On a small island with such an obviously limited pool of resources, the removal of goods or people from a village must be substituted somehow to restore balance (Strathern, 1984).

Marriage

Ideally, a twenty-year-old boy will marry a cross-cousin (the classificatory mother's brother's daughter or father's sister's daughter) near his own age. Young men and women get some say in the matter, and invariably have more than one choice. In every case of arranged cross-cousin marriage that I observed, the young woman first refused and ran away from home. However, within months she returned and assented. I'm not sure if this is a culturally patterned case of "playing hard to get" or simply a handful of examples of young women who initially did not approve of their father's arrangements, but eventually gave in to the pressure.

When, exactly, the two are considered married, is fuzzy. First, the two are "promised" with a gift of kava and a *tamafa*. They later begin living together. Months later, the father of the groom holds a feast (literally, "he does a feast toward a person"), and gives scores of taros, manioc, and other crops, plus several pigs and perhaps a cow or two (all killed on the day of the feast) to the bride's parents. Male members of the groom's family stand and say something to the effect of: "Marriage is like a garden. We're planting a new garden today." That is as if to say, "We've begun a new family today." The bride's family returns the gifts with a prestation of scores of baskets and mats. Males from the bride's family make similar speeches, "This is the first of many feasts. This is life. This is goodness. These two need to live at peace with each other."

It is notable that this feast is held at the hamlet of the groom—not in the *imaram*. Marriage has stronger ties to the clan than to the village structure at large. However, later in the evening, at the *imaram*, the father of the bride hands the groom a tuber pudding placed on the leaves of a nukra tree. This symbolizes that the marriage has been sealed "in the leaves of *nukra*."

Church weddings utilize Western symbols such as a white bridal dress, rings, and a wedding cake.

The bride and groom cover their face with cloth at a traditional wedding feast.

During the prestation, the bride and groom have their faces covered with a cloth. The bride is then marched around the hamlet, wailing all the while. One explained, "She is wailing because she is sad to be leaving her father and mother." Another said, "No, she is wailing because she's afraid to get married." Whatever the reason, the wailing is part of the modern ritual. The couple is then seated in front of their new home, and they are unveiled, but they retain somber faces. Virtually everyone in attendance presents them with a small gift such as a bar of soap, a plate, a paring knife, or some cloth.

The kastom marriage ritual is not particularly objectionable to the Christian churches on Tanna, although typically the church would like to have the line between unmarried and married be made more clear, and would not permit the bride and groom to cohabit until after the feast. Further, the church typically would encourage the feast to be seen as a happy occasion, rather than a time to wail and put on a somber face. However, the most significant objection that the church has raised about kastom marriage is not the ritual itself, but the insistence on arranged marriage. Many churches prefer that their young men and women be allowed to choose a worshiping spouse (of the same denomination).

Birth Rituals

There are five small-scale rites of passage in the first year or so of life. These are (1) new-born hidden in a special house until the father makes a *tamafa* for the in-laws, (2) naming of the newborn, (3) fallen-umbilical-cord ceremony marking that the child may now go in public, (4) first-tooth ceremony, and (5) first-word ceremony. Each of these is a "growth payment" (Strathern, 1984) for the father to present kava and gifts to the in-laws, serving as payment for the bride who was removed from her clan. These are small-scale events, and are not as costly as the puberty rituals or weddings. I predict that the ceremonies around the fallen umbilical cord and first haircut have to do with anxiety about contagious magic. When body parts fall off a newborn, he is susceptible to the tricks of a sorcerer who may obtain the exuvia. To safeguard any maliciousness, the family holds a small ceremony and disposes of the "leavings" in order to ensure health and prosperity of the child. Since circumcision involves the intentional removal of a body part, as opposed to the tooth or umbilical cord which falls off naturally, it alleviates the same sorts of anxieties about sorcery. But the circumcision rite is more than a celebration or disposal of "leavings"; it is Tanna's "coming of age" rite of passage.

Circumcision

Circumcision is similar to an age-grade ritual, since all boys between the ages of five and eight are circumcised together. The night before the circumcision, the fathers "fill up the children's baskets." That is, they "carry a *tamafa*" for the children's health during the ceremony. The next morning the boys are led to the *imaram*, where a special house called "the house of the arrow" is erected as their dwelling for the liminal phase of the ritual, which lasts two to four months (long enough for the wounds to heal). Then they are circumcised. Traditionally, boys are circumcised with a piece of bamboo by a man who is known to specialize in this procedure. However, many villages are now asking someone from the hospital staff to perform the circumcision with a scalpel.

While the circumcisions are being performed, adolescents blow conch shells "so that the mothers will not hear the crying." Afterwards, herbs are placed on the wound, and a pandanus penis wrapper holds the leaves in place. The herbs are not particularly considered efficacious in aiding in the healing or management of pain, but rather to ensure that the boy will become a strong young man. In fact, the purpose of the entire ritual is to

Boys alternate blowing conch shells during a circumcision ritual.

Women gather to greet their boys at the agregation phase of the circumcision ritual.

ensure that boys will be strong. "If you don't circumcise Tannese boys, they will become lazy," one father told me. The partial circumcision is optional nowadays, but undergoing the circumcision rite is nonnegotiable.

Once the operations are over, the boys' penises are wrapped in boiled leaves to stop the bleeding. The leaf is fastened and remains in place for two days. On the third day, the boys each stand in a specially constructed stall where they are lathered in coconut extract called *tafa*, and the leaf bandages are changed. This is painful for the boys, so the adolescents blow conch shells to obfuscate the cries of pain. The melody has three movements. The first movement is produced by each shell producing a different tune, being blown in half notes. The second movement is the same tune, with quarter notes. The third movement is a series of whole-note blasts of all the shells in unison. This melody resounds throughout the mountain range, signaling to the women that they must stay away from the trail, as the boys will be heading to the river to rinse. Before heading down the trail, the boys exit the circumcision house backwards and are whipped gently with sticks or wild cane.

Once circumcised, boys may no longer touch food with their hands. This is true not only during the liminal period of hiding in the *imarəm*, but for the rest of their lives. Circumcised males on Tanna may not squeeze coconut pulp, strain kava (which would require touching it), or handle any food with their bare hands. Instead, the initiates handle their food with leaves. All leaves used for eating are stored and burned at the end of the liminal phase.

Boys sleep next to their sponsors, usually their fathers, in the *imarəm*. The foreskin is wrapped in a leaf and dangles on the thatch roof above their heads. At the end of the ritual, these packages will be burned along with the leaves that have been used to handle food. The entire ritual sleeping house will be burned as well, in a large bonfire, while all males look on and cheer for the boys who have finished the ritual.

The day after the boys bathe in coconuts is called a "cold thing"—nothing happens. Two days after the initial bathing, though, is a "hot thing"—another ceremony. The boys line up in their individual stalls and repeat the bathing in *tafa*, the conch shell blowing, and the walk to the river with the whipping along the way. Once again, in the evening, the fathers take a "small *tamafa*"—a repeat of what was done two days before—for the boys' health, and roast a chicken for the initiates and give kava to the families of their respective wives.

At each of the "big *tamafas*," the fathers of the circumcised boys give gifts of kava, tuber pudding, and two chickens to the in-laws. This makes the circumcision ritual the most expensive event in the lifetime of any family. Immediately upon marriage, a couple begins raising pigs for the eventual circumcision of their firstborn boy. It is preferable, if boys are born close enough in age, to circumcise two or even three boys at once to save on costs.

The bathing ritual, feast, and libation is repeated every other day. The only change is the style of bathing in coconut oil. After two sessions of bathing in *tafa*, the boys bathe in uncooked coconut extract, called "white coconut." The next two sessions will be "green coconut" extract, which is from a less mature coconut. On the last two sessions, the boys will bathe in ash of roasted coconut, called "black coconut." At this point, the libations and gifts of chickens and kava to the maternal uncles is completed. However, the boys continue to bathe in the river twice a day, every other day, for two or three more months, until their circumcision wound is healed.

During this entire liminal period, the boys may not see their mothers, nor any other female. This will help them become strong. Their return to their families is called the "body, or meaning, of the circumcision." Alternately, they say the "circumcision goes out." On the night before the "circumcision goes out," two bonfires are lit. One is constructed in the *imarəm*, where the men burn all the leaves that the boys have used for handling food during the liminal period. The women also light a large fire in the village, with *nases* leaves that they have previously picked and left out to dry. They refer to this fire as "burning the *nases*" or "burning the bad *monapitəg* (banana leaves)." There is festive dancing around the fire, and shouting and blowing of conch shells. As they dance, the women stamp out the fire. The women of the initiates are whipped lightly with the stems of banana or taro[22] leaves.

Then the men and women gather in the *imarəm* for all-night dancing by the light of a full moon, followed by a large feast in the morning. The boys construct tree houses in the banyans around the *imarəm* so they can see the dancing, but the dancers (including the mothers) cannot look up and see the boys throughout the night, who are taboo until morning. At daylight the dancing ends, and the boys leave the liminal phase and are reunited with their families for the feast.

The feast takes only a short time to consume, but the final prestation of foods and gifts lasts all day, suggesting that giving, and not eating, is the core of the "body of the circumcision" ceremony. The prestation goes not only to the maternal uncle, but to his entire fam-

---

[22] They use the stems of *napikao* (*Xanthosoma sagittifolium*; Bislama: *taro fiji*).

ily; therefore it is said that the gifts are given to the "roads"—that is, they will go back along the road by which the uncle and his family traveled. A pillar of sugarcane is erected in the *imarəm*, one for each receiving uncle, around which the other gifts are placed in a particular order. At the base is a mound of taro. Large amounts of a special tuber pudding cooked in bark called *napwək* (rather than leaves) is carried in on stretchers and placed above the taro mounds. Flattened mats and cloth are placed above the tuber pudding. Then rolled mats and baskets are tied together and placed at the top of the heap. The flattened mats are shared with family members, but the rolled ones are meant to go only to the uncle. Lastly, ceremonial kava (*topugə*) is placed near the sugarcane pillar. The receiving uncle will take the *topugə* first, signifying that he accepts the whole prestation.

The Christian church easily identifies with the act of circumcision. However, the two- to four-month kastom ritual has significant deviations from that of the Judeo-Christian tradition. Missionaries and indigenous church leaders find it difficult to determine how much of the ritual, beyond the actual act of circumcision, is desirable for Christians to per-petuate. Does kastom circumcision have connotations of a covenant? Is it helpful to per-petuate the magico-religious thinking that the ritual strengthens boys? Should boys leave their mothers for such a long period of time? Should the couples be expected to lavish so many resources on their in-laws? Does the focus on *tamafa*, the gifts, the bathing, take away from focus on their relationship with God and emphasis on their spiritual growth?

Female Puberty Rite

The female puberty rite is an ordeal of scarification which is mandatory for firstborn girls. One father explained, "If a girl did not go through this ordeal, she would be called a *yoyerin*." A *yoyerin* is actually a noncastrated animal, but in this case it is a rather pejorative term suggesting that the girl is not mature.

When Violet started her first menstruation cycle, her mother informed the paternal uncles and aunts, "We're going to give Violet 'bigness.'" "Bigness" also means a title—they will recognize her as a big woman, rather than a child.

The maternal aunts led Violet to a hut located outside of the village boundary where she would stay in isolation from her male relatives for two weeks. The first step is referred to as kamapiəg *kɨm* ɨn (she is grass-skirted). Her aunts had her wear a skirt made from the leaves of a *mənowitəg* tree and began an ordeal of cutting tattoos onto her back and arms. The tattoo cutter searched for a sharp bottle shard, and blew off the dust to get it clean. Her aunts pinned her firmly while one began cutting deep patterns. Violet winced and cried from the pain. "Don't let your voice be heard by your family in the village," her aunts told her.

Patterns are cut into the girls' backs in four horizontal lines: two on the left side of the spine and two on the right, plus one horizontal line at the waistline. Additional pat-terns are cut into the shoulders. Each pattern is symbolic. The four common patterns in South Tanna are (1) *jihi mənmav*, (2) *nɨhu* man (meaning "chicken's foot," and resem-bling a chicken foot as well), (3) *mɨtək mɨtək* (shaped like the letter V), and (4) *kiko iko* (crooked crooked).

A woman's ritual scarification.

After the scarification ordeal, Violet was bathed in coconut extract and led to the river to rinse. Her aunts whipped her gently with branches along the way. Every other day during the isolation period, this ritual of bathing in coconut extract and then rinsing in the river is repeated, hence the entire rite of passage is referred to as "doing her coconuts."

Once bathed, Violet was led back to the isolation house and fed. During the entire isolation period, she may not prepare food or touch it with her hands. In fact, she will observe the same food taboo during menstruation throughout her life—until menopause.

At kava time, Violet's father fed the paternal uncles a chicken for *nohunu* and provided kava for the *tamafa*. The entire rite of passage also serves as an exchange ceremony where the father repays his in-laws for his bride. He has received a valuable gift from the in-laws' village—that is, his wife—and with every rite of passage that his children pass through, he will repay the in-laws for that gift. It is said that during these rites of passage the father's *tamafa* goes to the in-laws. In this case, *tamafa* refers not only to the libation of kava but to the entire prestation of pigs and chickens that the father will give to them.

The second day of Violet's isolation was unceremonious. There was no *tamafa* and no bathing in coconut extract. But on the third day she took off her skirt made from *məniwitəg* leaves and was given another one, made of the same kind of leaves. She was bathed again in coconut extract and taken to the river to rinse off. Her father killed one chicken for *nohunu* in the *imarəm*, and another one for the females in the village. The males again "carried a *tamafa*" for the girl's well-being.

The fourth day was unceremonious, and on the fifth day Violet took off her grass skirt of *məniwitəg* leaves and was given a new skirt made of *nəvir* leaves. She bathed in coconut extract and was led to the river. Her father again took *tamafa* saying, "I'm taking *tamafa* for the *nəvir* leaves." The *tamafa* was not actually for the benefit of the leaves, but for Violet's well-being during the period while she is wearing the skirts made of those leaves. Her father again gave the same meals of chicken to his in-laws. The same ritual of changing skirts, bathing, and *tamafa* for the leaves was repeated two days later.

This pattern continued as Violet's aunts sewed new skirts made from *mənətuən* leaves and lastly from *mənpirpəs* leaves, to be worn for two days, and then another of the same type for two more days before changing types. The same gifts of chickens were offered, and her father took *tamafa* for the leaves. However, Violet's last two trips to the river did not involve bathing in coconut extract, rather in *nikien apɨg*—a charcoal powder made from roasted coconut. The ash was painted on her face and her still-healing wounds. (The ash ensures that the scarification will be more apparent.)

After two weeks, Violet had worn each of the required skirts in the right order, had bathed in each of the coconut oils, and the proper *tamafa*s had been taken. She was returned to her parents, and her father offered a final gift of two pigs to the in-laws, as well as kava, baskets, cloth, and tuber pudding. He made a speech where he indicated that the in-laws were free to eat the pudding and pork, but Violet's brothers could not—it was taboo for them.

As with the circumcision rite, the Christian church has had to grapple with the female puberty ritual. Is it right to cut girls in this way? Would dedicating the young women to the Lord be a functional substitute for the puberty ritual?

First Shave and First Kava

When a teenage boy has enough of a beard to be shaven for the first time, his father must provide another *tamafa* and gift of kava to the in-laws. It is a small-scale ceremony, but is still a nonnegotiable rite of passage in kastom.

Nasara summoned his in-laws from Yenfitana village to come observe Nasara Jr.'s first shave. He bought two large pigs and excavated some kava roots. The boy's maternal uncle shaved Nasara Jr., and everyone presented him with mats and calico. In the evening the uncle uttered the first *tamafa*, promising that some day he would reciprocate the gift. Reciprocation is possible because the uncle married one of Nasara Sr.'s sisters. When they have a boy old enough to be shaven, Nasara will come and receive some pigs of equal value, and will make his own *tamafa*, promising yet another exchange when the next generation of boys are born and ready to be circumcised.

The first-shave ritual also signals the time when young men may drink their first shell of kava. The ceremony is usually scheduled at a time when a young man's in-laws will be holding a circumcision ritual for his own boy(s)—along with the other boys of circumcision age in the village. It is held in concurrence with the circumcision because, like all other rituals on Tanna, it is an opportunity for exchange.

Kilion had two boys taking part in the circumcision ritual in Yanemilen in 2005. At about that time, Johnson had reached kava-drinking age—somewhere between twenty-two and twenty-five years old. Being Kilion's in-laws, Johnson and his family were receiving pigs and kava from Kilion at this time. Kilion's gift of the first kava to Johnson was an additional gift during this time to his in-laws.

Johnson arrived at the *imarəm* unaware that this was his special day. He saw a kava stump with the highest leaf of a banana tree fastened to it—the "eye of the banana" (which is also the term for a firstborn). This sign signaled to Johnson and everyone else in the *imarəm* that someone would be having their first kava. "Whose is it?" "It's yours, Johnson." Usually the kava drinking order is from oldest to youngest, but Johnson was given the right to drink first on this night.

Because of its link to kava and *tamafa*, even a seemingly "harmless" ritual like a boy's first shave or a girl's first menstruation present a challenge to Christianity. Could the coming-of-age rituals be maintained without the animistic implications of kava and *tamafa*?

Death Ritual

As with most non-Western cultures, the death ritual in Tanna is a public ceremony involving speeches, accusations of sorcery, and wailing that lasts for at least two weeks. And, as with all Melanesian rituals, it is an occasion for exchange. It also brings out the familiar basics of folk religion, including sacrifice, libations, fear of spirits, and taboos.

When Arlis died, people did not outright say so. They said, "Her breathing flew," or "She turned," or "She left us." Kilion explained, "We don't want people to feel bad, as they would certainly feel if you said, 'She died,' so we soften the blow with euphemisms."

The men carried Arlis' body to her hamlet and placed her in a house where the mourners began to smash out the back wall in order to make room for more mourners. In fact, by the end of the mourning period this structure, which I would call a "makeshift mourning house," has only posts and a roof. Gifts of baskets, kava, chickens (alive), and pigs (dead) arrived. They were not heaped up as would normally be done in a prestation such as a birth celebration or a marriage. Instead they were tossed randomly; in fact, they were thrown down in some cases.

The mourners arrived from villages further and further away. One man said, "Do you hear that wailing? It's coming from people up the mountain. They're coming here." I did not hear them, but did see them arrive about twenty minutes later. Arlis' dearest relatives yelled, "Mama! Beloved mama! Mama? Mama, you've left us!" They slapped each other and her. New arrivals also slapped one another. Later I asked Kilion if they were slapping out of grief or punishment. He said that those who slapped the family members were doing so to say essentially, "You idiot, if you'd taken better care of her, she wouldn't have died."

After four hours, six men began digging the grave. Each donned only a sheet at the waist, and each had a shovel. I have never seen six shovels in one place before on Tanna, nor six men dressed in such a "uniform." How were these gravediggers chosen? Was the cloth mandatory? What was their pay for digging the grave? What other responsibilities did they have? I'd get these answers the next day, when it was more tactful to ask. They dug in shifts, working five minutes or so in pairs, until the grave was about seven feet deep. The other four men gave directions. "Clean it up down there, patch that part. Straighter now."

They began to work on the horizontal chamber. Tannese do not lay the body directly in the pit. They dig a chamber along the length of the pit, where the body is to be placed.

That way, when the dirt is tossed into the grave, none will directly hit the body.[23] (Since there is no dirt directly above the body, in the next heavy rain, this porous soil, rich in volcanic ash, will collapse a bit.) Two gravediggers took wild cane and measured her body—length, height, and width, so the chamber would be proportioned correctly. "Did you measure her width from the shoulder or the waist?" "The waist." "Good." They measured twice, and dug once.

Elder Hiwa gave a one-minute speech about Jesus' death on the cross that saves us from the penalty for sin, opening the door for us to go to heaven at death, and he offered an even briefer prayer. Then her body was moved from the makeshift mourning house to the grave—a distance of about four yards—and was lowered and placed in the chamber.

About three hundred people proceeded to the grave. Her husband, Tom, made as if to jump in the grave with her, but two men held onto him slightly. He slightly tugged away as if to jump in the grave. But they spoke tenderly to him, "Dada, don't think about the dead. Think about the living. We're all still here. Don't leave us."

The gravediggers immediately and quickly pushed all the dirt back in. Two stood at the bottom of the pit. As each shovelful of dirt hit the bottom of the pit, they lifted up their feet and patted down the ground—thus raising themselves up another inch with each shovelful. With this manner, as the last bits of earth were shifted back into the pit, they had been elevated up to ground level, rather than having to climb out of a seven-foot grave before filling it.

The mound was made directly above the horizontal chamber where the body lay, and a wooden fence was constructed. (After a month the fence was completely destroyed, the mound was smoothed out, and there was no longer any visible gravesite.) Mourners took some pots and pans that Arlis used to cook with, smashed them, and tossed them onto the mound. This is in contrast to an inheritance—rather than passing things on as a memorial to the children, her goods were destroyed. Her old clothes were burned and placed in the grave area. "But I kept her pillow as a memorial," her husband told me, "and her children took some of her nicer things for their own, as a memorial."

The wailing continued well into the night. The men went to the sacred dancing place to have kava. A fire was constructed in the makeshift mourning house. "We'll stoke this fire every night until we complete the mourning," one woman explained to me. "Otherwise, this house would be cold." That is, Arlis' spirit would wonder why nobody was mourning her. The close family members would not leave the mourning house or its vicinity for the entire mourning period (about two weeks). They would not bathe, shave, nor sweep out the mourning house, nor even shake out the mats. "At the end of the mourning period, we'll clean out this house."

The next day Kilion explained that the six gravediggers represented six customary exchange "roads" or general directions. Two came from "on top"; that is, from the other side of the mountain range, where many spouse exchange partners are chosen. Two came from the coastal road, one came from the northern road, and one from the southern. These

---

[23] Interestingly, early missionary George Turner found a resemblance between this practice and that of the Assyrians in Ezekiel 32:23 (1861, 93).

representatives were given gifts of pig and kava, and they directed events throughout the rest of the mourning ritual for the next two weeks, until the large "stand-up feast" was held. Mourners must "sit" (refrain from work) until the "stand-up feast." Regarding the cloth that the gravediggers donned, Kilion explained that it is indeed a sort of uniform. I submit that this is a recent cultural accretion.

Like the other life-cycle rituals, the death ritual has posed challenges to Christian faith and practice. As this anecdote shows, churchgoers are incorporating some Christian practices such as grave-digging and the eulogy into animistic mourning rituals of wailing and warding off the deceased's ghost.

SUMMARY OF RITES OF PASSAGE

Rites of passage are more than mere celebrations like birthday parties or graduations in the West. They ensure health and proper growth. Additionally, they are the vehicle by which the groom pays back his bride's family for the gift of the wife. While the church has raised objections about aspects of each of these rituals, Tannese find it difficult to imagine abandoning these rites. Why relinquish something that ensures health, growth, and good ties with the in-laws?

Table 9 summarizes the rites of passage and their expressed and implied meanings. There are commonalities in each of the rites: Each has a liminal period, though the length of that period varies significantly. Each involves gift-giving to the bride's family. With each, the expressed motive is somewhat different than the inferred ultimate goal.

Table 9: Aspects of rites of passage

RITUAL	MARRIAGE	CIRCUM-CISION	FEMALE PUBERTY	FIRST SHAVE	DEATH
PREPA-RATION LENGTH[8]	1 year or so	5–8 years	Fairly spontaneous	Several weeks	Spontaneous
DURATION OF LIMINAL CEREMONY	1 day	2–4 months	15 days	1 day	2–4 weeks
EXPRESSED MOTIVE	"A new garden/life"	"Make the boys strong"	"Make the girls strong"	Happiness	Respect the family
INFERRED ULTIMATE GOAL	Exchange	Exchange, health	Exchange, health	Exchange, health	Keep the ghost at bay
RELATION BETWEEN PRINCIPALS	Husband's family gives gifts to the bride's family	Father gives gifts to the mother's family	Father gives gifts to the mother's family	Father gives gifts to the mother's family	Deceased's family gives gifts to the deceased's mother's family

---

[24] Preparation time includes learning songs and announcing the date and venue, but excludes gardening and purchasing of items.

SUMMARY: KASTOM ON TANNA

It should be clear by this point that kastom is more than superstition, as the nineteenth-century missionaries to Tanna described them. Nor is kastom a religious choice—one does not switch from kastom to Christianity the way one changes denominational affiliation. Kastom is not an activity compartmentalized to Sunday mornings and Wednesday nights; the *imarəm* is not simply another house of worship, and the ceremonies are not simply holidays. Kastom is something that, as I mentioned in the beginning of this chapter, Tannese believe they "cannot do without." It provides an epistemology, defines exchange partners, delineates boundaries in social relationships, reinforces social structure, explains origins, ensures healthy crops, explains the source of tragedies, empowers parents to teach ethics, transmits knowledge about healing, establishes sovereignty of land, and provides a way for settling disputes.

If by "heathenism" the early missionaries meant kastom, how did they plan to bring the Tannese out of heathenism? How can the Tannese reconcile the ecocentric nature of kastom with the Israel-centric nature of Judeo-Christianity? Could the Tannese imagine a world without kava, as Christendom would encourage them to do, without denying established patterns for reciprocity, homage of ancestors, and modeling of gender and age roles? How would the Tannese respond to the missionaries' urging them to leave their ancestral inland villages and gardens and take up residence on coastal mission stations, thus facilitating classes in literacy and religion? Could the Tannese imagine teaching ethics to the children without the myths? Would identifying with Adam as the first ancestor mean a denial of identity with the clan and totem? Can alliances be maintained without rituals of exchange such as the *nier* and *nokiar*? Christianity would raise a number of objections about kastom (see Table 10). The next chapter shows how Christendom has dealt with traditional religion over the past century and a half.

Table 10: Challenges to kastom by the early Christian church on Tanna

CHALLENGE	RATIONALE	DIFFICULTY PRESENTED
Myths discouraged	Considered false	Hearers were unfamiliar with the church's pedagogy, which was propositional rather than narrative
Nokiar, nakur, nier, rites of passage, and other exchanges discouraged	Considered licentious, linked with heathenism	"Worshipers" were perceived as unfaithful in fulfilling duties to in-laws

CHALLENGE	RATIONALE	DIFFICULTY PRESENTED
Encouraged to leave inland villages and live at the mission station	Facilitates teaching literacy and civilization	Kastom places provide identity (names are linked with place) and ensures property (gardens are linked with place, as is access to resources such as healing herbs and knowledge of myths)
Kava and *tamafa* discouraged	Considered a libation to ancestors/spirits	Totemic stones ensure health and prosperity
Tupunas (totems) discouraged	The Bible teaches that the first ancestors are Adam, Noah, etc., not totems	Denial of the totem was a denial of clan identity

PART 3

KASTOM AND CHRISTIANITY ON TANNA

T HUS far I have given a description and theoretical analysis of the traditional religion of the Tannese—that is, of kastom. I have described its ideology and shown
how it is manifested in everyday life. I ended the last chapter by intimating that if the missionary pioneers attempted simply to displace kastom with Christianity, they would not
only be unsuccessful, but would face harsh opposition. In Chapter 10, I attempt to reconstruct early missionaries' approaches toward animism, which would in turn shape Tannese
Christians' approaches. Although missionaries have produced less literature in the more
recent decades, I will attempt to bring the study into the present day to see how missiological approaches have affected present-day attitudes of Tannese Christians toward kastom.
Then, in subsequent chapters, I report on how Tannese Christians describe for themselves
their interaction with kastom. Tannese fall into two groups regarding this issue: kastom-
retainers and kastom-relinquishers. The marked differences in church life and worldview
between the two groups can teach us a number of important lessons about how to effectively contextualize the gospel for animistic background believers.

CHAPTER 10

Mission History and the Integration of Kastom and Christianity

THE various missiological approaches employed by early missionaries to Southern Vanuatu can be described using Friesen's (1996) five approaches that were characteristic of Protestant missions during the colonial era. Friesen shows that missiology at that time was informed by the anthropologists of the day (e.g., Müller and Tylor). It is notable that missionaries at that point were not privy to the economic model of Radin, the social model of Durkheim, or the structuralism of Levi-Strauss, who all came later. Instead their missiology reflected early anthropologists' understanding that animism is primitive religion, based on ontological and epistemological fallacies. Basically the missionaries saw animism as fetishism and, therefore, idolatry.

Based on missionary accounts at the beginning of the twentieth century (cf. Armstrong 1909; Callaway 1868; Fraser 1911, 1914; Nassau 1904; Warneck 1954) and the anthropologists who influenced them, Friesen found five paradigms that characterize Protestant responses to tribal religion during the colonial era: (1) displacement, (2) radical displacement, (3) moral reconstruction, (4) fulfillment, or (5) affiliation (Friesen, 1996, 18). Displacement vis-à-vis Warneck predicted that if tribal peoples converted to Christianity, they would leave behind their animistic worldview. Radical displacement vis-à-vis Armstrong saw animistic religions as a product of satanic influence—there was nothing worth keeping. The moral reconstruction model vis-à-vis Fraser emphasized civilizing or, to use a less volatile term, development, as a means for culture change. If missionaries could put an end to tribal wars and teach literacy, magico-religious thought would wane, and Christianity could take hold. Fraser believed that missionaries were called to "fix the broken lights" of tribal religion and to live exemplary lives (ibid., 115). "The new ethical standard of the missionary's life is the first and most startling doctrine he brings" (ibid., 117). Callaway's fulfillment model saw "religious sentiment" in tribal religions: a latent and sometimes vague notion of a creator God. Christianity is to be presented as the plenary fulfillment of these partially true religions (ibid., 66). The affiliation model vis-à-vis Nassau is similar to Callaway's model in that it presumes a sentiment of the Creator within all religions. Nassau saw all religions as degradations of Yahweh worship that need to be restored. Contrary to the cultural evolutionists (cf. Tylor, who believed religion evolved from animism to more complex religions and eventually monotheism), Nassau believed that religions began as systems for worshiping God, and subsequently either degraded or experienced accretions. Each of these five models were paradigms for Western Protestant missions at the turn of the century, and the missiology of the missionaries to Tanna can be described by these paradigms.

Table 11: Five twentieth-century missiological models

	DISPLACE-MENT	RADICAL DISPLACE-MENT	MORAL RECON-STRUCTION	FULFILL-MENT	AFFILIA-TION
MOTTO	"Lord of Lords"	All other religions are satanic religions	Light in the darkness	General revelation evident in tribal religions	Original monotheism; folk religions are corrupted but have vestiges of Yahweh worship
SPOKESMEN	Warneck	Origen, Armstrong	Fraser	Callaway, John Piper, Don Richardson	Nassau, Schmidt, Corduan
SUPPORT-ING VERSES	Deuteronomy 10:12–22	Isaiah 44:1–8; Romans 1:18–23	Psalm 67; Matthew 5:16	Isaiah 49:6; Acts 17:16–31; Romans 1:18–2:1	Psalm 22:27; 72:8–11; Acts 14:16,17

Because missionary accounts from the early years are usually autobiographical rather than missiological, it is somewhat difficult to assess the early missionaries' evangelistic methods, but there is enough information to discern some missiological trends. For each of the missionaries and mission periods, I will attempt to determine which of Friesen's approaches characterized the missionaries. Did they essentially perceive inherent value in traditional religion because of general revelation, and theorize that Christianity's specific revelation was a fulfillment of that knowledge? Or did they view traditional religion as a corrupt product of man or Satan, where Christianity must replace the traditional religion? And did they see civilization as a prerequisite for evangelization?

Vanuatu, whose motto is "In God we stand," may accurately be called a Christian nation. This is remarkable for a country that just over a hundred years ago was replete with reports of cannibalism and warring tribes (W. Watt 1895) that were virtually inaccessible, both linguistically and geographically. Today Vanuatu boasts numerous denominations, some theological training institutes, and a government that is sympathetic to Christianity.

Scottish Presbyterian missionaries brought the gospel to Tanna as early as 1842. However, in many of these coastal villages, animism and cargo cults are flourishing today while the church struggles. Mission work can be strategized, planned, and executed; expansion and renewal cannot. Expansion—and its corollary, recession—are dependent on many factors that are beyond any one person or agency's control. It is alluring to try to find a key redemptive analogy or missiological approach that led to a breakthrough on Tanna, but such a report cannot be given. Contrary to sensationalized reports (Green 2007; Rush 1997), there has been no widespread revival on Tanna similar to that which the Mouks in Papua New Guinea experienced, or that of the Sawi in Irian Jaya. Tanna has no Bruchko. Instead there has been a gradual chipping away at the strongholds of animism. The veneer of Christianity exists in many villages, but the animistic worldview is virtually universal.

As I have studied missions on Tanna, five distinct eras have become apparent: Martyrs, Pioneers, Maintainers, Recession, and Partners. (See Appendix B for an exhaustive list of long-term missionaries on Tanna and their respective eras.) Remarkably, these five eras resemble rather closely Whiteman's model of revitalization in Melanesia. Nida predicted that acculturation in Melanesia would follow five stages: (1) steady state, in precontact times; (2) reaction to challenge after contact; (3) defeat; (4) revitalization or absorption; and (5) a new steady state, or time of autonomy (Whiteman 1983, 274). As with churches on other islands in Melanesia, the church on Tanna was rejected in the early decades, was dealt a serious blow during a period of nationalistic pride, and has recently expanded and, to some extent, become enculturated.

CONTACT

Tannese are ethnically and linguistically Melanesians. Several millennia ago, their seafaring ancestors left the Malay Peninsula in canoes in search of new land. Perhaps a clan or two landed on Tanna somewhere in the fifth century BC[25] (R. J. Gregory 2003, 67), bringing pigs, chickens, dogs, taro, yams, and spinach to an otherwise "green desert" that was home to no land animals and very few edible plants (MacClancy 1980). Inhabitants flourished there, hidden from the outside world for centuries.

Sadly, the first one hundred years of European contact on Tanna involved less than reputable visitors. After Cook's discovery of Tanna and its glowing red volcano in 1774, Tannese had occasional contact with whalers, sandalwood traders, and "blackbirders" who tricked islanders into working multiple-year contracts on sugarcane plantations in Australia (Bonnemaison 1994, 39–42). The Tannese impression of Europeans was not favorable; white men were known to use alcohol, firearms, and deceit. They took, but did not give. They were a threat to the island.

CANNIBALS

Islanders were suspicious of Europeans, and in 1839 the first missionaries to the New Hebrides,[26] John Williams and James Harris, came face to face with islanders' mounting hostility. They stopped briefly at Tanna's Port Resolution where they placed three Samoan teachers—Lalolangi, Salamea, and Mose—to see how they would fare (J. G. Miller 1978, 33). If they were successful, they would later be joined by missionaries from the London

---

[25] This date is based on carbon dating; the scientist apparently had the audacity to round to the nearest ten years, giving a date of 420 BC.

[26] In order to avoid anachronism, I refer to the nation as New Hebrides in this historical section.

Missionary Society (LMS). Having commissioned the Samoans, Williams and Harris set out for Erromango,[27] twenty-five miles north of Tanna. They were martyred immediately upon landfall.

> Instantly, within a few minutes of their touching land, both were clubbed to death; and the savages proceeded to cook and feast upon their bodies. Thus were the New Hebrides baptized with the blood of martyrs; and Christ there-by told the whole Christian world that He claimed these Islands as His own. (J. Paton 1889, 123)

Paton was right; the martyrdom of Harris and Williams triggered an interest in missionary work in the South Pacific, beginning with George Turner and Henry Nisbet who arrived within a year of the martyrdom.

> By the following August, we were on board ship and off to the New Hebrides—a proof to these benighted savages of the forgiving spirit of Christianity, and of the unflinching determination of the friends of the Saviour to carry out his dying command, however much opposed by Satan and his heathen servants. (G. Turner 1861, 9)

Paton himself was inspired by Harris and Williams' martyrdom, arriving on Tanna nineteen years later. What Paton could not have known was that his own missionary work would become a far more significant impetus for worldwide interest in missions than the martyrdom at Erromango. Paton's influence for missions in the New Hebrides has lasted more than a century. Numerous books have been published about his work, championing the cause of Melanesian missions (A. M. B. n.d.; J. Allen [1905?]; Cromarty 1997; Lange 2005).

The three Samoan teachers commissioned by Williams and Harris enjoyed more success than the white men. They were eventually joined by two others: Pomare and Vaio-fanga. Salamea and Pomare fell ill, and within six weeks of their arrival died (J. G. Miller 1978, 33). The other three remained. Turner and Nisbet joined the Samoans in 1842, but after only seven months they feared that the incessant warfare became such a threat to their own lives that they fled with the Samoans. In 1845 Upokumano came from the Cook Islands, but fled to his homeland (Lange 2005, 249). The next year more Polynesian teachers came to carry on the work. One teacher, named Vasa, was martyred, and the others fled to Aneityum (J. G. Miller 1978, 36). Three other Polynesian teachers were sent between 1847 and 1850, who also eventually fled (G. Patterson 1864, 372).

We know a little about the missiological approach of the Samoans and Nisbet and Turner. We know from Nisbet's letters that the Samoans' mission focus was literacy, but they encountered "non-earnesty [sic] to acquire reading" and "little progress in evangelisa-tion" (Jersey 1978, 165). Langridge is fairly optimistic about their success: "Native [Sa-moan] teachers really prepared the minds of the people to receive the white Missionaries"

---

[27] Numerous spellings (or misspellings) of island names in Vanuatu abound. Here I have used the Bislama spelling for island names.

(1934, 40). From Nisbet's letters, it is evident that the success of their mission rested on the "willingness to hear the message and the desire of the chiefs to receive teachers" (Jersey 1978, 168). They were able to create an orthography, preach in the local language, and set up a printing press (G. Turner 1861, 11).

Adams records two apparent missiological approaches of the Samoans. First, they promised the Tannese at Port Resolution that "when they cast off their gods and worshiped Jehovah, white missionaries would come and live among them." Second, rather than teaching monotheism, they taught Jehovah as supreme over the other gods, (for they believed Jehovah to be over the Samoan deity Tagaloa) just as many today are inadvertently guilty of the heresy of henotheism; i.e., presenting God and Satan as if they are involved in a dualistic cosmic battle (Adams 1984, 53–55). This is the displacement model of Warneck, or the "competitive pluralism" of the Old Testament described by Corduan (see Chapter 2).

PIONEERS

The pioneers who achieved at least partial success were Scottish Presbyterian missionaries. Most of them were prolific enough writers to leave a trail of their missiological approach in letters (M. W. Paton 1894), reports, or autobiographies (F. Paton 1903; J. Paton 1889). What follows is a brief history of their methods.

John G. Paton resumed Turner and Nisbet's work at Port Resolution in 1858. He eventually learned the language, loved the people, and won a convert named Abraham. A small pamphlet from the Australian Mission Board records Paton's introductory comments: "My love to all you men of Tanna. Fear not; I am your friend; I love you and every one, and am come to tell you about Jehovah God, and good conduct such as pleases Him!" (A.M.B. n.d., 4).

Sadly, Paton's wife, Mary Ann Robson, and son Peter Robert, died within four months of their arrival on Tanna. And after four years of continual threats on his life, Paton feared martyrdom was at the door. He prayed for an escape, and the Lord sent a ship to rescue him. He left the island and eventually returned to the nation's only atoll, Aniwa, about twenty miles east of Tanna, where he worked for the next forty years and had a remarkably successful ministry to the handful of villages there.

Fortunately Paton gave us an idea of his missiological approach. He said that Tannese must understand

> the idea that man disobeyed God, and was a fallen and sinful crea-
> ture,—the idea that God, as a Father, so loved man that He sent His
> only Son Jesus to this earth to seek and to save him,—the idea that
> Jesus so lived and died and rose from the dead as to take away man's
> sin, and make it possible for men to return to God, and to be made
> into the very likeness of His Son Jesus,—and the idea that this Jesus
> will at death receive to the mansions of Glory every creature under
> heaven that loves and tries to follow Him. (J. Paton 1889, 121)

Paton also clearly taught that Tannese must "renounc[e] their heathen customs, getting rid of their idols and fetishes" (ibid., 125). For Paton, Christianity allowed little room for kastom.

> When we began to teach them that, in order to serve this Almighty and living Jehovah God, they must cast aside all their idols and leave off every heathen custom and vice, they rose in anger and cruelty against us, they persecuted every one that was friendly to the mission … It was the old battle of History; light had attacked darkness in its very stronghold, and it almost seemed for a season that the light would be finally eclipsed, and that God's day would never dawn on Tanna. (ibid., 122)

However, preaching in the local language was not enough to ensure successful communication of the gospel. Would these foreign theological concepts get across in the tribal language? Undoubtedly the Tannese found it difficult to understand many of these new fundamental concepts of Christianity through the lens of their own conceptual categories. Paton taught that God lives in *neai*, which means "heaven" but is also a village high on the mountain. Satan (*Tiapolo*) was, for better or worse, paralleled to their local deity Karpapeng. Speaking in the vernacular about the "Holy Spirit of God" made it seem like God had a disembodied spirit floating around. Using *yermaru* for God as a ruler simply seemed to make God out as a high chief (Adams 1984, 62–65). Of course Paton did not have any other choice. He was attempting to speak of Christian categories in a language that did not have the faculty to express those categories.

Despite the difficulty in communicating these unfamiliar concepts, Paton and his colleague on the neighboring island of Aneityum, John Geddie, had an evangelical faith, and they considered their main work to be proclamation which led to life change.

> However, for these early Protestant missionaries, the preaching of the gospel was a necessity to bring the people "out of the darkness and into the light" … Conversion to Christianity was measured by a rather dramatic change of culture—from their own traditional way of life to the culture and way of life represented by the missionaries. (Prior 2006b, 9)

The "dramatic change of culture" and the "way of life represented by the missionaries" would include the new concept of love of one's neighbor (rather than cannibalism, infanticide, and strangling widows), service instead of retribution, education, and clean health practices that could eradicate malaria, tuberculosis, and venereal disease. To this day, visitors to Vanuatu hear refreshing speeches of gratitude from the ni-Vanuatu regarding the way that the early missionaries raised their standard of life and brought them out of a cycle of tribal warfare. This is the moral reconstruction of Fraser.

Like Paton, John Geddie, who pioneered the missionary effort in the southern New Hebrides, saw coming out of heathenism as an essential part of coming into Christianity:

> In the midst of all our troubles we have much to encourage us. Super-
> stition is declining fast among the heathen themselves. In the district
> where I reside there has been a great destruction of sacred groves. The
> Christian natives are now cultivating these spots. The time is not far
> distant when all traces of the ancient worship will be lost. The sacred
> stones likewise which were worshiped as gods are despised by the na-
> tives. They may now be found strewed about in all directions, none
> caring for them, and none afraid of them. Offerings to *natmasses* [spir-
> its] have ceased in a great many places. Even the very heathen are
> ashamed to be seen in any act of worship. (in R. S. Miller 1975, 112)

Geddie, based on the island of Aneityum, required his teachers, including ones sent to Tanna, to agree with a creed regarding the true triune God, the Scripture, sinfulness, and propitiatory sacrifice (Adams 1984, 74). Like Paton, his missiological approach emphasized a radical displacement of the tribal religion. He stayed on Aneityum long enough to see the evangelization of the entire island. A wooden tablet in one of the churches there used to read: "When he landed in 1848, there were no Christians here, and when he left, in 1872, there were no heathens" (Steel 1880, 108).

Mary and John Matheson were on Tanna the same time as Paton, from 1858–1862. In a span of one year, the three Mathesons perished. Their daughter Minnie died in 1861 while they were still on Tanna (J. G. Miller 1981, 23). After Mary and John fled with Paton and the Samoan teachers, Mary fell ill and died March 11, 1862, on Aneityum at Geddie's house. John died June 14 of the same year in Mare, Loyalty Islands (Steel 1880, 168–69). We learn of Matheson's missiological strategy from his letters. Like the others, his strategy was to learn the language, set up schools, dispense medicine, teach practical skills like literacy and sewing, and to hold worship on Sundays (G. Patterson 1864, 383). He clearly taught that to become a Christian was to leave kastom. He reported, "There is no native yet who has abandoned heathenism . . . We often feel cast down, yet not discouraged hoping that brighter days may yet dawn upon Tanna, and that 'the time to favour her may soon arrive'" (ibid., 387). Their missiological approach involved radical displacement, but also community development, or Fraser's model of moral reconstruction.

Samuel Fulton Johnston and his wife, Elizabeth (O'Brien) Johntson, joined Paton on Tanna in 1860. Samuel died of fever in 1861 after an attack on his life (J. G. Miller 1981, 29) and Elizabeth escaped with Paton and the rest in 1862. Bishop Patterson records Johnston's missiological approach:

> Though my experience of heathen lands is only commencing, yet I
> have seen enough to make me realize in quite a new sense, the awful,
> the dismal darkness, the consummate degradation, and awful wretch-
> edness of heathenism. Such is Tanna! Poor Tanna! Long has she re-
> sisted the efforts which have been put forth to give her the light and
> blessing of the glorious gospel. Some have been driven from the field;
> others have suffered cruel death; others have fallen on the field; others
> have endured trials seldom equaled. Still they resist, still they refuse to

receive the gospel message, and threaten the destruction of all connected with this work. Shall all this loss of life, these sufferings, trials,
labours and prayers be lost? Surely not. Doubtless the happy harvest
will come, when the sheaves shall be gathered with great rejoicing.
But it still looks dark. (G. Patterson 1864, 244)

The "message" is a recurring theme among the pioneers. Their mandate was to present the Tannese with the gospel. It is clear from Johnston and the other pioneers that the
appropriate response to this message would be a withdrawal from kastom such as the radical displacement of Armstrong.

William Gray is a bridge between the era of Pioneers and Maintainers. He came to
Tanna in 1882 and began working in Waisisi Bay. Tanna had been without a missionary for
twenty years, and Miller records an anecdote about the state of Christianity after this long
hiatus. When Gray arrived, he noticed some Tannese men wearing shirts, albeit threadbare
ones. Upon inquiring about the shirts, they said it was part of their "worship." "How do
you worship?" Gray asked. "We put on our shirts, and we sit round with the young men,
and say we will not work . . . and we say: How happy we shall be when someone comes to
tell us about the Jehovah God!" Miller says, "The shirts lasted more than twenty years. The
mysterious *misi* was John Paton. His work had not been in vain" (J. G. Miller 1986, 261).

Ferguson (1918) records one of Gray's reports on his mission, in which he describes
extensively the building of a mission station. He compares the infrastructure of the mission to the skeleton of a bridge, and the planks on the bridge are the parts of the language:
the suffixes, prepositions, etc. (ibid., 9). To get across the bridge, he would have to put
the planks in place—i.e., to learn the vernacular. Critics of his mission asked him why he
did not just teach the natives English, and his response tells us a good deal about his missiological approach.

Our commission from Christ is to evangelise these people, not to
teach them the English language; to Chistianise them, not to Anglo-
Saxonise them! . . . There is such a thing as thinking in a particular
language; and before you could get a South Sea Islander to receive the
truth through the medium of the English language, you would have to
Anglo-Saxonise his habits of thought. In his own language, we have
the medium, we have the means of conveying to him any truth he, as
a human being, is capable of receiving. I would go further than this
and say that, except through the native language, it is impossible to
convey to these people at once such truths as Christianity embodies
. . . Everyone knows that people are most powerfully influenced by
truth spoken in their own language. (ibid., 11–12)

Gray's mandate was to learn the language and communicate a message—a truth encounter. He made the distinction between a "heathen" and a "savage." The Chinese were
heathen, he said, but civilized. Missionaries need not concern themselves whether a people group is savage or civilized; they are to evangelize the heathen. "Our object is to Chris-

tianise them; the civilising of them will take care of itself" (ibid., 12). Because Gray was so careful to dignify the culture, while emphasizing conversion, perhaps it is accurate to say that he was more in line with Warneck's displacement model than Armstrong's model of radical displacement. Sadly, he saw little fruit. "The Grays, after twelve and a half years at Weasisi,[28] without any baptisms, returned to South Australia" (J. G. Miller 1986, 264). The MacMillans (see below) soon picked up work in their region.

MAINTAINERS

The era I call "Maintainers" began at the turn of the twentieth century. For the most part, the maintainers were able to remain on Tanna much longer than the pioneers did, and they enjoyed a boom in church attendance (and perhaps even in conversions). It is difficult to determine what factors led to the change in popular attitude toward the church, but it can be no coincidence that the church expanded precisely during the decades that Christianity was becoming the state religion in the New Hebrides. Tanna was administered in these decades by the British and French. While the resident commissioners may not have been personally sympathetic to the Christian cause, Christianity certainly had political legitimacy (Lindstrom 1981, 198). Constantine's principle remains true: Christianity does well when the state greases the skids.

Thirty-two years after John G. Paton was run off of Tanna at Port Resolution, his son Frank, having been raised in the southern New Hebrides, took up residence on the other side of Tanna, in Lenakel. Frank Paton's primary concern was conversion of the natives, as evidenced by natives giving up kava, heathen dances, and *netik* (magic) or discussions about *netik*. He joined preaching with caring for the sick, translating hymns, showing gospel pictures, Bible translation, raising up elders and deacons, clothing the heathen, ringing bells for worship, having natives live in settlements, establishing outstations, and preparing candidates for church membership (cf. F. Paton 1903). In other words, Frank Paton understood the Gutenberg principle: The church expands when information flows freely. Whereas kastom natives lived in sparsely populated mountain villages, the Christians were encouraged to live on coastal settlements where education could be more regular. These are examples of attempts at both displacement and moral reconstruction.

Dr. J. Campbell Nicholson was at Lenakel from 1903 until he left to serve in the war in 1917. His letters to his mother have been recently published (Mayne 2006). He was a medical missionary and was responsible for opening Lenakel hospital, which operates to this day. His missiological strategy was a power encounter of sorts. "Dr. Nicholson's first work was to build a small hospital to demonstrate that the superstitions of the witch doctors were of no avail against the skill and medicine of the white doctor" (Langridge 1934, 132). In other words, by healing with Western medicine, he was not directly showing that the power of God is supreme over the power of shamans, but he intended to show that the ancient wisdom of kastom was perhaps questionable in light of the missionary's apparently superior knowledge. Nicholson was one of twelve doctors, serving a cumulative total of

---

[28] The old spelling is maintained because this is a quote.

128 years, who were sent by the Presbyterian Church to the New Hebrides between 1883 and 1920.

Medical work was not Nicholson's only missiological strategy. He taught the 107 questions of the shorter catechism (in the vernacular) to the congregation in Lenakel "and several did not make a single mistake" (J. G. Miller 1986, 389). He was joined by Mr. and Mrs. Charles Christian, from Norfolk Island, in 1912. The Christians stayed three years. A letter from Mr. Christian indicates the Tannese needed to have a communion "token" in order to go to the Lord's table (ibid., 392). Unfortunately, we are not sure what the criteria were for receiving the token.

Though he was not trained in medicine, J. Campbell Rae took over the work in Lenakel from 1918–1922, largely expanding on the foundation that Frank Paton and Dr. Nicholson laid. His work was to strengthen the church. Miller says Rae was responsible for introducing the ideas of Christian holidays to Tanna (ibid., 403). The church held political sway, and Rae thought the Tannese should observe its holidays. We see in Nicholson, the Christians, and Rae an establishment of Christianity as a culture that is separate from kastom, with its own holidays and rules.

William Watt lived forty-one years amidst the coconuts on the wave-beaten southern coast of Tanna between 1869 and 1910. His first wife, Agnes, died in 1894 and left a descriptive diary that included both ethnographic notes and information about their mission. (Later Watt married Jessie Paterson.) We get a good picture of the Watts' missiological approach from Agnes' letters. She traces her and her husband's interest in missions to "the great revival that swept over Scotland in 1850" (A. Watt 1896, 19). A revival in the old Hebrides had, in the same generation, an impact on the spiritual awakening in the New Hebrides.

Unlike the non-anthropologically-minded traders that visited Tanna, the Watts were concerned with learning the culturally proper way to do things on Tanna, such as exchanging goods for help (ibid., 88). They took careful ethnographic notes regarding indigenous houses, myths, polygamy, use of magic and totems, and the meaning and preparation of kava (ibid., 105–9). They were motivated to learn the Kwamera (South Tanna) language as quickly as possible. However, Watt ran into the same problem as Paton—even though he was linguistically apt, he could not find the right vocabulary to accurately teach doctrine; if Tannese were going to hear the message in their language, they would need to fit it into their conceptual framework.

While the Watts did not understate the primitive condition on Tanna, they esteemed the nationals as having the same potential as any other race for coming to repentance and a knowledge of God. Most remarkably, they were not content simply to put clothes on the natives and have them attend worship. They desired evidence of true conversion, and found this evidence elusive. The Aneityumese, upon conversion, burned their kava, and the Watts wondered whether the Tannese would ever follow suit. Kava is used for communication with ancestral spirits, and the Watts saw this practice as incompatible with Christianity. Therefore, Watt would not baptize kava drinkers (J. G. Miller 1981, 44). The early missionaries were looking for a clean break from kastom.

At one point, Agnes and William visited the grave of the Mathesons' daughter who was lost on Tanna several years before. Agnes wondered in a letter whether the missionary effort, after costing so much in human lives, would ever see fruit.

> Yet they are immortal, they have souls to be saved; they are degraded, it is true, but Jesus can save unto the uttermost . . . Many have died during those eight years and those upon whom their highest hopes were set have as yet manifested no desire for instruction. I feel sad when I think how long [the Mathesons] laboured, and yet so little sign of permanent success. Perhaps we may have to do the same. (A. Watt 1896, 91)

During his time on Tanna, Watt translated numerous hymns and the New Testament into the Kwamera (Nɘfe) language. Ferguson (1918) has compiled a bibliography of scores of pamphlets produced by Watt, et. al., which were published by the Mission Press.

Rev. Gillies and his wife were at Port Resolution and Kwamera for three years, from 1898–1901. They saw a number of people baptized and "admitted to the Lord's table," which apparently were marks of conversion. Gillies wrote, "Several of the Kwamera people, unable to make the final decision, have yet been of great service, going regularly to the outlying districts to hold services" (J. G. Miller 1986, 272). Unfortunately, we cannot be certain if what he meant by the "final decision" was a decision to be baptized, to leave kastom, to pray the "sinner's prayer," or something else. Nevertheless, conversion is clearly emphasized here over merely identification with the church community, and Gillies was probably endeavoring to displace kastom with Christianity.

Thomson MacMillan initially came to Waisisi in 1896, and again with his wife in 1900. Like the Watts, he had a remarkably long career in Tanna, lasting thirty-six years. MacMillan's missiological approach is evident in his catechism in the Whitesands language. He intersperses salvation by faith with obeying the Law, including the Sabbath (MacMillan n.d.).

It was in MacMillan, Watt, and Nicholson's day that Christianity saw what Langridge calls the "conquest" of cannibal Tanna, effected by the translation of Scriptures, ending of polygamy and warfare, making the roads safe, and encouraging civilization, trade, and interisland travel (1934, 166–167). These are perhaps indicators of a cultural or political shift toward Christianity, but to the early missionaries, the indication that Tannese were converting was their removal from kastom. "Times of Pentecost were brought to mind when converts delivered up idols that they had for generations regarded as sacred, and proclaimed themselves servants of God" (ibid., 149).

Little is known of Holton Forlong's ministry on Tanna from 1894–1900; he was an early tentmaker. "There he came to the conclusion that he would be able to get to the hearts of the Tanna people best by being a Christian trader, and we gather that the Watts encouraged him in that approach" (J. G. Miller 1981, 41). Forlong worked in North Tanna and saw converts and appointed elders. He eventually moved to Malekula, serving a total of fifteen years in the New Hebrides in "self-supporting missionary evangelism," and he influenced at least eight others to do the same (J. G. Miller 1986, 307). This model closely resembles Fraser's moral reconstruction.

ROMAN CATHOLICS

After sixty years of Presbyterian missions on Tanna, the Roman Catholics arrived. They chose the beautiful coastal spots for their missions. Father Durand did reconnaissance to determine where the first mission would be built; it was constructed at Lowanatum in 1925 (R. J. Gregory 2003, 70). In 1932 a house was built for a bishop, and the first mass was celebrated on May 26, 1933, with Father Durand and Pierre of Baie-Barrier (Monnier, 1988, 137). Father Pierre Bochu was the first missionary; the catechist was Pierre Batik. Bochu said, "Short of divine intervention, the conversion of the Tannese will be a long and exacting task" (ibid.). Being on less than agreeable terms with the Protestant missionaries, the fathers' idea of conversion was different from the evangelical idea.

Father Martin spent seventeen years on Tanna. He "left behind him only a handful of baptized Catholics but the seeds had been sown" (ibid., 138). By 1987 there were 1,328 Catholics out of a population of 17,600, with stations in Imaki, Ipekel, Loono, Lautapuga, Lamlu, Imaru, Lonelapen, Loanatom, Lenakel, Isangel, Ikiti, Green Point, Yanavateng, and Yapkapen (ibid., 137–38). The Ikiti church has remained since at least 1968,[29] and is the longest standing church in the Southwest Tanna language group (all other churches in the language group were rendered defunct between 1950–1990 due to the John Frum cult). Catholics have not enjoyed rapid expansion in Vanuatu like the Protestant groups have, but they have had a steady presence.

The missals are printed in French and sent over from New Caledonia, just 230 miles to the south. Mass, rather than preaching, is central to the service. Other than the Mass, there are few symbols: there are no icons; saints and Mary play a minimal part in the Catholic theology in Vanuatu. Conversion is marked not as much by a statement of faith as by receiving the sacraments. In Catholic missiology, the *character indelibilis* of baptism is salvific, even if the baptized is ignorant of doctrine or if he backslides (Bosch 1991, 219). Therefore, proclamation is not the primary means for evangelism. Love encounters through community development are the primary Roman Catholic evangelistic methodology. They establish schools and agricultural schemes such as copra plantations (Bonnemaison 1994, 76). Trade centers and hospitals are part of the missionary compound. Faith is joined with good works and community development. This is the moral reconstruction model of Fraser.

TANNA LAW

At some point in the early life of the church on Tanna, nationals, or missionaries, or both, got the idea that church rules, rather than faith, were paramount. Ecclesiastical laws were zealously enforced. Even nonworshipers were required to comply with church rules. Today Tannese remember this era as "Tanna Law" (Guiart 1956, 130–45). Historians are not sure who was more responsible for the system of Tanna Law: the missionaries or the national believers. Calvert, a Presbyterian missionary on Tanna from 1967–1979, reckons the missionaries and the Tannese are both responsible. The missionaries created a political

---

[29] According to the catechist in Ikiti.

environment where chiefs had unusual power, but the worshipers conceived the notion of such harsh prohibitions. MacMillan and Nicholson, not understanding the limited nature of "big men" on Tanna, set up two Polynesian-style paramount chiefs

> in a situation where chiefs were not part of the cultural pattern. These Chiefs, taken from the coastal tribes of the east and west sides of the island of Tanna and given the background authority of European influence rapidly built up an integral legal system known as Tanna law. (Calvert 1978, 212)

In the heyday of Tanna Law—the early twentieth century—ceremonial dances and polygamy were banned. Kava was outlawed, but secret trails were cut for the smuggling of kava from village to village (cf. R. J. Gregory, Gregory, and Peck 1981; Lindstrom 1990a). Work was banned on the Sabbath, including feeding pigs (Bonnemaison 1994, 201). Offenders were brought to court and jailed. Dogma had become law; Christianity had become Christendom.

Brunton argues that Tanna Law was not as much a construct of the LMS or of MacMillan and Nicholson, but a result of the Tannese worldview (1989, 117). Legalistic rules fit well into their religious system, so did prophetic inspiration. Frank Paton's champion convert, Lomai, had a dream in which he got sick from drinking kava, and subsequently began speaking against kava and the transport of kava on LMS ships (ibid., 114–15). If the missionaries were partly responsible for Tanna Law, local believers certainly encouraged it.

However, MacMillan was probably not endeavoring to institute a rigid system of laws; he was experimenting with Fraser's moral reconstruction. Calvert gives a picture of how MacMillan hoped civilization would make Tannese open to the gospel:

> He encouraged feasts and customs which he thought preserved tribal alliances, although no important tradition of feast and custom existed. He banned the prostitution system, and with Nicholson ... he improved standards of health. He used his influence to allow in only traders of good moral standing, and he alienated French interests by surrounding land-grabbing plantation owners and traders with a barrier of registered land held in trust by the Presbyterian Mission. He and his earlier colleagues translated and upgraded the three major local languages and tried to turn one of them [Whitesands] into a lingua franca. He translated the Bible and hymnbooks, and refused to teach English in the well-organized school system he set up. (Calvert 1978, 213)

However, MacMillan's plan backfired, according to Calvert. MacMillan tried to implement an ideological notion of a Melanesian paradise, and the Tannese became suspicious of his paternalism. "What was supposed to be an island paradise became a paternalistic prison with no key to the outside world. MacMillan held it all together, but cracks appeared in the system" (ibid.). Instead of protecting the Tannese church, they thought he was alienating them. They began to consider Catholicism and newer sects such as the

SDA church, but the majority of Tannese believed they had found freedom in the John Frum cargo cult.

RECESSION AND ENCULTURATION OF THE CHURCH

The mid-twentieth century marks a time of recession of Christianity on Tanna. In 1939 a census had counted 4,109 Christians on Tanna (71 percent of the population). On the "fateful Sunday" of May 11, 1941, only eight people attended Presbyterian church services (ibid.). By 1942, "less than a hundred Christians remained, the other Islanders being either undecided or enthusiastic advocates of John Frum" (Bonnemaison 1994, 225). This marked a 98 percent drop in numbers for the Christian church—a devastating blow.

Many Tannese identified with the John Frum cargo cult because it promised a new economy of money without work. A road would magically join America and Tanna, and cargo would begin to flow in. White ships bearing guitars, trucks, and especially ice boxes would come to shore (Jebens 2004, 20). John Frum, the son of the Tannese god Karpapeng, would return and usher in a millenarian age of health and prosperity. People would shed their skin and be young again, there would be no sickness or drought, and gardens would mature without work.

By 1950, 40 percent of the island still identified with the John Frum cult, and many more were Frumers secretly (Bonnemaison 1994, 235). In line with Latourette's theory that Christianity expands and recedes with the political and social tides (Walls 2002, 27–34), the church on Tanna experienced one of the most significant recessions of Christian history proportionately. It took four decades for the church to begin to recover. It has been said that we are only one generation from atheism: all we have to do is neglect to tell our children. The Tannese church did essentially that: the generation of WWII deliberately silenced the voice of the church. It took more than fifty years for some villages to begin considering Christianity again. Here is Kilion's story about how his village dissolved the church and replanted it half a century later in his village:

> Once, well, ancestor Wako began worshiping in like 1947. He worshiped, and so on, and then, like, John [Frum] appeared up above [Green Point]; [so] the [church] house was empty. They'd all left. They went and all dispersed entirely. He'd strike the bell, [but] there wasn't a single person listening to it, that he would see worshiping with him inside. So he cried.
>
> Therefore, like, he took some kava and a pig, and had it represent the church. He took it and sent the church off toward the coast, in the hands of Daniel Keasi and ancestor Nakahu. So, we went on and went on and we're here, and the church has disappeared. The fathers didn't worship. We lived like that continually until we came to the year 2001. And I reckoned that whatever the ancestors had, or did [got rid of the church], we must bring it back.
>
> Therefore, I summoned the church to come. Along with deacon Kai,

we lived and went on, but some chiefs only paid attention to the ceremonial pig that ancestor Wako killed, forbidding the church. Like, his prohibition was still [in effect]. [So] many of them didn't come to church. They simply thought about the pig and the kava.

And we went on to the time when Eliud [the church planter] came and we lived with him. He stayed until 2003. Eliud returned. He left us and returned [to his hometown] and many people still talked about the pig. When it was time to worship, well, people were afraid of ancestor Wako's prohibition of the church through the ceremonial pig and kava.

Then I figured that I'd undo the kava and pig. Or I'll take out the speech about it. Therefore, I figured I must take away the talk of the ancestors. And that's what I did on last Saturday. Kai took a pig, and my uncle Karmi took kava [and] I took kava. And we summoned people in the Presbyterian Session—starting in Isaka, then to Yelkenu, then to Samaria. They came on Saturday and I took away the pig and the kava. I took away the talk of ancestor Wako which he'd set down beforehand, sending the church out of the mountains. Now I've taken it away.

Before, the prohibition of the church stood on the kava and pig, but now I've taken away the talk of like ancestor Wako. Now the church is [rooted] deeply and stands on the ground, deep; the roots hit the bedrock.

And now, and tomorrow, the day after tomorrow, the people who don't worship must come and worship, never ceasing. They must come and worship. Therefore, that's the talk which I set down on last Saturday.

Kilion's narrative addresses the recession of the church due to the John Frum cargo cult and shows how at least one village has been innovative in reclaiming the church. Kilion and his peers found a way to embrace the church without blatantly disrespecting the previous generation that forbade it. The village's reclamation of the church incorporated indigenous symbols of covenant (a pig and kava gift to the *imarəm*) with new Christian meanings.

It was in these decades of enculturation that the Presbyterian Church became a national, rather than foreign, institution. The Presbyterian Church of Vanuatu (PCV) established its own seminaries and budget, and ordained its own leaders. This indigenization is a sign of true missionary success; the baton was passed by the expatriates to the local church. However, as the church became enculturated, approaches toward kastom and conversion changed. Going to church was emphasized, but little was said about the clash between Christ and culture. National Presbyterian Church leaders ceased emphasizing a break from kastom (cf. Barker 1990, 28). Animism and churchgoing became compatible de facto, though it was not explicitly stated. Lindstrom says, "Even Christians have revalued positively traditional magical knowledge" (Lindstrom 1990b, 49). There was a return to kastom—not a full-fledged revival like that which cargo cults instigated in the mid-twentieth century, but an attitude of permissiveness that is characteristic of a pluralistic society.

The expatriate missiological strategy of the missionaries continued to be that of Fraser's moral reconstruction. They avoided direct confrontation of kastom, relaxed their rules on kava drinking and dancing, and focused on community development. They installed water supplies in villages and focused on their schools and economic development (Calvert 1978).

While the church was relaxing its stance on traditional religion, Tannese steeped in kastom were also making traditional religion more popular and accessible. They allowed ceremonial kava, topuga, to be drunk by anyone, thus using special kava as an incentive to gain more kava drinkers. They also began drinking a less formal daylight kava, kwatini (small one), thus permitting churchgoers to have kava in the day and attend church in the evening (Brunton 1989, 119). "Pagans" had to ease restrictions on power and prohibitions of kava in order to make it more accessible; and in the process, they made it more accessible to Christians (ibid., 127–28).

Expatriate Presbyterian missionaries maintained a presence, but more as servants. Ken and Anne Calvert joined their church leadership responsibilities with community development projects on Tanna from 1967 to 1979—in the thick of nationwide struggles for independence. Calvert says one of their goals was to make people's lives easier by giving them knowledge for processing copra, operating sawmills, driving trucks, growing crops commercially, and later, growing coffee. Like the pioneers and maintainers of previous decades, they encouraged Christian converts to make a break from animism, while maintaining the positive sides of the culture, but they did not overtly set policy. The indigenous church leaders had "big men" status, and they tended to be more permissive of kastom (pers. comm., March 20, 2008).

Concerned with helping the PCV become truly indigenous, Australian pastor Randall Prior has been encouraging national church leaders to become self-theologizing and to publish their work—or at least to articulate themes of the gospel in terms of their cultural heritage. Presbyterian pastors have attended work groups and written essays to address kastom cosmology, the use of language, and conversion (Prior 2003). Elsewhere, a national church leader published an essay on Jesus as the great chief, the defender and helper, who cares for the poor (Prior 2005, 42). Recently, Prior has encouraged the church to give voice to women leaders (2006a).

Self-theologizing will become more important in the future as the prosperity gospel floods the islands of Vanuatu, along with numerous cults, secularism, and world religions such as Islam. Each of these sects will take on their own indigenous flavor, and the Christian churches must work out their particular response to these sects.

EMERGENCE OF SECTS AND DENOMINATIONS

By the 1980s, long-established Presbyterian churches had recovered substantially from their recession, and new denominations began to spring up. What dynamics led to a renewed interest in Christianity? Three factors are likely:

1. The promised cargo of John Frum did not come; the cult did not deliver the goods. Tannese lost interest in the cargo cult and began to be interested in Christianity again.

2. More Tannese received education and traveled to the capital city. They understood the world better than their parents; they understood the genuine (rather than imagined) benefits, both spiritual and material, of Christianity.

3. Well-established churches from other islands became self-propagating and exported themselves to Tanna relying on ni-Vanuatu leadership and theology.

The SDA church is a good example of a sect that gained popularity because of these three factors. It was established without a resident foreign missionary as early as the 1940s (Hook, n.d., 23; cf. Bonnemaison 1994, 77). Perhaps the establishment of SDA churches was possible because of the mobility of young men who traveled from Tanna to the capital city, Port Vila, on Efate Island. Perhaps young men lived for a time with their cousins and brothers in Port Vila, while performing menial labor. There they converted to the SDA church, and they eventually returned to Tanna with their newly acquired saucepans, mattresses, machetes, and the SDA faith. Occasionally they persuaded enough of their clan members to allow an SDA church to be built, and at times ni-Vanuatu SDA members came from other areas to help establish the church.

Brunton suggests that the success of the SDA church is due, at least in part, to its emphasis on legalism. The Catholic church, with its casual attitude toward traditional religion, experienced very little growth, while the SDA church grew to 10 percent of the island's population (1989, 120). People from animistic backgrounds expect religion to be about rules, and the SDA church lived up to that expectation. It is also likely that the millenarianism in the SDA church was a good match with the Tannese worldview. Melanesians have apocalyptic expectations. Their folklore anticipates the return of the golden ages, when the old will shed their skin, gardens will flourish, and sickness will be no more.

In the past few decades numerous denominations, especially Pentecostal ones, have sprung up on Tanna in exactly the same way that the SDA church did seventy years earlier. Assemblies of God (AG), Foursquare churches, Neil Thomas Ministries (NTM), Upper Room, Apostolic, and independent Pentecostal churches have been established with little intervention from expatriates on the island. It is interesting that the newer denominations did not experience the same life cycle (Martyrs, Pioneers, Maintainers, Recession, Enculturation) that the older denominations experienced. Perhaps the more than one hundred years of contact that preceded the arrival of these denominations prepared their way. A Melanesian metaphor would say that the earlier churches "broke bush" for the later ones. Within twenty years, the newer denominations were experiencing a "decade of harvest" (Larson 1997, 400).

One of these harvesters was the AG church. The AG came to Tanna through a mixture of indigenous multiplication and short-term expatriate evangelism campaigns. Ron Killingbeck was stationed in New Caledonia in the sixties, where he became acquainted with a ni-Vanuatu community. Several ni-Vanuatu, including AG pastors Obed and Wili Nais, became believers and brought the AG church back with them to their islands in Vanuatu. In 1968–1969 Killingbeck held "good news crusades" in a number of John Frum villages on Tanna. His missiological method was to hold revival meetings where he would preach the gospel through an interpreter and make an invitation for people to be born again.

> For these people it would be a night of decision. Would they accept Christ or continue on in heathenism and spiritual darkness? . . . We share the simple gospel of Christ with them. The rewards are tremendous as you see men and women who were bound by superstition and fear changed by the power of Christ. (Killingbeck 1978, 22–23)

Killingbeck reports that Chief Laufa in Launipiktuan prayed the sinner's prayer. "When the chief comes to Christ, it opens the door to the village . . . Today every member of this village has received Christ as Savior" (ibid., 29–30).

Emphasis was given to the point of decision, but coming out of animism was also stressed. In order to ensure long-term viability of the churches, Fijian missionary Seru Naiviqu came to Tanna to pioneer an AG church. In 1969 Fijian missionary Kiniviliame (Vili) Railau and his wife, Melaia, came to Tanna and remained for several years to offer more in-depth discipleship training and enjoyed "phenomenal" success (Larson 1997, 372) as they witnessed to the John Frumers (ibid., 380) and observed people "receive the Baptism in the Holy Spirit" (ibid., 390). "The field was ripe and being harvested" as people

AG church members at a baptism ca. 1969.

made "decisions for the Lord" (ibid., 392). What was still lacking, however, was local train-ing for pastors. If they were to be educated in the AG, they would go to Fiji. Tom Ironga was trained in Fiji and returned to Tanna to pastor (Killingbeck 1978, 50). Later, Joy Bible Institute was established in Port Vila to train AG pastors.

RECENT MISSIONARY EFFORTS AMONG
THE CARGO CULTS

Despite the enculturation of the established church and the emergence of new denomina-tions, the John Frum cargo cult continues to be a vital religious community on Tanna. Ev-ery Friday islanders who identify with the movement celebrate their taboo day. Adherents sing songs about cargo that will soon come from America, perform séances, and speak their orders of cargo into flowers that symbolize telephone links to Honolulu. The number of John Frum adherents has drastically dwindled since its heyday in the 1940s. Only a couple hundred people identify with the current John Frum prophet Isak Wan,[30] in Ipuekel village. However, the cargo-cult ideology (i.e., maintenance of kastom, political indepen-dence, and magico-religious thinking) is still pervasive, if not islandwide.

Fred Nasei, one of Isak Wan's followers, went on to found his own nativistic move-ment. While he was fulfilling a contract on a fishing boat in 1999, he had a vision: He would be the one who would combine John Frum and Christianity. If he didn't hurry back to Tanna to start his movement, there would be a catastrophic volcanic eruption. Claim-ing to be the one who will unite kastom and church legitimates someone as a prophet on Tanna. But further evidence of Fred's qualifications as a prophet came when Lake Isiwi's bank gave way and the water emptied into the sea in 2000. He claimed that he had proph-esied this catastrophe beforehand. A supernatural event, plus a sense of call, showed he was the legitimate leader of the John Frum movement.

Because of Fred's strong personality and sense of purpose, he could not remain in Isak Wan's shadow. He brought thousands of John Frumers with him to nearby Yenkahi, where they built a large settlement and started their own movement called "John Frum, Christ, Unity." Unlike the John Frum movement, which is an affront to the church as a representa-tive of colonial rule, "John Frum, Christ, Unity" tacitly condones both church and kastom. Having formed an alliance with Pastor Tarwei in the original John Frum village of Sulfur Bay, the movement has two religious days per week. On Sunday they attend church, and on Wednesday they gather to hear short chiefly speeches, to sing proprietary church songs and songs about the birth of their movement, and especially to perform "glass." "Glass" is a metaphorical looking glass or a crystal ball that allows them to look into the spirit world. They spin around ecstatically with their hands raised to the sun until they become entranced, allowing them to receive "reports" from the sun about the source of illness or about the future. Thus the movement has everything a modern religious movement needs: its own day of worship, its own corpus of songs about their history and beliefs, a prophet, a growing group of churches, and even a truck with a "Unity" logo.

---

[30] Isak Wan means "the first Isaac" in Bislama.

Women perform "glass:" A mildly ecstatic dance.

Fred's movement had its enemies—Tanna cannot accommodate thousands of people living together in such a small place. In April 2003 the Vanuatu Mobile Force came from Port Vila and handcuffed the men in Yenkahi, and burned down the settlement. Fred, Pastor Tarwei, and so many other men were put in prison that there was "standing room only." They were released and never arraigned. To this day, they lament (through song) that they have not had their day in court to exonerate themselves. Some accused Fred of being mentally ill but, the modern legend has it, "the government drew his blood twice and found him to be mentally stable."

Assuming "Unity" continues on its current trajectory, it will arguably be considered Tanna's indigenous religious movement *par excellence*—having found a solution for the cognitive dissonance Tannese feel about the bifurcation of church and kastom. While it will be popular, it is not biblical Christianity. Evangelical missions such as Campus Crusade for Christ (CCC) and Youth with a Mission (YWAM) have focused on these cargo-cult villages, engaging in various short-term discipleship and evangelism campaigns (Green 2007; Lessard 2003; Rush 1997).

CONTEMPORARY RESIDENT MISSION EFFORTS

During the height of nationalistic pride and cargoism, missionaries kept their distance. It is to their credit that they did not force themselves upon islanders who were reluctant to host them. Recent missionary efforts on Tanna have begun again only by invitation from a host village.

After this long hiatus of expatriate missionary presence, mission sodalities and denominational missions began to arrive on Tanna. The Summer Institute of Linguistics (SIL) sent a translator to North Tanna: Joan (Blaymires) Finlay. After five years (from

1984–1989), she transferred to Papua New Guinea and was replaced by SIL translators Greg and Beth Ann Carlson, who stayed in Lomakaun for seventeen years, completing the New Testament translation in 2007.

Other contemporary missionary efforts have been a church plant by the Presbyterian Reformed church in Lonapkiko (Tim and Ruth Zylstra, 1997–2006), a three-year effort by the Australian Foursquare Church to start the Tanna Island Bible Institute in Kito (Ian and Georgina Hamilton), and an attempt at starting an AG school at Lonapakel on the northern coast of Tanna by John and Abi Blake and Wayne and Jackie Hindson (2004–2006). My wife, Mendy, and I began the translation of the New Testament into Southwest Tanna in 2003, and Erik and Michele Stapleton began a retranslation[31] of Watt's New Testament in Kwamera in 2004.

The Missionary Baptist mission near Lonialu requires special mention for their connection to the cargo cults. The mission began in the 1994 under Neil Morley (Zocca 2006, 250), who established some churches in the Southwest Tanna language group from Greenpoint to Yelkis. Morley, unlike the pioneer missionaries that preceded him decades earlier, apparently did not learn the language or culture, and did not sanction magic, kava, or ancestor worship. Meanwhile, the John Frum cargo cultists were awaiting an American who would come in the spirit of John Frum and would "join kastom and the church." Because of his acquiescence to kastom, Morley seemed to the Tannese to be joining the two "roads." As a result, Missionary Baptist churches on Tanna (especially Southwest Tanna) are not only syncretistic but evidence cargoism. Morley left, and David Bennett took his place. He is, to many Baptists on Tanna, the new John Frum. He drinks kava, does not speak against animism, and believes that he is at least a partial fulfillment of these prophesies. Indigenous Baptist preachers envision Jesus as an ancestral type, and Bennett to be the one who will usher in a millennial age of cargo, peace, and eternal life. Bennett's missiology resembles Callaway's fulfillment model, since he believes that the partial understanding of Christianity can be made complete through the apparent fulfillment of cargo-cult prophesies (pers. comm., August 2005).

Recent evangelistic methods of short-term missions involve a brief proclamation of the gospel and a call to make a decision (vis-à-vis Evangelism Explosion, YWAM, or CCC), whereas the early pioneers planned on living in traditional villages for a number of years, learning the language and, through proclamation and silent witness, encouraging the receptor culture to come out of "heathenism," "paganism," or "fetishism"—that is, out of animism. In other words, the early pioneers focused on culture change, but the modern movement of short-term missions focuses on an individual's conversion experience. I would argue that the history of missions on Tanna has shown that conversion is not merely an individual decision; when one person converts, the entire clan fears that there will be negative consequences—either sickness or disaster. Therefore, individual appeals to conversion must also take into account the group-oriented culture and the animistic background of the convert.

---

[31] A revision was found impractical, so a retranslation was necessary. See Stapleton 2008.

Women in the Prince Philip Movement look at pictures of the Duke.

INLAND

As early as 1930, the three "church" languages on Tanna (Whitesands, Lenakel, and Kwamera) had their hymnals, New Testaments, and established churches. North Tanna did not have an orthography, but it had some Presbyterian churches. However, being largely inaccessible, tribes in Tanna's mountainous interior received little attention. Among them were the Yasurmene (currently spelled *Yahuri mine*), living west of the volcano, whom Frank Paton called "the most evil-looking cannibals one could wish to avoid" (F. Paton 1903, 52). Having lived and worked with this tribe for eight years, I would disagree with Paton. They are arguably the most wonderful and pleasant people to work with anywhere!

The Southwest Tannese have developed a cargo cult of their own: the Prince Philip cargo cult. Though perhaps thirty years newer, this cult has many of the same characteristics as the John Frum cult, including nationalism, a rejection of the West (including clothing), and a reification of kastom.

Because of misinformation regarding Prince Philip, Duke of Edinburgh,[32] more than five hundred inland Tannese came to regard Prince Philip as the son of the Tannese demigod Karpapeng, who will eventually take up residence on Tanna. Some say that he will run a profitable small business and distribute the proceeds to the islanders. Earlier myths about him said he would land at Blacksands beach and the much-coveted kava plants will spring up. The old will shed their skin,[33] and men will be permitted to marry without having to pay adultery fines (Shears 2006; Tabani 2009). Tannese are aware of the duke's age, but they have not lost hope that he will return.

---

[32] Prince Philip visited Vanuatu in 1971 and Aneityum in 1974 on his royal yacht. He is aware of his peculiar status among the Southwest Tannese and, to his shame, has done little to discourage the cult. Five men from Tanna were permitted an audience with him in 2007, as part of a British reality show called "Meet the Natives."

[33] This is common in cargo-cult mythology.

CONCLUSION

God's redemptive mission on Tanna has been worked out under two paradigms: First, by individual missionaries sent by the Scottish Presbyterian church, then, in the past fifty years, by multiplication along denominational lines. Sodalities such as SIL, CCC, and YWAM have also played their part in recent years. Here I have attempted to reconstruct the approach toward kastom of the missionaries, denominations, and parachurch organizations over the years.

Turner, Nisbet, Paton, and Mary Matheson were run off the island; their long-term goals are unclear to us. We can assume, based on early twentieth-century missiological trends, that they would have preferred to remain in the mission field for decades like the Watts and MacMillans; and they would then have hoped to have been replaced by other expatriates. From the extant documents, it seems that each of these early pioneers made preaching about Christ their first priority. Secondary work would have been education, leadership development, and community development. It appears that it was their intention all along to establish self-supporting and self-propagating churches, even if Venn's model was not available to them. It was their understanding that Christianity would displace heathenism.

By 1940 the John Frum cargo cult had such a hold on the island that foreign missionaries were not as welcome. If the church was going to expand, it would have to be by multiplication—through ni-Vanuatu witness and direction.

Numerous denominations, employing various missiological strategies (or lack of strategies), have flourished on Tanna in recent years. Early missionaries learned the language and translated the Scriptures in an effort to plant authentic Christian churches. Over time, due to nationalism, institutionalization, lack of leadership, and cargoism, many of these churches became syncretized (if they were not so all along). On the other end of the spectrum, the Missionary Baptist missionaries did not learn the language or translate the Scripture and guaranteed the establishment of syncretistic churches. SIL translators took a servant leadership role, learning the language and culture, and translating the Scriptures, but not establishing churches or teaching doctrine. Also, numerous denominations and cults were planted quite without missionary effort, but due to self-multiplication.

It is difficult to reconstruct the methods of persuasion that the pioneers used to achieve their goal of displacement. Today we theorize that in order to evangelize animists, a mixture of methods is necessary: power encounters, truth encounters, and love encounters (Hayward 1997). To the pioneers and maintainers, conversion was a change in worldview; evangelism was done through truth encounters. In the more recent indigenized church, love encounters and power encounters have been more prominent.

We have seen that a new model, not mentioned by Friesen (whose study was limited to early twentieth-century evangelism), must be added. In place of the association model, which was not a salient movement in Tanna's missiological history, we note the "proclamation-decision model" employed by sodalities that engaged in short-term mission work on Tanna. Table 12 shows the five prominent missiological models tried on Tanna, who tried each model, and how each of these models dealt with kastom.

Table 12: Missiological models on Tanna

	DISPLACE-MENT	RADICAL DISPLACE-MENT	MORAL RECON-STRUCTION	FULFILL-MENT	PROCLAMA-TION/DECISION
MOTTO	"Lord of Lords"	All other religions are satanic religions	Light in the darkness	General revelation evident in tribal religions	Hold evange-listic cam-paigns, call for decisions
MISSION-ARIES WHO ADVOCAT-ED THIS MODEL	Gray; modern evangelical and Pentecos-tal movements such as AG, NTM, Chris-tian Outreach Center, and Apostolic	Early Presbyterian missionaries such as Paton, Watt, Geddie, Matheson, Gil-lies, Johnston, Watt, Gillies, MacMillan, SDA church	Calvert and other later Presbyterians, Catholics, Matheson, F. Paton, Nichol-son, Forlong	John Rush, David Bennett	YWAM, CCC, and other short-term missions
NUANCED APPROACH TOWARD KASTOM	Culture esteemed, conversion emphasized; kastom dis-couraged but not prohibited	Kastom banned, conversion emphasized	Community development is a major part of mission emphasis; less emphasis on relinquishing kastom	Kastom is reified and esteemed as a forerunner to Christianity	Ignorant of the nuances of kastom; kastom not addressed

The extent to which the church has been truly contextualized remains to be seen, but she has yet to demonstrate the eleven elements of contextualization in Hayward (1995). Missionaries and local church leaders have had to work out together the interface of kas-tom and Christianity. As Walls predicted (2002, 67), the cross-cultural process of missions in Melanesia has invigorated the church, bringing up tough questions about involvement in kastom rituals, and issues that never before challenged Christendom, such as how to deal with magic, myths, or kava.

Christendom as an institution is well-rooted on Tanna. It is the established religion, but the kastom worldview is ubiquitous. In virtually every village, men get intoxicated on kava daily for religious purposes. People trust in magic for rain and crops. They turn to shamans and clairvoyants for healing. Illiteracy is a deliberate choice for some village lead-ers—it is a passive-aggressive way of rejecting the church and Western influence. More than 70 percent of inland villages[34] do not have a church—many by design. Villagers are afraid that if they adopt Christianity, sickness or disaster will befall them.

Tanna is no longer the land of darkness, nor is it the land of light. It is not clear how long animism will have a stronghold on the island; we may assume that orthodox Chris-

---

[34] By "inland villages," I mean in the Southwest Tanna region. Illiteracy rate comes from personal field notes.

tianity, cargo cults, syncretistic movements, and cults will survive or even thrive. We are more certain that the expansion of the church will no longer be largely dependent on the efforts of Western missionaries. It is now in the era of partners—missionaries, theological schools, and indigenous church leaders share the task of realizing the kingdom of God. Urbanization, globalization, and growing literacy rates are new forces that affect the growth of the church.

There remains a great need for missionary efforts on Tanna. Future efforts will need to focus on leadership training, Bible study methods, cults, and, of course, the integration of gospel and kastom. The current church needs to work out a plan for contextualizing the gospel in a way that all of the societal needs (social structure, alliances, exchange, gender roles, respect) are met but which maintains orthodox doctrine and practice. However, before we work out that plan, we need to understand how Tannese Christians relate to kastom, and what factors have been important in shaping their attitudes toward kastom. And that is the subject of the next chapter.

CHAPTER 11

The Gospel-response Axis

I ASKED twenty-five churchgoers on Tanna to tell me how they relate to kastom. I began by saying, "Some churches encourage kastom while others forbid it. Why is that?
And how are you involved in kastom?" In some ways, the answers I received were not
surprising. People who were affiliated with churches that characteristically discourage kastom were more likely to avoid it, and were less likely to reflect an animistic worldview.
People affiliated with churches that are typically sympathetic to kastom saw kastom and
the church as compatible.

This was expected, but I was also received some unexpected answers. An educated elder discounted the myths outright because of scientific reasoning, including the theory of
plate tectonics. Similarly, another pastor theorized that myth contains vestiges of truth, as
it is an oral record of prehistory. Many islanders' ideas about atonement for sins were new
to me. I discovered that the way Tannese integrate Christian faith and kastom is complex
and innovative. With each interview, I attained new insights into how Tannese respond to
kastom.

The journey was invigorating. Not only did I hear fascinating responses, but I have
concluded that a study of the function of animism (Chapters 1–9), the history of local missions (Chapter 10), and emic attitudes toward animism (the present chapter) is essential
for engaging in missions in an animistic setting.

It became clear that the churchgoers I interviewed fell into two groups: (1) those
who were vague about the nature of salvation, conversion, and the distinction between
Christianity and kastom; and (2) those who had specific conversion experiences, articulated a concise explanation of soteriology, quoted the Bible, and were aware of functional
substitutes. The former type of participants were more likely to retain kastom, while the
latter uniformly relinquished much of it. There were, in the end, ten prominent differences
between the two types of participants. These ten factors are the body of this chapter. However, before discussing those, I must address the influence that denominational affiliation
and family history have on attitudes toward kastom.

DENOMINATIONAL INFLUENCE ON ATTITUDES
TOWARD KASTOM

This chapter does not list denominational affiliation as one of the ten factors that affect attitudes toward kastom. Why not? It seems a given that people in an SDA village would be far less inclined to eat pig or drink kava, precluding them from participating in kastom. Similarly, we would expect people in a Roman Catholic village to be more likely to drink kava and not to frown upon shamanism or totemism. Isn't denominational affiliation a significant influence on people's attitude toward kastom?

It turns out that denominational affiliation does not directly affect people's attitude toward kastom. There are kastom-retainers and kastom-relinquishers among Baptists, Presbyterians, and Roman Catholics (see Figure 5 in Chapter 13). Denominations are not homogeneous groups; instead their constituents can be quite diverse regarding their attitudes toward kastom. This is true for two reasons. First, some denominations do not have a clear stance regarding kastom, leaving people to determine their own course. Second, determining what denomination people belong to, and the degree to which they reflect their denominational teaching, is fuzzy.

No two people in the same denomination responded to my interview questions in the same way. This is largely because many people do not have a background in only one denomination; instead, they have been involved to varying degrees in a number of different denominations. Pastor Walter went from Presbyterian to Apostolic, to Baptist, to Baha'i, to SDA. His attitudes about kastom and Christianity are different from Horace, who was born and raised in the SDA church. Marilyn was raised Roman Catholic, chose the SDA church as an adolescent, and married into the Presbyterian Reformed Church (PRC). What denomination is she, then, at heart? We would be misguided to think that people simply adopt or reflect the same attitudes toward kastom that their current denomination officially teaches (if it even has an official stance).

However, people in some denominations, such as the PRC, SDA, and AG, have a high degree of homogeneity. Do these denominations affect their members' attitudes? Perhaps, but only indirectly. The people I interviewed did not mention their denominational stance; they didn't cite official church policy. If denominations influence kastom, it is not by dogmatically condemning or condoning, but by emphasizing the ten gospel-response factors that I will present in this chapter. For example, people who associate with denominations that stress conversion and that have a high view of the Bible and emphasize atonement will likely be kastom-relinquishers.

FAMILY HISTORY AND ATTITUDES TOWARD KASTOM

While denominational history does not have a direct effect on one's attitude toward kastom, one's family history may affect his or her attitude. For those who set out on a quest to answer what role kastom will play in their lives, family history had minimal influence. But for those who did not set out on such a journey, and who simply mirrored the attitudes of those around them, family history had a significant, indirect influence. People pattern the values and behaviors of those to whom they are close. Horace was born and raised in the SDA church, in an area where there were no other churches. His doctrine is akin to official SDA doctrine, and his attitude toward kastom is similar to many others who are affiliated with the SDA church. His sons live on the same land and only know the SDA church.

Meriam married into the (French) Protestant church. She worships where her husband does, and her understanding of kastom and Christianity is affected by her identification, through marriage, with that denomination. Likewise, Nancy was born and raised Presbyterian and has only lived in villages with a Presbyterian church (or no church at all). Her approach toward kastom is, to an extent, a product of the ethos of the local Presbyterian churches. Neither Horace, Meriam, nor Nancy arrived at their current understandings of kastom and Christianity through introspection, intentional discipleship, radio programs, individual Bible study, or through an existential experience of personal transformation. Instead, they reflect the approach toward kastom that they have seen modeled in their communities by their churches.

However, there are some churchgoers who, like Daniel (in the Introduction), did embark on a personal search; they are seekers. They separated from their village's denomination, and their attitudes toward kastom are significantly different than their close neighbors'.

Therefore, we conclude that denominational affiliation and family history may indirectly influence one's attitude toward kastom, but only to the extent that such influences reflect the factors listed below.

FACTORS AFFECTING APPROACH TOWARD KASTOM

My interviews with Tannese churchgoers revealed ten factors unrelated to denominational history that distinguish kastom-relinquishers from kastom-retainers:

1. Discourse about kastom
2. Theology of local cosmology
3. Social obligations without idolatry
4. Conversion
5. Purpose of the church
6. Nature of salvation
7. Use of the Bible
8. Selection of church leaders
9. Prayer substituted for magic
10. Plausibility structure for evaluating truth

It is these ten factors that separate churchgoers whose worldviews have been transformed through a "full gospel response" from those who evidence a "low gospel response" (that is, those who continue in an animistic worldview).

FACTOR 1: DISCOURSE OF KASTOM

As a result of the interviews, I was most surprised to discover that for the previous eight years of mission work I had been misunderstanding Tannese discourse about the reason to avoid kastom. Perhaps I had been projecting my own reasoning onto others' evaluations of kastom. Many Tannese speak of kastom as something that faithful Christians would do well to avoid. One woman said, "I trust the blood of Jesus, I don't do sacrifice." Another said, "Christians shouldn't do *kajiə* (harvest ritual), they should just thank God." I mistook this to mean that churchgoers see kastom as sinful, and therefore something to be avoided. It turns out that this was not the case. When I interviewed churchgoers, I discovered that many Tannese think that kastom is a good thing, but it is inherently dangerous and therefore worth avoiding, if possible. It is not that Christians should avoid kastom because it is wrong; rather, if faith in God is sufficient for providing health and happiness, why handle magical stones that can do the same, yet with an added element of danger? Others suggest avoiding kastom, but purely for pragmatic reasons. Some Tannese, however, do see kastom as sinful. It is this bifurcation of discourse about kastom that seems to be the most salient difference between Tannese who have relinquished animism and those who retain it.

Kastom Is Life

Kastom-retainers talk about kastom as "life." It is a blessing, or at least a way of attaining blessings. They also see church as a way of showing the good life or attaining blessings. Therefore kastom-retainers see no major difference between the church and kastom. One church leader, Joshua, told me, "When I preach, I encourage people to hold on to their kastom." For him, the church and kastom are both about teaching respect and love, and about trying to have healthy gardens and healthy bodies. I asked him, "Why then would you go to church? Why would you want the others in your village to go to church?" He said, "Because kastom is about this life, but the church helps us for the life to come [heaven]." Joshua believes that kastom is helpful for this present life, but is not clear about what happens to the souls of people when they die. The church provides answers for the afterlife. He wants people to utilize kastom for the present life, and to be baptized so they are safe in the life to come. He said, "The church should promote the parts of kastom that are good, and block those that are bad." This is a common maxim on Tanna. One catechist referred to the "good kastom" as "white kastom" and bad kastom as "black kastom."

When I asked him to be more specific about what parts of kastom are good, Joshua explained, "The church should promote *tupunas* and *tamafa* ... but not poison." Poison, in fact, is the only aspect of kastom that is widely considered to be wrong in Vanuatu. Christians may also choose to avoid other "good" aspects of kastom because they are dangerous, but not because they are inherently sinful.

Kastom Is Dangerous

To many, kastom is a mixed blessing. The taboo stones grow gardens and send rain, but if one has anger in his heart or breaks the taboos, the magical stones will cause severe illness, disasters, or death. Why dabble with such a dangerous thing when faith in God alone is enough? Yes, it may be necessary to turn to kastom when faith in God is not enough. But when one turns to kastom, he is walking on dangerous ground.

I asked people what the difference is between God and kastom. One woman, Nancy, said, "When we had a mudslide, the garden continued to produce sweet potatoes. God was blessing this garden." "But," I asked, "don't the magical stones produce gardens too?" "Yes," she said, "but if you have anger in your heart when you go to the stones, your garden will

not produce." For Nancy, the difference between God and kastom is that God is not considered as dangerous as the magical stones. God is always beneficent; the stones are not.

Therefore, many Tannese worshipers reckon that the church should not explicitly
prohibit kastom, but that Christians may be safer not to engage in it. Doug, a Presbyterian
youth leader with theological training, said, "Kastom is for those who don't have enough
faith. If a man does not have enough faith for God to heal, or for God to make the garden to
grow, he goes to kastom. But it's good for worshipers simply to trust in God." Why would it
be more desirable for them simply to trust in God, rather than trusting in kastom as well?
Because kastom is dangerous.

Another woman, Rebeka, said:

> I believe that God approves of [kastom] because he created every-
> thing, but I am afraid to do the things of kastom. I like [kastom], but
> I'm afraid to touch it or do it. So I don't know if it's good or no good. I
> don't know . . . Other people can do it, but they want me to do it, but
> I'm afraid. I did not learn about it [when I was young, so I'm unfamil-
> iar with it].

Many churchgoers who speak about exclusive personal faith in God still consider
kastom to be a good thing: it teaches respect, is efficacious in healing, and ensures good
crops. Meriam's response is typical of many kastom-retainers. "Kastom and the church are
the same. They both teach love and respect. But we don't follow [those principles]. We go
the wrong way. But [kastom and the church] are good." For many on Tanna, kastom, in
itself, is not bad. It is only bad or dangerous when people misuse it, or neglect to follow its
guidelines.

Kastom Is Bad for Your Health or a Waste of Time

Janice's discourse about kastom-relinquishing is pragmatic, focusing primarily on utilitar-
ian reasons. She sees kava as bad because it is bad for one's health and makes people lazy.
Further, kastom places a heavy burden on people with its perpetual demands for large
feasts that must be reciprocated. "The church is much easier. If you want to have a meal
with someone, you just invite them over for a meal. Kastom requires such large feasts."
Kastom-relinquishers certainly have ideological reasons for leaving animistic practices
(discussed below), but the pragmatic reasons also factor in. For instance, kastom dancing
may be discouraged because it is a waste of time. One said, "There seems to be no meaning
to it."

My point in exploring the pragmatic discourse about kastom-relinquishing is that I
predict that these reasons are not as potent as ideological reasons. Even staunch kastom-
retainers may jokingly suggest that dances are a waste of time or that kava is bad for one's
health; only the serious kastom-relinquishers will have deep-seeded ideological reasons
for abandoning animistic practices. I suggest that the pragmatic arguments for kastom-
relinquishing are weak ones because they are not held with fervor.

Kastom Doesn't Work Anymore

Another weak argument (that is, one held with low conviction) for kastom-relinquishing is kastom's apparent inefficaciousness today. Pastor Perry's discourse about kastom-relinquishing is multifaceted, including ideological reasons, but he also discourages it because it is no longer relevant. "*Tupunas* doesn't work anymore . . . because the belief is melting. It's not powerful. There are so many people in church now." With so many people in the church, belief in kastom is dwindling; as a result, kastom's efficacy is diminishing as well. Pastor Perry explained that there are plenty of people in his village who are not Christians but nonetheless have relinquished parts of kastom simply because "there's nobody around anymore to support them in kastom." To do kastom sacrifice or *tamafa* requires a support system that is dwindling in his thoroughly evangelized part of Tanna. Kastom's relevance is limited there.

Indeed, ni-Vanuatu speak of the golden ages when the kastom really worked. It was an era when the ancestors could simply speak to the volcano to send forth stones to light their cigarettes, and it would obey. One could follow a prescribed ritual and turn chickens into money. People followed the rules of kastom closely in these days, so people lived harmoniously, kava was drunk sparingly, and children obeyed their parents. It was only in the more recent dispensation that kastom was lost, resulting in a period of tribal warfare, excessive kava drinking, and sickness. To add insult to injury, the church came at this point and further suppressed kastom. Today, many ni-Vanuatu explain, the ancestral rituals and magic are no longer efficacious because the church has overtaken kastom. Tomlinson (2009) has referred to the lament of these days when kastom was efficacious as the "discourse of loss." Missionaries in Papua New Guinea have noticed the same sort of lament regarding the loss of "all their sorcery and magical objects and their secret knowledge that had allowed them to go on to success and prosperity in life." There is a "suspicion" that missionaries "took our culture and our valuable objects" (Zocca, 2009, p. 137). The sentiment is predicated on the belief that some aspects of kastom are valuable—as some Tannese preachers say, "We should keep the good kastom but do away with the bad." Jack Urame appears to agree with a distinction between good and bad kastom when he asserts that "missionaries failed to distinguish between their good and bad traditional beliefs and practices" (p. 138).

The irrelevance of kastom today is Pastor Manny's primary way of speaking about kastom. "Kastom is changing. Even women can drink kava now. We've nearly lost *tamafa*. But the Bible doesn't change. That's why I believe the Bible." Pastor Manny doesn't see kastom as inherently wrong, but simply passé. "It is the Old Testament, and now we are in the New." Catechist Neil said, "The taboo places worked in the olden days. But you can break taboos now and not get sick." This autochthonous form of dispensationalism easily complements the fulfillment model of Callaway discussed in Chapter 10. For many Tannese, the era of *tamafa*, *tupunas*, and divination has been replaced with a Christian era where only prayer works.

Kastom Is Idolatry

Kastom-retainers cannot understand why churches such as the SDA or AG would prohibit

their rituals. Indeed, if kastom is "life," why should the church prohibit it? Why would
the church keep people from respecting their in-laws, from creating strong alliances with
exchange partners, from maintaining their rich cultural heritage? Of course, their understanding of why the church would sanction kastom is determined by their own worldview.
To many, the only reason for prohibiting something as beneficial as kastom would be a fear
of spirits. I asked an elderly Presbyterian woman, Nancy, why churches like the SDA and
AG would prohibit *tupunas* and dances and *tamafa*.

> I don't know why. I'll just say that. I did not ask them. But I'll say that
> they are afraid of eating pig—the SDAs.[They think] that there's a
> spirit in pigs. And I asked them about that. But they said kastom—
> songs and such, whatever [people in kastom] do—is darkness. Dark-
> ness. They do it in darkness. I don't know why, but they prohibit [kas-
> tom] dancing. Dancing is darkness. It's bad. They will not do it.

Some islanders hold conflicting ideas about why they should relinquish kastom.
Doug said that the problem with kastom is that it competes for our worship. This leads
to double-mindedness. Kastom is undesirable, not necessarily because it is sinful, but because double-minded faith is inefficacious:

> If kava is first in your life, and God comes afterward, some day you
> will not be able to go to God's place—to his big house . . . Because
> nowadays . . . we worshipers don't really have God in the forefront of
> our hearts. So, therefore, if the church forbade *tamafa*, or releasing
> sickness [with sacrifice] then our thoughts would be two-faced. On
> the one hand, we must do it, and on the other hand, we must not do
> it. But if your thoughts are only one, to lift up only God—and you
> don't do sacrifice or do *tamafa* . . . and you only look to God, God will
> help you. But if your faith is not strong, when the time for sacrificing
> for sickness or taking *tamafa* comes, then you must join in. Because
> your belief in God doesn't exist. Or it is there but is small . . . There-
> fore, it would be tough if the church prohibited it.

When I asked Doug why anyone would want to prohibit kastom, he said, "Because it's
a bad road. Stones, if you touch them wrongly, can give you a sickness. If you touch them,
and your heart is bad, you can become sick. And the church sees that. The worshipers see
that. If God is in you, you will not touch those things."

Doug's response left me wondering, does he see kastom as a sin, or just dangerous?
He said:

> People say that it's not sin. But I say it's sin because I see in the Holy
> Book of God that it says, "Don't make your god another one than me.
> I alone am God; only believe in me." But if you believe in another god,
> that's a sin. I see it that way, that it's bad, because, if you've done it, and
> believed in it, you've made it your god. That's your god . . . If you touch

those things, and you put them first in your life, you might as well not be going to church [worshiping]. You're going to church for nothing. God is not in your heart.

While Doug is a kastom-relinquisher, he argues that the church cannot practically prohibit it, because people will continue kastom practices anyway. It is significant that he does not dismiss kastom outright as superstitious or inefficacious. It is just undesirable to continue practicing it. In fact, I've never heard a Tannese person dismiss kastom as superstition—not even the most educated and "Western-influenced" ones. What varies is the reasoning that worshipers employ for articulating why kastom is undesirable. Churchgoers who evaluate kastom as "life" would only discourage kastom because it is dangerous, costly in terms of time and resources, or *passé*, but they would not consider it wrong. For them, kastom is valuable, so they are more likely to retain animistic practices and worldview.

However, other Tannese see kastom not only as dangerous but also sinful. In fact, for many of these it is not only sinful but a deception from Satan. They not only want nothing to do with the "gods" of kastom, but maintain that these spirits are agents of Satan. To them it is precisely because kastom is sinful that it is dangerous. It is not dangerous because some mechanistic force such as the loss of *mana* will bring punishment. Instead, they fear that to engage in kastom is to invoke God's wrath. In fact, some say that God will punish (in this life) anyone who practices kastom. One Presbyterian youth, Nellie, said she will not prepare *nohunu* (food eaten with kava), because it is like a sacrifice to the devil. I asked, "Why would that be bad?" "Because [God] would take away the blessing of my garden." For her, kastom is dangerous, but it is dangerous because it is sinful. Pastor John said:

> When kastom was against the church, there was a Tanna-wide famine. Then the church came, and now there are clothes, a dispensary, education, a hospital. God healed the land. Now, even though the population is growing, there's enough food. But in the days of cannibals, there was famine. Even though there were few people, there wasn't enough food for them. God healed the island.

Nellie and Pastor John see kastom not only as dangerous, but wrong. They want to avoid kastom, not simply because it grieves the heart of God, but because it will invoke his wrath. While their reasoning initially seems to show they have made a clean break from kastom, there is a vestige of the animistic worldview. Many Tannese churchgoers say something like, "Don't work on Sunday or you'll get sick. If you break a taboo of a garden or a tree, you'll be sick." I wondered if Elder Tom saw things this way. So I asked him, "Do you obey the Bible's laws so that God will not punish you?" Tom's response showed that he understood the Fall; a concept not articulated by kastom-retainers.

> We all know that we are people of sin. Everyone. We all sin. We have sinful hearts all the time. All the time in our lives, our hearts are still no good. Our hearts are no good. We think about plenty of things that are not straight. We break God's word. And, I think, regarding your question, when a man says if you break God's talk about Sunday, may-

be God will punish you. Ken, I think that if a man talks like that, it's a
bit like he is still halfway in [kastom]. He is still halfway in [kastom]
. . . if a man says, "If you break God's law, then God will ruin you" . . .
that's just the way [kastom] works.

This is foundational. Evangelical church planters may be pleased to see that their
congregations deem animistic practices as undesirable, and no longer participate in them.
However, we have learned here that their reasoning for not being involved in such practices
is also an indicator of whether they truly have a transformed worldview, or whether animism remains deep down. Elder Tom has noted that ceasing kastom out of fear of retribution is an indicator of an animistic mindset. It reflects a mechanistic worldview which says
that if you do something wrong, you will inevitably suffer the consequence. Because Elder
Tom has internalized the doctrine of the Fall, he sees the logical absurdity of a mechanistic
view of retribution. To make his syllogism explicit: if we sin every day in our hearts, and
must suffer consequences for every deed, none of us could survive another day. Elder Tom
has not only relinquished kastom, but has a transformed worldview; this is indicative of
what I term here a "full gospel response."

Kastom-retainers and kastom-relinquishers alike use negative discourse when describing kastom. They both refer to the stringent demands of kastom, its outdatedness,
and the ill effects of kava on the body. Only the kastom-relinquishers, though, conceptualize kastom as sinful or idolatrous. Therefore, the distinction between kastom as dangerous
and kastom as sinful is the starting place for any church attempting to contextualize the
gospel in an animistic setting.

In light of this, church leaders and training institutions must pose these questions to
those they are discipling: Is kastom indeed "life"? Does God relate to us the same way that
taboo stones do? Is kastom only dangerous because it is powerful enough to hurt us, or is it
dangerous because it causes the displeasure of a supreme God who requires and deserves
our exclusive worship? Church leaders must study the discourse of kastom and determine
whether parishioners see animistic practices as merely dangerous or pragmatically undesirable, or if they see them as sinful.

FACTOR 2: CHRISTIAN/KASTOM COSMOLOGY

Christians who have a biblical cosmology will likely relinquish kastom. Tannese churchgoers hold to one of two cosmological scenarios: either the traditional one or a diabolized
one. In other words, there is no Tannese cosmological scenario that denies the existence of
local deities, nor one that simply ignores them. Tannese either maintain the kastom view
of local deities or they contextualize them in light of biblical cosmology.

Worshipers who hold to the traditional cosmology have what Hiebert, Shaw, and Tienou (1999) referred to as split-level Christianity. They affirm that God created the world
and is supreme over creation. At the same time, they obey the taboos of local deities for
fear of the consequences if they do not. Here is how Nancy put it:

As far as Matiktik and Karpapeng go, be afraid of them, and let go of
anger. Don't be angry, and don't slander. Don't hate someone. If your
insides are bad, a *kughen* (deity) will come into you, and you must get
sick. [The shamans] will have to spit on you . . . and don't enter the
taboo places because [evil spirits] live there. If your heart is good,
you'll be fine; but if anger is in your heart, a kughen will come into
you. You'll get sick. And [the shamans] will have to spit on you.

Nancy has a split-level Christianity. She prays to God, comes to church regularly, and
affirms that the Bible is true, but is compelled to observe taboos about local deities, believing them to be powerful and retributive.

Many kastom-retainers have a cosmology that includes the creator God. God is sovereign and works through all the aspects of kastom, including totemism, shamanism, and
divination. Since they believe in a benevolent creator, they imagine that God gave the
magical stones for our benefit.

On the other hand, worshipers who have relinquished much of kastom contextualize
traditional cosmology by diabolizing local deities. Diabolizing them brings them lower on
the cosmological ladder. They are subservient not only to Jesus but to humans. Pastor Steven said Genesis 1:26 was God's greatest gift to humankind—authority. "It is we who have
authority over our gardens, not the demons who do. Why let the demons steal that from
us? They don't have authority to send rain and make gardens grow. We have that authority."
Steven does not deny the existence of the local deities; he just wants nothing to do with
them. To fear them is to hand authority over to them, as if they have the power to harm
and bless. Steven has turned indigenous cosmology upside down by placing humans over
the local deities. In this transformed cosmological scheme, only God is above humankind.
This is the hierarchy of heaven we learn from King David.

Then I ask, "Why do you care about us humans? Why are you concerned for us weaklings?" You made us a little lower than you yourself,
and you have crowned us with glory and honor. You let us rule everything your hands have made. And you put all of it under our power.
(Psalm 8:4–6 CEV)

Pastor Manny said he believes that the local deities exist and are demonic. "Would
you spit on them to make them leave?" I asked. "No. I've seen plenty of people try to spit
out demons, and it doesn't work. But when I pray for people, if they believe, they are always
healed." Pastor Manny does not ignore his kastom cosmology, he just sees the demons as
inferior to Jesus.

Churchgoers who have not worked out a Christian answer to local cosmology retain
kastom practices and worldview. They obey kastom taboos and fear local spirits. On the
other hand, people who have a transformed cosmology relinquish kastom. They are open
to the possibility that local deities exist as a threat to those who pay attention to them. But
they do not observe taboos about local deities and do not fear them. They know that Jesus
is more powerful than territorial spirits.

Van Rheenen's thesis is that to communicate the gospel in animistic contexts we must not only present the way to heaven, which is a primary concern for many Westerners, but we must also show how God defeated Satan, since this is a felt need by most animists (Van Rheenen 1991, 131). Nancy has a split-level Christianity because she is not aware that the good news of the gospel is that God defeated the powers of evil. This needs to be a central part of the church's teaching if they wish to transform the worldview of animists.

FACTOR 3: SOCIAL OBLIGATIONS WITHOUT IDOLATRY

Christians who are able to fulfill social obligations without engaging in totemism are most likely to relinquish kastom. Many Tannese reconcile the totemic system and their faith by saying that God must have established the totemic system. The reasoning goes like this: God made all things, therefore he made the totems. God called all things good, so he must call the totems good. Noel is a Presbyterian who shares this logic.

> Noel: God gave [the totems] to us. I believe that. Like the taro stone, yam stone, kava stone—God made all of those things.
>
> Ken: And God is happy about that?
>
> Noel: Yes. He gave them to us, and people use them.
>
> Ken: And do you figure that God showed us how to use them?
>
> Noel: He showed the road.
>
> Ken: How did he go about showing us the road? Did he speak with some man about it?
>
> Noel: It must have been like that. He talked with an ancestor, eh? Long ago. But he gave us those things. And you see that it's like that. He showed the leaves that complement [the totems], eh?

Other worshipers on Tanna are aware that the totemic system is idolatry. Even though Elder Tom is a member of the banana clan, he will not participate in the annual harvest rituals and totemic exchanges.

> When I started worshiping, I understood that the Bible says that as far as kivir (totems) are concerned, you can't worship two gods at the same time. You must worship the high God who is the true God. I understood this. As far as I was concerned, and my family, we are the people of the banana [clan or totem]. When they performed the magic on the stone, and the food was ready, they would send a message to me that I should go with kava, and a pig, and a chicken, and kill these things to make sacrifices to the stone, so the banana crop would come. At that time, I completely ceased such things.

While Elder Tom "ceased such things," it is not clear if he has a substitute for meeting social obligations that the kajia (harvest sacrifice) is meant to fulfill. He may be sacrificing social ties for his convictions. Meeting social obligations is part of the enculturation continuum, which is the content of the next chapter. Here we take note that what distinguishes kastom-relinquishers from kastom-retainers is the conceptualization of the totemic system. Those who see the totemic system as idolatrous are kastom-relinquishing. Those who see it as beneficial or instigated by God are kastom-retaining.

FACTOR 4: SALIENT CONVERSION EXPERIENCE/ VAGUE CONVERSION EXPERIENCE

A salient conversion experience is a positive indicator of who will leave animism. Hiebert's discussion of conversion (2008) raises three factors that affect the nature of conversion in tribal settings. First, like many other concepts in the mind of animists, conversion is a "fuzzy phenomenon" (ibid., 309). Secondly, most animistic religious movements are set in highly group-oriented societies where conversion is not an individual decision; it takes place in multiple-individual movements (ibid., 326–29). Conversion, at least initially, may be a communal event, but may become genuine in a second stage of individual reassessment (ibid., 327). Third, for the animist, conversion is more of a process than an event. Hiebert has appositely framed conversion as a change of allegiances. If we synthesize these three factors, we can say that conversion in the animistic setting will likely be a process where individuals and their societies change their allegiance from false gods to Christ.

Churchgoers who are vague about a conversion experience were more likely to be sympathetic toward kastom. I asked Elder Whale how to become a "worshiper." He said, "You must obey. Come inside [the building]. Have goodness [in your life]. Come to church. Agree with what the church says. Work together." This is vague, since it is not particularly measurable. How much does one need to obey to become a worshiper? How does one have "goodness" in his life? What if someone no longer has "goodness," does that mean he is no longer converted? Conversion is not a salient experience for Elder Whale.

Similarly, Nancy said that to become a Christian means, "You must be humble, not puffed up . . . You should help your wife; feed your family. Don't bring fighting into the home." For Deacon Whale and Nancy, the qualifications for identifying with Christ are no different than the qualifications for being a good kastom person: join the group, agree with group consensus, work for the group's benefit.

Indeed, kastom-retainers do not speak of personal conversion experiences. They remember joining the church, but they do not relate their spiritual journey in terms of typical evangelical phrases such as lost to found, sinner to saved, making a decision for Christ, taking him as their personal Savior, etc. Kastom-retaining women, especially, simply worship at the church where their husbands worship. I asked Rebeka, "Why are you a Baptist?" "Because my husband is." Meriam said she ended up in the Protestant church "because my husband goes there." I asked Elder Whale why he changed from Presbyterian to Apostolic. "Because I moved inland, and there was no Presbyterian church. But there was an Apostolic pastor that came around."

Some kastom-retainers recall a change—a time when they began attending church—but the change in their life is not about conversion; rather, about fulfilling hopes. Some began attending church and were baptized in hopes that they would no longer be sick. One began attending church after having a dream about a man who would show him where cargo would come from. The man in the dream pointed him to a certain denominational church.

Other churchgoers, however, recall a period in their lives when they were looking for a church that looked different—one that acted different. They wanted a church where people stood out—a church that asked for something of them. They wanted to find a church where people repented from something. One SDA pastor, Walter, was a genuine seeker. He went from denomination to denomination (including Baha'i) looking for a fellowship where people not only believed right but behaved right. He had determined that right behavior meant they did not drink kava. Eventually his quest ended in the SDA church, where people had a strict set of rules and followed them. This had the appearance of genuine religion to him.

The islanders who articulated conversion experiences were universally the ones who also relinquished kastom. To them, becoming a Christian meant leaving kastom. Christianity, for them, was about a decision—a life change. The very power of their faith is rooted in their changed lives. Pastor John, an AG pastor, was a seeker like Pastor Walter. He was disillusioned by the lives of those in his own church.

> They were immature; they prayed but did not grow. They did not do what the pastor said. They did not do what the Bible says. I asked God, "What's the deal?" And God said to me, "You must make a decision" . . . I stopped chewing and squeezing kava, smoking . . . and I went to Bible school. I was born again on November 11, 1987. The pastor [Tom Ironga] was preaching about Nicodemus in John 3. He said, "Take Jesus as your passport—your personal Savior."

Participants in this study who have relinquished kastom, but not all, remembered a specific time that they converted. A conversion experience is a strong indicator, then, of those who will relinquish kastom. Churches that wish to foster a full response to the gospel, and to aid people in coming out of animism, must emphasize the conversion experience as normative for the Christian, as the New Testament indicates (cf. Mark 1:15; Acts 2:38; 2 Cor 7:9; Rev 2–3). In societies that are group-oriented, perhaps a community-wide "kastom-leaving ceremony" would be a meaningful expression of conversion. Converts in Ephesus brought their fetishes and burned them to demonstrate that to follow Christ was to relinquish traditional religion (Acts 19:19).

FACTOR 5: CHURCH FOR FELT NEEDS/ CHURCH FOR KNOWING JESUS

Ecclesiology is another indicator of who will relinquish or retain kastom. What is the church good for? What is the point in going to church, or in trying to persuade others to come? I asked twenty-five islanders what value they saw in the church, and received twenty-five different answers. In general, though, there was a bifurcation between the types of responses the kastom-retainers offered and the responses that the kastom-relinquishers offered. Those who saw church as primarily a place to meet felt needs were more likely to retain kastom. They saw church as a place to teach proper values, to ensure the "good life," or to bring Western prosperity. Those who had Christo-centric purposes for the church (such as a place to worship Jesus or proclaim salvation through him) were kastom-relinquishers.

Church Is for Teaching Values

As I mentioned earlier, most kastom-retainers see no fundamental difference between the church and kastom. The church and kastom are, as many Tannese worshipers have said, one road. They both bring goodness, as they both teach the two most important values in kastom: respect and love. In fact, a number of Tannese villages have sought out the Presbyterian or Catholic church as a way of maintaining kastom values. One Catholic catechist told me how his village endeavored to set up a Catholic church in order to safeguard kastom. I asked a catechist, Joshua, what it meant that the church can "hold on to kastom."

> There are some laws from other churches. We can see that some churches are cutting things from kastom that will affect our lives. We wanted the Catholic church because its law is like kastom. It does not block things. It blocks the bad things, but allows the things that are good.

I asked Joshua what sorts of good things he was referring to. He said, "The things we do in the imaram, like tupunas, these things, tamafa. In my preaching I teach that you must do kastom."

But how does a church go about proactively reinforcing this notion that the church "holds on" to kastom. Joshua explained:

> I preach, "What you're doing, keep it up. Don't stop." Many churches are coming to our island in Vanuatu. But I see that two churches, if they weren't here, the kastom people would lose kastom. In my opinion, the Presbyterian and Catholic churches are holding on to kastom. If they weren't here, people would lose their kastom, the other churches would snatch everyone. But the Presbyterian and Catholic hold onto kastom.

The church is valuable precisely because it maintains all that kastom stands for— not because it is different. Elder Whale agrees. He participates fully in kastom. He takes tamafa, participates in the new harvest ritual, and uses the services of diviners. I tried to determine what he sees valuable about the church.

Ken: How does the church give goodness?

Elder Whale: Its teaching.

Ken: What teaching?

Elder Whale: It lays down what the imaram teaches. Goodness. Don't steal. Don't slander people. Don't be lazy (waiting around). Therefore, I want the church to come and help the *imarəm*.

Rather than envisioning the church and *imarəm* to be at odds with each other, kastom-retainers expect the church to help the *imarəm*. The church is simply another road for achieving the goals of kastom. Kastom-retainers also talk about the church as a place to network, like a club.

Church Is a Club

Kastom-retainers also see the church as another social group to belong to. I asked Nancy what she must do as a worshiper.

> In order to feed my family, I go a long way to the Port and bring food back on the day of rest—Sunday. But [I regret doing this] because I feel in my insides that, no, I must prepare some food in advance for my family, eh? And I should sew clothes for the children. When I was young, I did this work, PWMU [Presbyterian Women's Missionary Union], and sewed clothes. But when I got older, my husband prohibited it, saying I shouldn't do that kind of work; I must stop it. I had bad insides because of that, because I did not talk about these things. He said I shouldn't do the work of the church. I wanted to do a work, and my husband prohibited it. [He wanted us to] just stay quietly in the village.

Some islanders believe that it is the duty of churchgoers to help the church accomplish its goals. They should attend committee meetings and fundraisers so the church's functions will be successful. In other words, they do not frame their church duties in terms of worship, fellowship, evangelism, and discipleship; rather, churchgoers fulfill their duties when they help its programming run smoothly.

Church Is for Bringing Western Goods

Melanesians recognize that when the church arrives, prosperity and development come with it. When people recount how a denomination arrived in their village, the story is often intertwined with the establishment of education and hospitals. Tradition-maintaining ancestors who were against the church were also against hospitals and schools. And forward-thinking ancestors saw the church, hospitals, and schools as a package deal.

I asked Deacon Nako why he decided to bring the church into his village, which is a hub for the John Frum cargo cult. He said, "Because I saw that the church would bring us trousers and shirts." "What happens if [the missionaries] leave and those things stop coming in through the church?" I asked him. He said, "I'm not sure if we'll keep going to church or not."

Along these lines, the collective memory of a cannibalistic past is part of the Melanesian discourse about the benefits of the church. The comment goes something like this: "Without the church, we would be not be able to sit here together. We wouldn't be able to travel more than a kilometer away from our villages. Certainly white people wouldn't be joining us." The church brought about a Melanesia-wide transformation of culture—an end to the era of darkness, epitomized by tribal fighting and cannibalism. Many people speak of this as the primary contribution the church has made to their island.

Church Is for Christo-centric Purposes

On the other hand, islanders who had relinquished kastom saw church primarily as a place to worship and to spread the news of salvation through faith. For Doug, church is primarily about securing salvation.

> My mother worked it out for us to go to church because some pastors or missionaries said we'd go to a new era, when God gave us eternal life. So they told us to worship, because God is coming, and will give us eternal life . . . I worship today because I saw that if I did not worship, my knowledge/ability would come to nothing. But if I worship, my knowledge will grow . . . I'll have knowledge of how to help my family, and knowledge/ability for when God comes back. I worship today because when God comes back, and sees me worshiping, he'll let me go to heaven.

Pastor Perry's purpose for the church is Christo-centric, but more holistic than simply attaining salvation. It is about proclaiming the kingdom of God.

> On Tanna, they talk about ships—*nimrukuwen* and *koyomera* [the moieties]—the different ships. So, the work of the church on Tanna is easy. It's easy for people to understand, because they already talk about ships. That is, the different time periods. We call them ships. The work of the church is to show the true kingdom/ship, of Christ. Mark 1:15 says, "The kingdom has come." The kingdom has come. So the church's business is to make awareness, to teach, to preach the kingdom . . . where Christ is in charge, and everyone knows not to be afraid. Where fear doesn't rule us, because Christ is there . . . Let's help them not be afraid; let's show them that Christ is the ruler. He gives peace and joy.

While kastom-relinquishers are aware that the church brings development, and are aware that the church often teaches the same values as kastom (namely love and respect), they see these things as peripheral benefits of the church; Christ is central. Churches must be Christo-centric to bring people out of kastom.

FACTOR 6: SALVATION IS FREEDOM FROM PAIN/ SALVATION IS ATONEMENT

Soteriology is another indicator of who will be a kastom-relinquisher or a kastom-retainer. Animistic views of salvation are about mitigating "badness," while salvation for Christians is a release from the penalty of sin.

Biblically speaking, sin is both an offense to God and the community. Westerners emphasize that sin makes us guilty in God's sight. Animists emphasize that sin is a social problem, rather than a break in one's relationship with God. Therefore, for animists, salvation is about restoring horizontal relationships, not particularly about atoning for sins (Van Rheenen 1991, 290). The judicial aspect of atonement is clear to Westerners, so when we talk with Melanesians we think it is clear to them as well. However, it is completely lost on some, like Noel.[35]

> Ken: What do you mean, "God will take away your badness"?
>
> Noel: That he'll scatter it, so I won't have a punishment, so I'll be healthy.
>
> Ken: When you say punishment, do you mean sickness?
>
> Noel: A sickness. That he'd take out all my sins. I'd turn from them.
>
> Ken: What kind of sickness? A boil? A disaster?
>
> Noel: I've heard the taboo talk, so I must turn from badness and hear his Word, so he'll take these things out of me, so I can be healthy, and not feel the guilt of having done those things. If those badnesses were in me, I'd be sick from them. Like I've done a bad thing, so someone hates me. Or I stole, so someone gossips about me. I must repent from those things and obey God's word.

Kastom-retainers see their relationship with God like a game of "tit for tat." The animistic idea that taboo objects are potentially beneficial and potentially dangerous is projected onto Jesus. Jesus is another taboo object—a fetish. I asked Elder Whale how Jesus treats us.

> Elder Whale: Jesus is the man of life. Goodness . . . He's a god. They say he's a god. And if you go to him and if you treat him well, he'll treat you well. If you treat him badly, he'll treat you badly.
>
> Ken: He'll hurt you?
>
> Elder Whale: He'll hurt you.
>
> Ken: Why would he hurt you?
>
> Elder Whale: Because you've spoken badly to him. He'll hurt you. If you speak well to him, he'll treat you well.
>
> Ken: If you break a law of his . . .
>
> Elder Whale: If you break a law of his, he'll give you badness.
>
> Ken: Then what does "God saves" mean?
>
> Elder Whale: Goodness. God saves us; that means goodness. Goodness. Respect. Love. You go to him, ceasing bad behavior, and he will

---

[35] This is more of a paraphrase than a translation. Noel's discourse was highly contextual and used a good deal of implied information, making a strictly literal translation useless for this present study.

help you.

Ken: How?

Elder Whale: He'll help with whatever you say or do.

Ken: That it'll be good, or . . . ?

Elder Whale: That it'll be good.

For many Tannese, salvation is about the moral example that Jesus provided for humankind. The vernacular term for "salvation" is "God gives us life." I asked Tannese to explain what that means to them. Janice said that it means God enables us to do our work for him. Deacon Whale said that it means God will help people in whatever they say or do for God. Martha said it means, "If you find it difficult to do God's work, he will help you."

In contrast, other churchgoers understood well the motif of judicial atonement. Doug's explanation of salvation was in accord with the traditional understanding of substitutionary atonement:

> Jesus is God's Son. If you know that God will give eternal life to you,
> or you believe in God, all the time you must know that Jesus is God's
> Son. It's not that he's a man like us. He's God's Son. He came to help
> us, and take us out of the bad place, and take away our sin. He's God's
> Son . . . If you believe in Jesus, you've become like a family member of
> God's. But if Jesus is not in your heart, or you don't know him, you're
> like an outsider. Like a stranger.

While the judicial motif of atonement is not commonly understood on Tanna, Doug and others have grasped it. If churches wish to transform the worldview of their audience, they need to be explicit in their teaching about the judicial aspect of atonement. To say to an animist that "Jesus takes away the punishment of sins" invites the possibility of miscommunication. The church needs to explain that taking away the punishment does not mean that Jesus will only treat us as well as we treat him. Nor does it mean that we are "saved" because we are no longer sick as a result of a feeling guilty for sins we have committed. It means that we once deserved eternal punishment for our sins, but now we will no longer receive the punishment we deserve.

> In the past you were dead because you sinned and fought against God.
> You followed the ways of this world and obeyed the devil. He rules the
> world, and his spirit has power over everyone who doesn't obey God.
> Once we were also ruled by the selfish desires of our bodies and
> minds. We had made God angry, and we were going to be punished
> like everyone else. But God was merciful! We were dead because of
> our sins, but God loved us so much that he made us alive with Christ,
> and God's wonderful kindness is what saves you. God raised us from
> death to life with Christ Jesus, and he has given us a place beside
> Christ in heaven. (Eph 2:1–6 CEV)

FACTOR 7: BIBLE EMPHASIZED/ BIBLE NONSALIENT

The 15 kastom-relinquishers I interviewed referred to the Bible or explicitly cited it an average of 1.9 times during the interview sessions, whereas the nine kastom-retainers did not mention the Bible.

The Bible played a significant part in Joe's religious experience:

> I was just going to church—my father led me in devotions at home. Then I realized that I don't have anywhere else to turn to; I must give my life to God. Romans 12 says you must give a living sacrifice to God. Give your whole life to God. I read that verse, and was going to Bible studies, and then I said, "Yes, I must simply believe."

It should not be surprising that those who have a good background in the teaching of Scripture relinquish kastom. As I point out in Chapter 3, the Old Testament has a great deal to say about animistic practices. Joe cites the Bible as an authority for relinquishing kastom:

> I see that one of the commandments, number one, said you must not take a picture of something in the sky or ocean or land, and make it, and fear it. God says you must worship only the God who created everything. If you fear a [magical] stone, you take away respect for God and put it on the stone.

Joe went on to quote the Bible three more times in our short interview. He quoted James 2:19; 2 Timothy 3:16; and 1 John 1:7. I asked him (and everyone who cited the Bible as an authority) why the Bible, above any other book, is to be trusted. The reasoning was elusive and circular, and went like this: "I trust it because it is God's book." "How do you know it is God's book?" "Because it says so." "But what if other people say they have God's book? How is the Bible different than those?" "Because the Bible is true." In other words, the argument quickly became circular. Joe, however, clinched the discussion with a more refined argument:

> The canon agreed on what should be in the Old and New Testaments ... The elders in the Mormon church, or the SDA—(Ellen White is their mother)—there are some books that they wrote through their own power. I don't agree with them.

Kastom-relinquishers have a high regard for Scripture. Therefore, they have learned the Bible well and are willing to let it challenge them. They are aware of the Bible's condemnation of animistic practices, and they try to heed its words on the subject.

FACTOR 8: STRINGENT LEADERSHIP SELECTION/ LOOSE LEADERSHIP SELECTION

Many kastom-relinquishing leaders often underwent stringent leadership selection training. In contrast, several kastom-retainers found themselves in church leadership not because of a personal quest—i.e., not because they were Radin's "religious thinkers" (Chapter 2), but because the village appointed them. Joshua related his entrance into ministry:

> Sometime in 1983 or so, I was in Port Vila; one of my uncles, his plan
> was to secure the Catholic church. At that time he went to Imaki. He
> summoned them and asked for the Catholic [church], and the imarəm
> agreed to it. At that time, I had just finished [6th grade at] Yenaula.
> They said, "We have something we want to get hold of [i.e., the Catho-
> lic church], but we don't have a person to lead the church. So you
> must go." But I said, "I don't speak French." They said, "We want this,
> you must go." So, in 1985, I went to Pentecost Island. I went to Pente-
> cost and came back, and am here to this day. When I came back, the
> elderly people became Christians. They were baptized.

For Joshua, and for Nellie, another church leader, entering ministry is not about calling or unction, but about fulfilling duties for the village.

Christian workers who want to plant contextualized churches would be well-advised to take a look at how their students end up in theological school. Is it that the students had conversion experiences and want to evangelize others? Or are they sent at the behest of village elders to return with a church that will bring cargo, or to establish a church that is sympathetic toward kastom, thereby counteracting the influence of churches that are antagonistic toward kastom? Or, was the reason vague? Training centers may see it as a great opportunity to receive any willing person—as an opportunity to "plant seeds." However, training centers must remember that their students will soon matriculate and return to their villages. Will they return to evangelize, or simply to maintain kastom?

FACTOR 9: DIVINATION, SHAMANISM, TOTEMISM, SORCERY, RELIGIOUS USE OF DRUGS, OR PRAYER?

Most people I interviewed, whether kastom-retainers or kastom-relinquishers, see prayer as efficacious in the same way divination, shamanism, totemism, sorcery, and the kava ritual are; however, only kastom-relinquishers actually replace these kastom practices with prayer. For them, prayer is an adequate functional substitute for the animistic practices, so they do not need to practice "split-level Christianity."

However, by relinquishing animistic practices, these people have had to pay a price. For example, by not participating in the kava and tamafa ritual, or by not exchanging kava with in-laws, or by not swapping birth children with their wives' families, they inevitably create tension in their social relationships. They sacrifice relationships for their convictions. How they will meet those social obligations without engaging in divination, shamanism, totemism, sorcery, or the religious use of drugs, depends on whether the church has a functional substitute that meets those obligations. This will be discussed in Chapter 12.

FACTOR 10: TRUTH BASED ON FEASIBILITY/ TRUTH NOT AN EVALUATIVE CRITERION

What plausibility structure people employ shapes their attitude toward kastom. Plausibility structures are the systems that people use to evaluate the truthfulness of propositions (see Sire 2004, 112). While historical evidence, compliance to scientific laws, and logical tenability are components of Westerners' plausibility structures, these components are not necessarily elements of the animistic plausibility structure.

Horace, an elderly SDA man, said he believed in the myths as a child, but the more he learned about science, the more he came to doubt them. For example, he said he does not believe the myth of the volcano taking a hike around the island, because volcanoes are the result of the earth's mantle bursting through the crust. He could not reconcile science with myth, and the scientific plausibility structure was more acceptable for him.

This is not to imply that exposure to the scientific method makes acceptance of biblical narratives easier; indeed, it can cause additional problems for the believer. But Western-style education does make Tannese more skeptical about the veracity of myths and the efficacy of sympathetic magic. Doug is educated. While lacking the vocabulary for explaining Frazer's law of contagion (Chapter 2), he sees that as the basis for sympathetic magic on Tanna:

> God made stones. But when we [Tannese] see that a stone resembles a thing, we put our spirits into it, and our belief, saying, "That stone will do this." But that's not something God said [to do]. We [humans] alone put the names on those stones, and make them [magical/efficacious].

Pastor Perry, who attended school in Australia for several years, was dumbfounded when I asked what totem his family belongs to. He said, "That sort of thing is fake." He has relinquished kastom for a number of reasons, including the biblical injunction about idolatry. Additionally, his (Western-influenced) plausibility structure cannot allow him to believe in totemism.

Some kastom-relinquishers say that the myths are not true because they are not in the Bible; the Bible is their authority. However, many kastom-relinquishers were not willing to say that the myths are false, but that they are "not sure" about them. In their plausibility structure, the Bible and scientific explanations were far more feasible than kastom stories. Kastom-relinquishers are interested in determining the veracity of the myths. They are not satisfied to simply say, "I don't know." They think that answers are out there for the curious.

Steven has demythologized the myths to make them fit his Christian worldview. He said that the myth of the volcano roaming around the island is true insofar as it represents prehistory. The entire island is volcanic, and different parts of the island have been mini-volcanoes over time. The myth of the shark living inland before the animals held a council to send him out to the ocean is true in that, before seismic uplift raised the island, the shark lived further up the mountain (that is, the mountain was actually the shoreline before seismic uplift). The myths recount prehistory, and Steven would not write them off entirely.

For him, the coconut-yam-man myth (Chapter 3) is true in that coconuts may have begun in one location on Tanna, and have spread across the island over time. This is, in fact, an ingenious way of contextualizing local mythology. Rather than dismissing it outright, Steven can see the value in the myths in his current post-Enlightenment worldview.

Kastom-retainers, on the other hand, simply do not speak about the truthfulness as a criterion for plausibility. Almost universally, their criterion for plausibility is, "If you believe it, it is true for you" (cf Zocca, 2009). The centrality of belief in ni-Vanuatu's plausibility structure has ramifications in every area of their worldview: Myth is a source of knowledge to those who believe in them; taboos are dangerous to those who believe they must be observed; divination works for those who expect it to work. Figure 2 shows how this ontology affects kastom-retainers' attitudes about other religious systems (namely Christianity).

Figure 2: Belief is central in the kastom-retaining plausability structure.

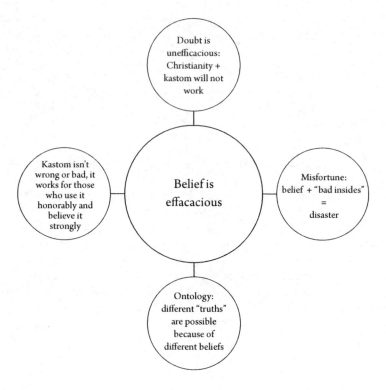

What makes something powerful in the kastom worldview is one's belief (rather than because a powerful spirit or God is at work). Belief, in and of itself, is the power. I have argued that belief is *mana* in Vanuatu. It is *belief* in magical stones that makes them taboo. Belief in certain off-limits places makes them taboo. Similarly, animistic background believers conceptualize prayer as powerful because one puts his belief into it (not particularly because God chooses to respond). When you pray for the garden to be abundant, it must be abundant if you believe enough, just like working magic on the crop stones will make an abundant crop, if you believe enough. If the crops fail, it is not because God or the stone has let you down, it's because you doubted, or were double-minded. The problem that kastom-retainers see, then, is not whether you pray to God or do magic, but whether your belief is wholehearted enough to be efficacious.

The job of the church will be to place God at the center of this plausibility structure, rather than belief. Ni-Vanuatu pastors have raised concerns about this. "What is the place of belief, then?" That's a valid point, since the command to have faith or belief is central in the New Testament. The point is not to take belief out of the equation, but to put it in its proper place. God is the center of truth, and our job is to believe in Him, rather than in the power of our own belief.

Figure 3: A transformed plausability structure.

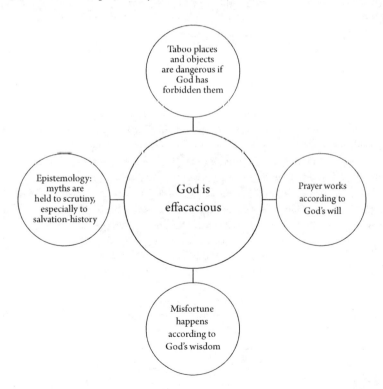

Since belief, rather than truthfulness, is the basis of the plausibility structure in Vanuatu, some consider the criteria of truthfulness an odd one—some have not even considered it before. When pressed on whether aspects of kastom are true or false, kastom-retainers may be caught off guard, left with nothing to say but, "I do not know." I asked Noel if the myths were true. Rather than answering outright, he cited proof that the deities are real. His proof was that people got sick. If people get sick, the deities must be true:

> Matiktik has his [myth cycle]. I don't know Matiktik; but Karwas, he's the one who stands for the gardens. He guards bananas. In Yepangkapier, they put the stone there, and Karwas is there. They put the stone for him to think about it [i.e., to be the security guard or punish offenders]. If they go there, he punishes them. They break the taboos and get sick like [the late] Puria, and Kowia.

The landmark rock formations are also "proof" to the kastom-retainer that the myths are true. The shark story is true because the rock about which the rock story speaks really exists. You can see for yourself!

Unfortunately, exposure to post-Enlightenment epistemology is the factor in the gospel response continuum over which the church has the least influence. Churches can (and have) set up primary schools to teach world history, geography, and science, and they are having some success in transforming people's plausibility structures. In fact, it is hard to imagine that anyone on Tanna has no exposure to the scientific method. However, the majority of people on Tanna are still only educated through "class six," which, as the interview data show, does not offer enough exposure to the scientific method to cause people to question the veracity of kastom origin myths, herbal-spiritual healing practices, kastom epistemology, etc. However, secondary education does seem to distinguish kastom-retainers from kastom-relinquishers. None of the kastom-retainers I interviewed had secondary school education, while five of the kastom-relinquishers had been in secondary school.

To bring people out of kastom, the church needs to present worshippers with a new plausibility structure, and undoubtedly needs to develop education. The church needs to challenge the plausibility of such statements as, "If you believe it, it is true for you." Further, the church should equip people to have convincing answers about why they trust the Bible rather than the circular argument "because it's God's Word." I admit this may be a naïve statement. When I taught about plausibility structures at a theological college in Vanuatu, the pastors said, "That's how you convince dichotomistic thinkers in the West; but we just want to tell people that the Bible is true because it's God's word, and leave it at that."

SUMMARY: RELINQUISHING KASTOM IS NOT THE POINT

I have listed ten ways that kastom-relinquishers are different than kastom-retainers. In fact, the main focus of this book has been to determine the difference between these two types of worshipers. However, throughout the study, I was regularly reminded that simply to pull people out of animism is not the goal of Christian missions. A number of Tannese reminded me that just because one lets go of kastom does not mean he is going to heaven. Doug said:

It doesn't matter if you let go of kava; if you don't have God in your heart, God will not know you. Some of us attend church and pretend like it is genuinely our own. But if it isn't in our heart, then God isn't in our heart. I'm a Presbyterian, and I don't drink kava, I don't touch *tupunas*. But if I did not have God in my heart, stopping those things would be inconsequential. God would be vacant in my heart. If I figure that I'll stop kava, and go to church [worship], I must also take God in my heart.[36]

That is the goal of Christian missions—a change of allegiances from the things of creation to the Creator himself.

The chapter has made evident ten factors that distinguish those who have relinquished kastom from those who retain it. This suggests that if the church wishes to transform the worldview of animists, it would do well to address each of these factors. After reporting each of the ten factors above, I provided some practical application for the church. These applications are summarized here:

1. Emphasize that magical behaviors compete for exclusive worship of God.

2. Emphasize that local spirits are demonic and not to be trusted; Christ is more powerful than they are.

3. Frame the totemic system as idolatry.

4. Emphasize the conversion experience.

5. Emphasize that while the church does bring development, its work is for worship, evangelism, and teaching.

6. Distinguish between judicial atonement and simply avoidance of suffering in this life.

7. Use the Scriptures as an authority.

8. Give extensive prebaptismal training and develop a training program for church leaders that is stringent.

9. Emphasize that prayer is not only a substitute for divination, shamanism, sorcery, and the religious use of drugs, but that it is the only trustworthy power.

10. Help congregants develop critical plausibility structures.

These actions will help ensure a full gospel response. But for the church to be contextualized, it must also address the functional needs of kastom. I will tackle that challenge in the next chapter.

---

[36] Doug's discourse here was also highly contextual, relying on implied information. A literal translation would be abstruse.

CHAPTER 12

The Cultural-integration Axis

CHAPTER 11 presented the ten dimensions for bringing people from animism to faith in Christ. The findings show that the fuller the response to the gospel, the less likely a person will be to engage in animism. That is, their faith is less likely to be syncretistic. However, as far as contextualization is concerned, a transformed worldview is only half of the story. The other component is enculturation. The research in the present chapter provides ten dimensions of an enculturated church. Together, the ten dimensions of gospel response and ten dimensions of cultural integration form a two-dimensional model of ecclesiastical responses toward animism. The vertical axis plots a gospel response along a continuum, and the horizontal axis plots the cultural integration (see Figure 4). Neither one of these axes on their own is enough to foster a contextualized church—both are essential. Contextualization requires a church that transforms individual's worldviews while engaging them in the culture. Brown (2006) defined contextualization as conformity to the biblical worldview (represented here by the gospel axis) while honoring and maintaining native culture (represented by the cultural integration axis).

FACTORS OF ENCULTURATION

This chapter suggests that the following ten domains are necessary for a church to be enculturated:

1. Independence
2. Self-multiplication
3. Meeting social obligations
4. Indigenous leadership patterns
5. Vernacular liturgy
6. Local hymnody
7. Indigenous preaching style
8. Indigenous art forms
9. Indigenous metaphors
10. Healing practices

Figure 4

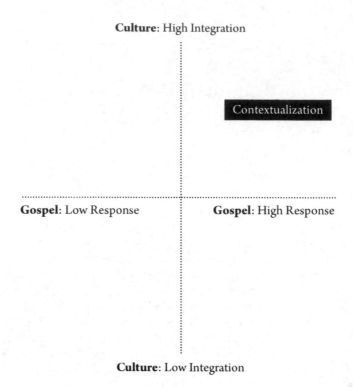

Culture: High Integration

Contextualization

Gospel: Low Response   **Gospel**: High Response

Culture: Low Integration

Factor 1: Independence

One of the first principles recognized by early missiologists was the need to foster churches in the field that are independent. Nineteenth-century missiologists Henry Venn and Rufus Anderson formulated the "three-self model," arguing that churches in the field must become self-governing, self-funding, and self-propagating (Shenk 1977). Venn and Anderson recognized that the missionaries' work was not finished until they had transferred full responsibility of the church to the host culture.

Independence is a mark of maturity and sincerity. As long as the church depends on foreign leadership, its own people will not grow in Christian thought and practice. As long as a church receives substantial foreign funding, people's motives for participating in the church will be suspect. Are they affiliating with the church for its goods, or for its good news? Will they continue to identify with the church if the funding dries up, or if they find a better offer somewhere else? A congregation in Isangel village left their denomination for a new one called "Great Lake Fellowship." Their price for switching: a sawmill. That is a high price—others have switched denominations for second-hand clothes. Indeed, the phenomenon of "rice Christians" appears as much on Tanna as it does anywhere else in the developing world.

Independence alone, however, is not a mark of enculturation. Early missiologists were focused on how to help the church become independent, but they had not yet begun to dialogue about how to help them become enculturated (Hayward 1995, 135). A church may certainly be self-governing, self-funding, and self-replicating, and yet be fairly irrelevant in cultural terms. While independence does not make an enculturated church, an enculturated church certainly must be independent. If a church relies on foreign funds for the sound systems, buildings, salaries, and outreach campaigns, it is not enculturated. If foreign mission boards set policy, it is not enculturated. Independence is the first step toward enculturation.

To bridge the gap between mere independence and genuine enculturation, Tippett expanded Venn and Anderson's three "selfs" to six: (1) self-image; (2) self-function; (3) self-determination; (4) self-support; (5) self-propagation; and (6) self-giving (Kraft 2005a). The logic is that if an indigenous church is independent to this degree, it will surely be culturally relevant. The earlier model recognized that an enculturated church cannot rely on foreign energy for multiplication, support, or function. Tippett theorized that if the indigenous church is responsible for its own self-image and determination, it will be enculturated.

Historically, expatriate church planters have been reticent to give the leadership over to the local church out of fear that the nationals will overly enculturate the church. That is, they are afraid that it will become syncretized. So expatriates hold onto the reigns. Twenty-first-century missiologists know that missionaries must pass the baton. They must have a strategy for transferring full control of the church to the local community (Steffen 1997). Obviously, the newer a church, the more it will rely on foreign funds and foreign leadership; but there needs to be a plan in place for churches to become independent if they are to become enculturated.

It is encouraging to note that the majority of Tannese churches are independent, as the next section, on multiplication, shows.

Factor 2: Church Is Self-multiplying

If a church relies on outside influence to reproduce, it is not enculturated. Multiplication is one of the main avenues for believers to practice their spiritual gifts. The fruit of Spirit-filled evangelism, teaching, prophecy, and administration is multiplication.

We have had the opportunity to watch indigenous church multiplication in action over the past nine years on Tanna. Of the nineteen churches in the Southwest Tanna language group, only one (the Catholic station) was established by foreigners. The other eighteen churches were planted in the past decade through the effort of Tannese. Whether SDA, Presbyterian, or AG, the multiplication worked the same: Someone caught a vision for having that denomination in their own village; then they arranged the acquisition of some land for the building, found someone to lead the church, and asked the community for permission. Within a matter of weeks, the new church was planted.

At times, these indigenous churches receive outside donations; some churches are led by elders or pastors from other islands within Vanuatu. However, each of these churches was established by locals. While most Tannese have known expatriate missionaries who are working on their island, expatriates have had relatively little to do with the establishment of new churches in the past thirty years.

It is fascinating that modern models for multiplication are not being experimented with in Vanuatu. I am not aware of any church using the cell-group model, the house-church model, the multiple-congregation model, door-to-door evangelism, or street evangelism for growth. These are models that have been successful in urban settings, but are limited in their application for rural villages. At a population of only fifty thousand, Vanuatu's capital, Port Vila, may not have reached a degree of urbanization for these models to be successfully implemented.

Instead, self-multiplying churches are using their own context-specific model that does work. New denominations are established on the outer islands through urban drift. Young men come to Port Vila, where cousins or brothers introduce them to the new denomination. When the workers finish their contract, they bring the new church back to their village. Short-term crusades, as well, have a long history in Vanuatu as a method of evangelism, but new churches are only planted when locals take initiative in leadership, funding, and direction.

Factor 3: Church Members Meet Social Obligations

Kastom practices such as divination, shamanism, the totemic system, and rites of passage, (marriage, birth, puberty, and death), serve dual functions. First, they ensure health and prosperity for those involved in the ritual. And second, they allow people to meet social obligations by exchanging gifts. In the previous chapter, I mentioned that kastom-relinquishing Tannese substitute prayer for such animistic practices, believing that prayer is efficacious and honorable in God's sight. However, what about the social function of kastom ritual—meeting obligations to affines? Unless the church provides rituals that fulfill social obligations, worshipers will continue practicing kastom, even if it presents difficulty for them theologically. Alternately, in the case of some kastom-relinquishers, they will practice a Christianity that is not entirely "in the world." They will neglect their social obligations because of their theological convictions.

However, there is apparently no scenario where a Tannese man can simply choose to neglect responsibilities to the in-laws. In more individualistic societies, this is certainly a viable option—perhaps the common one. If in-laws have demands that contradict one's religious convictions, he can simply ignore those demands. This scenario is not considered a solution in Tanna, though males are at times accused of shirking their responsibilities to the in-laws.

Therefore, obligations to the in-laws create a great deal of anxiety for Tannese churchgoers. They have essentially two options available. Either they can fulfill their duties to their in-laws regardless of personal convictions or what the church teaches about kastom ritual, or they can choose a spouse whose family will not put demands on them that contradict their convictions.

For those who retain kastom, the first scenario causes no problem. Worshipers enthusiastically prepare gifts of pigs, kava, and chickens for the in-laws throughout the couple's lives. They give proper homage to the *tupunas* of the clan; they take the correct *tamafa*; they fully participate in all the rites of passage. That is, they practice a split-level Christianity. They worship in a church that delegitimizes kastom, and yet they practice kastom at important moments in their lives.

Indeed, some churchgoers who relinquish kastom nonetheless continue to meet all of their social obligations regardless of the church teaching. Kejio, a member of the SDA church, cannot raise pigs or kava, but pays others to transport these gifts to the *imaram* as gifts to his in-laws at important events. I asked a group of students at a ministry training center if they would cease taking *tamafa* if they were convinced that God wanted them to. One student said, "Ken, you don't understand. We Tannese respect our in-laws more than God." To cease *tamafa* would mean slighting the in-laws; this is an infraction most Tannese are not willing to risk. The student may have been using hyperbole, but the chuckles from the other students indicated that he had struck a nerve. Tannese worshipers are under great pressure to fulfill their obligations to their in-laws.

Other social obligations, however, are a bit more negotiable—there is some latitude to redefine how they will be met. The church has had more than a hundred years to work out substitutes for kastom practices—what Hiebert (2008) called "living rituals." Some of these living rituals are so effective at meeting the social obligations that they allow churchgoers to relinquish the corresponding kastom practice all together. Other substitutes are still in the experimental stage—they are not yet widely practiced, and they may not fully replace the kastom practice. Below, I discuss a number of these substitutes.

Tupunas *and* Kəjiə *Substituted*

Innovative Christians have substituted the kastom harvest rituals with a thanksgiving service. Many Tannese churches schedule a thanksgiving service in April, about the same time that the *imaram* schedules the *tupunas* celebration where the representatives of various totems are given the firstfruits of the garden. Some churches are careful to schedule the thanksgiving service after the kastom one, in order to avoid offending the *tupunas*. Kastom says that the *tupunas* must be the first to eat his clan's crop, lest people get sick from the new harvest. Other worshipers are certain to give their crops to the church before the kastom celebration as a direct affront to kastom. This is a sort of power encounter. It is a deliberate reenactment of Elijah's confrontation of the Baal worshipers on Mount Carmel (1 Kgs 18).

The church thanksgiving service appears to be a functional substitute for the animistic ritual; however, the Christian thanksgiving service does not actually replace the tribal one. Many Tannese participate in both. They bring their crops to the church and the *imaram*. Both rituals are deemed necessary, because each one fulfills half of the function of ritual. The church ritual ensures prosperity as worshipers thank God for a healthy garden (hoping he will provide them with the same next year), and the kastom ritual solidifies clan boundaries and delineates ancestral exchange routes. Some worshipers, like Horace, Elder Tom, and Pastor Walter, surrender their ability to fulfill those social obligations by only participating in the church ritual. Their principle (i.e., that kəjiə is idolatry) takes precedence over kastom's social obligation. Most worshipers, however, participate in both rituals.

Recently, some pastors have suggested that the pastors be viewed as a substitute for the *tupunas* who mediates between men and the spirits at the time of the new harvest (Prior 2003, 19). Pastor Perry sees Jesus Christ as the fulfillment of the *tupunas* who offers propitiation, and as the fulfillment of the *yeni* ("big man"):

> Jesus is everything. Christ is the prophet, priest, and king—all in one man. The actions of *tupunas* are the priestly way. Christ fulfilled that. So, Christ has fulfilled the role of king, prophet, and priest.

Tamafa *Substituted*

Tamafa is a type of prayer or incantation. It is seen as a way of efficaciously effecting one's desires for, e.g., an abundant garden, healthy children, or good weather. Many worshipers easily envision prayer as a substitute for *tamafa*. Kastom-retainers participate in *tamafa* and prayer. Kastom-relinquishers replace *tamafa* with prayer because they see God as more powerful than kava or ancestors, or whomever the *tamafa* is directed at.

Kava Drinking Substituted

Interestingly, some Christians suggest that the worship service is a functional substitute for the kava ritual. The function of the kava ritual, in contrast to the *tamafa* ritual mentioned above (which is a libation), is largely to remind people where they stand socially (see Table 7 in Chapter 9). It is a time for announcements, problem solving, sharing a meal, and showing respect to elders. The worship service itself can substitute each of these social functions. In addition to worship and preaching, Sunday services are a time for sharing announcements and meals. Some churches not only block *tamafa* but attendance at the kava ritual. The degree to which churches consciously incorporate the functions of the kava ritual will determine how effectively the worship service can replace the kava-drinking ritual. In fact, many denominations in Melanesia hold an evening vespers service, which partially replaces the evening kastom gathering.

Sacrifice Substituted

Sacrifice is meant to pay for an infraction that may be causing illness. The payment does not go to any particular spirit or living person—it is more of a mechanistic metaphor than an organic one. The blood of pigs is simply meant to atone for sins. Kastom-relinquishers see the death of Jesus Christ as a substitution, "once for all" (1 Pet 3:18). They do not need any further sacrifice ritual; instead, they recall the death of Jesus and count on it to atone for all sins. One islander, Marilyn, told me, "People who worship shouldn't pull the blood of animals. They should only worship. Only pray. Let the outsiders do [sacrifice]. They don't worship; they sacrifice."

Birth and Puberty Rituals Substituted

Some churchgoers substitute the rites of passage with biblical rites. One man, Joe, told me, "Now, in my opinion, one sacrament that God said to Moses, a good sign, was to circumcise the children. But now I think that it's changed. Now we must baptize." For him, baptism is (theoretically) a viable functional substitute for circumcision. In practice, though, Joe will also have his boys circumcised. But, like some other Christian Tannese, he will not send them to the *imarəm* for three to five months for the kastom ritual; the boys will only be circumcised in the hospital, and then come home. Of course, the Christian replacement does not create an opportunity to pass on kastom myths and rituals, but pre-baptismal training does allow for parents or sponsors to teach about morality.

Cross-cousin Marriage Substituted

The church's answer to cross-cousin marriage, which inevitably leads to a lifetime of kastom obligations to the in-laws, is to marry someone within the same denomination. This way the bride's brothers will have no expectation on him to reciprocate the gift by offering *tamafa* during the puberty ritual, circumcision, first shave, etc. Jon and Annie are under no pressure to give *tamafa* and kava to Annie's brothers and father because he, too, is a pastor of the same denomination.

Steven's wife's family is a kastom-retaining family, but they have made some concessions for him. Whenever there is a rite of passage or significant event, Steven and the family fly to his wife's village on Aniwa with gifts for the in-laws. What he lacks in gifts of kava for *tamafa*, he makes up for with extra crops and pigs. Steven has altered the kastom ritual rather than substituting it. Alternately, Jon and Annie are able to substitute kastom rituals because they married into families that do not put kastom demands on them.

All-night Dancing Substituted

A potential substitute for all-night dancing is all-night revivals. Kastom-retainers participate in both, seeing no particular problem with the kastom dancing. Diehard kastom-relinquishers do not participate in kastom dancing, but are vague about their reasoning. When I inquire why, I commonly hear, "Because kastom dancing doesn't have any benefits; it's a waste of time."

Children-swapping Substituted

Some social obligations in kastom are out of the question; church members are adamant that they cannot fulfill these requirements. It is an example of Christ against culture, to use Niebuhr's (1956) taxonomy. One example is the requirement in kastom for couples to adopt out one of their daughters to the in-laws, as an exchange for the bride that has been taken away from the in-laws' clan. This is out of the question for strong kastom-relinquishers. Joe told me:

> It's our kastom, when you get married, like when I married Anita, I
> must exchange. I must give a girl [to her family] because of her. Since

I exchanged/married Anita, they wanted to take my small girl, Serah. But some Bible study I read . . . was against that. Other men don't have a right to teach my children, otherwise they might teach things that are against God. Therefore, I didn't allow that . . . So I just held a feast and gave my in-laws a pig, as if to say, "Take this pig and eat it in place of the child that Anita and I have . . . It's preferable to have this obligation be complete. The child is under my responsibility. I wouldn't agree to have her live a long way from me, or she might learn false things . . . I won't agree to that, regardless of the fact that many people asked to have one of my kids. I didn't want that. I said, "No."

Joe has not fulfilled his kastom obligation to adopt out a child, but he has tried to mitigate the offense by offering a feast instead of exchanging his daughter. The feast is a sort of functional substitute for Joe and Anita's family.

Summary of Functional Substitutes

In many cases, worshipers participate in the church's functional substitute and continue the kastom practice as well. This suggests that the function has not in fact been adequately substituted. For instance, church marriage is a potential substitution for kastom marriage, but it does not function the same way. It does not meet a need that kastom marriage does, because it does not provide adequate respect to the bride's family and does not provide enough control for the groom's parents. In kastom, the groom's parents run the show. In the church ritual, the elders or pastor do. The church ritual is a desirable addition, but not a substitute. For many, prayer does not adequately substitute for the kava ritual. Prayer is efficacious, but it does not meet the social obligation of meeting in the *imarəm* to hear the chiefs' speeches, and to chew and spit the kava that they will drink.

Thus, we have seen that Andrew Walls' theory rings true in Tanna: the cross-cultural process is the lifeblood of the church (2002, 67). Over the past century, the church has worked out substitutes for at least eight components of kastom. The Christian functional substitutes are a break from shamanism, sorcery, idolatry, and totemism. The substitutes are limited, however, in their ability to allow members to meet social obligations. For this reason, many churches have not yet grasped the utility of these substitutes. Some substitutes, like prayer in place of *tamafa*, are widely adopted. Others, like baptism in place of circumcision, are not implemented; virtually all Tannese continue in some version of the circumcision ritual. Table 13 shows the functional substitutes, the reasoning behind them, and the degree to which they are.

Factor 4: Church Utilizes Indigenous Models of Leadership

The introduction of the church into traditional village life on Tanna has created new leadership possibilities that could never have existed before. For example, these days young men and women organize events and plan budgets. Women speak in front of older men. Power brokers within the church are the ones who can read or speak the national pidgin, Bislama; whereas under the traditional paradigm they had no need for Bislama or literacy.

Table 13: Functional substitutes on Tanna

SUBSTI-TUTED	FUNCTION	SUBSTITU-TION	REASONING	WIDELY PRACTICED?
Kəjiə	Ensures that the new crop will not harm anyone	Thanksgiving prayer for new harvest	Kastom harvest ritual reifies stone idols and magicians	Some participate in both the kastom ritual and the Christian substitute
Tamafa	Connection with ancestors	Prayers of intercession	Considered prayer to false gods	Prayer is widely recognized as a substitute for *tamafa*
Kava drinking	Reminder of social standing, invoking "goodness," group cohesion	Kava drinking substituted with communion celebration of wine and bread	Kava is associated with demons, leads to drunkenness or laziness	No church overtly recognizes communion as a substitute for kava drinking
Sacrifice	Takes away punishment for sins	Prayer of confession, asking for forgiveness	Kastom sacrifice reifies local demons, ascribing them authority to forgive sins and heal	Some participate in both the kastom ritual and the Christian substitute
Birth or puberty rituals	Ensures that the initiates will be healthy, marks young people as "in group," marks initiates as mature	Baptism, confirmation	Threatens continuity of church involvement, may encourage return to kastom	Widely practiced by denominations that relinquish kastom
Cross-cousin arranged marriage	Fulfills exchange obligations	Choose a spouse who is a member of the same church	Considered idle, not edifying	Utilized, but not overtly recognized as a functional substitute

All-night dancing	Fellowship	All-night revival sessions	Considered idle, not edifying	Utilized, but not overtly recognized as a functional substitute
Swapping birth children with in-laws	Reciprocity, a form of bride wealth	Feasts in place of the child	Considered demeaning to swap children, considered irresponsible, potentially allows children to be raised in kastom families	Practiced by some

Even the traditional concept of leadership is elastic and evolving. Kastom in South Vanuatu does not comprise chiefs, per se; rather "big men." Foreign influences have acted throughout history to shape what a "big man" is. For instance, hereditary succession, an integral part of Tannese leadership patterns, may be an ancient residual element reflecting Polynesian influence (Capell 1938, 77). But the title "chief" was introduced only recently by the British colonizers for their own convenience. Early missionaries in South Vanuatu played a major part in increasing the chiefs' authority in order to establish law and order (Proctor 1999). The British and French governments were major agents of culture change in Vanuatu until independence (in 1980), but traditional leaders have been innovative in combining foreign and indigenous roles and expectations for leadership. Lindstrom notes, "If the state has to some extent defined what a *jif* can be, along with the proper compass of his powers and duties, men who call themselves *jifs* have influenced the expanse and effectiveness of state programs" (White and Lindstrom 1997, 211).

Here I identify ten aspects of leadership where the church and kastom either conflict or coincide. When the church's patterns coincide with kastom, it is enculturated. Where it conflicts or ignores kastom leadership patterns, it is either less culturally relevant or is a deliberate example of "noncontextualization."

Qualifications of a Leader

All aged men in a village are "big men." They all have power, influence, and wisdom—the marks of a leader. While Tanna is far from egalitarian regarding gender, all men, at least, are created equal. Agnes Watt observed more than a hundred years ago, "Chieftainship may be said to consist only in name. In a village of eight or nine men, six will claim to be chiefs" (1896). Most "big men" are respected, or *tabu* men, because they possess totems and the knowledge to perform sympathetic magic on those totems. Men who are able to go into a trance are *tabu*, and wield power.

Table 14: Duties of church and *imarəm*

DUTY	IMARƏM	CHURCH
Resources	• Natural resources of the village: roads, waterfall, volcano access • Input into use of the M.P.'s allocation and other political decisions • Enforcing taboos about sacred spaces, fasts from certain foods • Performance of sympathetic magic for rain, sunshine	• Road maintenance and access • Input into use of the M.P.'s allocation and other political decisions
Family life	Arranging marriages	Performing Christian marriages
Ritual	Traditional rituals: *nakur, nokiar, nier*, marriage	Church rituals: worship, baptisms, church openings, session meetings, outreach events
Education	Input into school decisions	Input into school decisions
Scheduling	• Work days in the garden • Planning of holidays: Independence Day, *Bonne Année,* Christmas	Planning of holidays: Independence Day, *Bonne Année,* Christmas, Easter
Discipline	Regarding domestic violence, disobedient children, breaking of taboos, incest	Regarding domestic violence, disobedient children, people who disgrace the church or break its "taboos"
Conflict resolution	Settling of land disputes; at an earlier date, planning warfare	
Illness	• Discerning causes of death or illness • Healing (bone doctors, herbal medicines, clairvoyance)	• Discerning causes of death or illness • Praying for the sick

There is a further distinction among "big men," though. Most villages have two inherited positions; one being the *yeni* (spokesman), and the other being the *yermaru* (ruler). Theoretically, the *yeni* speaks on the behalf of the *yermaru's* wishes. In reality, however, the gregarious or opinionated "big men," regardless of their title, dominate village politics, and the more reserved ones talk significantly less.

Aside from age and gender, the necessary qualification for a kastom leader is generosity, usually masked by the euphemism *nasituyen* (helpfulness). A leader gives his own resources to others. Leaders possess knowledge (e.g., bone doctors), titles, and power, but they are evaluated in terms of their generosity. Early missionary John Inglis noted, "The sin that would be visited with the severest punishment there was stinginess . . . and the virtue that received the highest rewarded was a generous hospitality and a giving liberally at feasts" (1887, 31).

The ideal of a "big man" is powerful on Tanna, but is only a partial influence on how Christians conceptualize a church leader. Other voices offering new ideas about leadership come from the West and from indigenous readings of Scripture. In accordance with New Testament models, they are expected to live exemplary lives, free from such vices as sexual immorality, gossip, stealing, and violence. They are men (and in some denominations, women) of any age. Like traditional chiefs, they have "copyrighted" knowledge—familiarity with the Bible and its stories.

Duties of a Leader

Certain activities of village life fall exclusively under the ecclesiastical realm: teaching doctrine, worship, church openings, outreach events, and planning of Christian holidays. Likewise, some activities fall exclusively under the auspices of kastom. Namely, settling of land disputes, scheduling of kastom events, and the almost daily scheduling of work parties in the gardens. In most domains, the village as a holistic organization—the church and *imarəm*—makes decisions. Whether the details are settled within the walls of the church, on the grass (neutral territory), or in the *imarəm* is inconsequential. It is misleading to say that the power is shared between the church and *imarəm*. The village is, instead, one organization with two venues. Table 14 summarizes the venues where various domains of decision making took place in the region where I did mission work from 2003 to 2010.

There is an overlap of duties, which creates solidarity between the church and *imarəm*. For instance, many churchgoers utilize both the *imarəm* and church for healing. They will take herbal medicines, "pull the blood" of a chicken in the *imarəm* to "release" the sickness, and go to the church for prayer. Most do not see this as syncretism nor as hedging their bets, but as a way of participating in the whole community.

However, at times, this overlap between *imarəm* and church's duties causes bitter disagreements. Church leaders have insisted that the taboos on certain foods or sacred places need not be observed—God made all things, and all things are clean. For instance, the *imarəm* in Yelkenu village prohibited eating of *kwənirghnə* (a nut like an almond) for a few months while the chief "flipped" his almond[37] stone. That is, he went into a period of

---

[37] This is the nut that is called *navel* in Bislama.

seclusion to perform sympathetic magic on the stone. But the church did not observe the fast from almonds. The chief of Yelkenu strongly rebuked the worshipers for not observing his taboo.

Pattern of Followership

Traditional patterns of followership are also being reconsidered by the church. Kelley (1992) suggested that the ideal follower is one who is actively involved in the group, but who thinks independently to solve problems. That is, the best follower is the one who proactively tries to solve problems while being a team player. Of course, Kelley's model is culture-specific. What makes a good leader in Kelley's culture makes a rather enigmatic character on Tanna. An exemplary follower in America does not make a good follower on Tanna, just as a leader on Tanna is not the one who casts vision or strategically solves problems. The ideal follower is not the one who troubleshoots; the ideal Tannese follower is one who fits in with the group and exemplifies group ideals, not drawing attention to himself.

Janet Gregory (1982) suggested that, even in a homogeneous culture like Tanna, there is not one single type of follower, but three: conformists, retreatists, and rebels. Rebels (members of the John Frum cargo cult) are alienated followers; they are highly motivated but not team players. The retreatists exclusively follow kastom, they lament the golden ages before contact, when kastom made children obedient and families cohesive, and when magic was efficacious. I suggest that to function well within each of these organizations (cargo cults, churches, or kastom) Tannese followers must be conformists. Members are not called upon to be proactive problem solvers; they do their job best when they conform. One pastor said, "Followers should be simple. They may ask questions, but they shouldn't challenge. They should simply follow."

Authority and Power

The locus of power under kastom has been the clan or village, or along alliances built between villages that lie on mythical concentric roads on Tanna (cf. M. Allen 1981; Bonnemaison 1994, 117). The locus of power in the church paradigm, however, is along denominational lines, extending beyond Tanna Island, and at times, throughout the South Pacific. It is not at all unlikely that a young man or woman from a village in Tanna may find himself in a church leadership position for a time in Fiji or Australia. This is completely foreign to the traditional village's paradigm of power.

Succession

Succession has been symbolized in kastom by the passing of a walking stick or a club. When a *yeni* (spokesman) or *yermaru* (ruler) dies, he may be buried in the *imarəm*. If his presumptive successor (a son) is still young—in his thirties or younger—it is said that the village has no *yeni* or *yermaru*—just young men. In another ten years, the village may formally recognize or "lift up" the heir as their *yeni* or *yermaru*. "Lifting up" would involve the exchanging of gifts and lengthy discussion, lasting several days, about how "it is good and right" to recognize this son as the new chief. These discussions serve to show that the new chief is legitimate, and that the village will support him. (Vernacular terms for support include "helping" or "following.") In contrast, the position of deacon or elder is not inherited. Nor is it particularly achieved. Anecdotal evidence suggests that numerous church elders have been "lifted up" as a plan for personal reformation. Rogues or petty thieves have been informed that they must become elders in order to straighten out their lives. After all, the logic goes, 1 Timothy 3 says that an elder *will be* a godly man. Surely, the reasoning goes, if they make a rogue young man an elder, he will become the godly man that an elder is supposed to be. In Yanemilen village, second-born males have been chosen to be church leaders, ensuring that the firstborn remain exclusively in the domain of kastom (traditional religion).

Selection

Just like kastom leadership, succession normally has no liminal period; the church rite of passage from member to elder is almost immediate, with no stage for initiation (i.e., training). The church discusses who will become the next elder, and if he is approved at the next meeting, he is commissioned.

Support and Legitimacy

Legitimacy is "a cultural potential about an authority; a law, an act, or what you will, to the effect that it conforms to 'recognized principle or accepted rules or standards'" (Adams 1975, 31). When a chief does what is expected of him, his power is legitimate; when he steps outside those bounds, he is seen as illegitimate. A Tannese chief may speak his mind, but he may not bark orders, spend village money, or give away village property. If he does, he is seen as using illegitimate power.

The same is true for church leaders. When they preach, cut the grass, or prepare the building, their power is legitimate. But they cannot speak for the group unless the group has already spoken its wishes. They cannot spend group funds or plan events without the church's consent. Church power, like chiefly power, is limited in an egalitarian society. Legitimate church leaders "lift up the thinking" of the people. That is, they encourage the people to do what the group has already determined to be normative.

The ceremony indicating support and legitimacy of an elder in the church involves the pomp and circumstance of speeches, liturgy, readings, prayers, and laying on of hands. Denominational support also legitimizes ecclesiastical titles. Church leaders from other regions, and even pastors from other islands, are called on to participate in the Christian ritual of laying on of hands to consecrate the new leaders. This is a stark contrast to the support and legitimacy given to kastom chiefs, who neither receive nor need the recognition of outsiders.

Church leaders are expected to "live straight" themselves. A major theme in the discourse of church leadership is the worthiness of a church leader. Churchgoers told me that it is not worthwhile to go to church and listen to an elder preach whom they do not trust. Conversely, Tannese indicate that the uprightness of their church leaders is an important factor in their own decision to participate in church life.

Table 15: Ten domains of leadership in the church and kastom

	KASTOM	CHURCH
Qualifications for a leader	Elderly male, generous, rightful landowner	Men or women, traveled, able to read, knowledge of national language, some education
Duties of the leader	Exemplify: Speaks on behalf of the group, maintains group's ideals, is generous with resources	Encourage: Reminds people of right behavior, brings unity and peace, "lifts up thinking" or "puts thinking straight," can bring in "cargo," and is generous with it
Pattern of followership	Conformist	Conformist
Power/ authority	Persuasion, nondirective	Persuasion, directive
Succession of leaders	Inherited	Chosen by the church, sometimes as a plan for "personal reform"
Selection of leaders	Bloodline, "plan of reform," known to be apt at getting and distributing material resources	Educated, young, not directly responsible for maintaining kastom, personal reform
Support of leaders	Speeches, exchanges	Commissioning service
Legitimacy of leaders evidenced and asserted	Family line, many generations on this land	"Blessing" of God in health and wealth, backing of the presbytery/session
Discipline of leaders	Gossip, saying "he talks a lot" (defrocking possible), claims that one has engaged in sorcery	Formal discipline, leave of absence, defrocking
Completion of term	Death	Death, or until leader relinquishes title for some reason

Discipline

Seldom is a chief defrocked. Performance appraisals are done through gossip rather than through promotions or formal evaluations. "Big men" who cheat, or act in their own self-interest, are slandered rather than formally disciplined. Gossip, it turns out, is an effective behavioral management tool.

The church has become an additional vehicle for the village to manage behavior. Church leaders can be defrocked or forced to take a leave of absence. However, they are disciplined more for their personal lives than for their ability to discharge their duties in the church. Elders have been asked to step down from their position for regular abusive outbursts of anger toward family members or for sexual promiscuity. In the *imarəm*, a strong rebuke may be given, but kastom does not strip a man of his title.

Completion

Ordinarily there is not a plan for "big men" to relinquish power or to complete their terms. They are succeeded at or near death, which makes the mentoring process somewhat less obvious. Church leaders, likewise, are expected to remain in leadership until death. They are called by God, and God's call is for a lifetime. A number of examples can be shown of Tannese men and women who remained in church leadership roles their whole lives. There are also numerous examples of people who stepped down from leadership positions to pursue other careers or because of "backsliding."

Contextualizing Leadership

I have briefly discussed where indigenous and ecclesiastical leadership patterns diverge or coincide. The degree to which the church is able to incorporate indigenous patterns of leadership (and followership), while remaining biblically grounded, will influence its ability to be culturally relevant. At times, the patterns are similar: generosity is expected of both church leaders and kastom leaders. Followers are expected to be conformists in both systems. Both kastom and church leaders are expected to remain in their roles until death. However, often the differences are significant: foreign, young, literate women can be church leaders, but only elderly land-owning men can be kastom leaders. Church leaders are appointed; in kastom, leadership is inherited. The degree to which the church conforms to indigenous patterns will determine its acceptability to kastom people. However, conformity is not always possible nor desirable. Table 15 shows the patterns of leadership in the church and *imarəm* across ten domains.

FACTOR 5: LITURGY IN VERNACULAR OR AT LEAST IN THE NATIONAL LANGUAGE

In order for a church to be culturally relevant, it must utilize the heart language of the worshipers. This may seem obvious, but it is easier said than done in a country like Vanuatu, with more than one hundred languages and almost no liturgy or Scripture in the vernaculars.

One Sunday I worshiped at a church where six languages were used. An order of worship was read in Tok Pisin (the trade language of Papua New Guinea). Formal hymns were sung in Bislama (the trade language of Vanuatu) and the South Tanna language. Choruses were sung in English, Bislama, and the South Tanna language, and one chorus even had a stanza from some African language that nobody could identify. A skit was performed by speakers of two related languages: Southwest Tanna and South Tanna. The majority of communication was done in languages that the worshipers understood well. Despite its use of six languages, this church did a good job of employing vernacular. People understood almost all of what was going on.

But there is no church in Vanuatu that completely uses vernacular—even those churches that have Scripture in their languages use English, French, or Bislama at times. Some churches, however, lean more toward vernacular while others lean heavily toward English, French, or Bislama. The Catholic liturgy is mailed quarterly from New Caledonia, and is recited in French. Likewise, the SDA churches sing many English hymns from well-used copies of Australian SDA hymnals. Therefore, the Catholic and SDA churches are not as culturally integrated as the denominations that are not as dependent on English or French.

FACTOR 6: LOCAL HYMNODY

Music style, choice of instruments, and language choice for worship songs also determine how culturally relevant a church is. However, it can be difficult to say whether certain musical instruments and styles are indigenous or not. For instance, guitars are not kastom instruments, but they are culturally relevant, as they are used in string-band music throughout the South Pacific, and many young men, and even women, can play some chords on the guitar. Although guitars are rarely manufactured within the country, one could argue that guitars, and certainly ukuleles and bass boxes, have become contemporary Vanuatu-style instruments.

It is notable that there are essentially no churches in Vanuatu that incorporate kastom music style or instruments in church. No church uses the conch shell or bamboo flute; in northern Vanuatu, the *tamtam* (drum) is the kastom instrument, but it is rarely, if ever, used for worship music. Additionally, while string-band music is now an indigenous Melanesian music style in its own right, essentially no church incorporates a string band in the worship services. (Nor does anyone use an organ as in the days of John G. Paton.)

What, then, would be considered indigenous music for the church domain? In fact, ni-Vanuatu prefer to compartmentalize their music style. Kastom music, including instruments, appropriate dress, vernacular, and the accompanying dance style, belongs in the *imarəm*. String-band instruments, Bislama, and casual clothes are appropriate for string-band concerts on public holidays. Church music has its own style, dress, and gestures. Guitars are used almost ubiquitously, but not ukuleles or bass box drums. In more urban churches, the guitars are accompanied by synthesizers, perhaps drum sets, and even expensive sound systems.

Because ni-Vanuatu are so comfortable with guitars and church hymnody sung in English or Bislama, it is unnecessary to force the issue of using kastom music style in church. The more important question is: are the churches writing their own songs from their hearts, under the inspiration of the Holy Spirit? The early missionaries had many hymns translated, which are still sung today. Translating Western songs makes the songs more culturally relevant, but does not indicate that the church has been enculturated. When local Christians write their own songs, that is a sure sign that worship has captivated the church at a deep cultural level.

The use of vernacular songs is encouraging—some were translated hymns from days of old; some have been composed recently by Christians who want to sing to God in their heart language. Indeed, there seems to be an increasing amount of indigenous praise choruses being written and circulated throughout Vanuatu, but there is not a large enough corpus of vernacular hymns in most areas to replace entirely the use of English or Bislama choruses.

FACTOR 7: LOCAL PEDAGOGICAL STYLE

In an effort to measure contextualization, Hayward (1995, 136) asks: is theologizing done only propositionally (a danger of transplanted churches), dialogically, or through narrative? All styles are biblical forms of theologizing, and should be utilized, but to be culturally relevant, the church must employ local pedagogical styles.

Indigenous pedagogy in Vanuatu is typically brief spurts of hortatory such as, "Let the husbands respect their wives," or "We need to watch out for our own lives." Such brief hortatory discourse has a great deal of implicit information, making it virtually impossible for an outsider to grasp the meaning without help. One elder repeated the exhortation, "We need to release our sickness." What he meant was, "We're arguing about land, and we need to settle this."

In church, the preacher's pedagogical style will be largely determined by the genre of the scriptural text he is reading. A psalm will require a different pedagogical style than the narrative of the gospels or the apocalyptic of Revelation. I conducted a longitudinal survey of one hundred sermon texts preached on throughout Vanuatu between December

Table 16: Genre of passages used for preaching one hundred sermons in Vanuatu

GENRE	PERCENT OF TEXTS CHOSEN
OT narrative	19
OT Psalms	6
OT prophecy	4
OT wisdom literature	2
NT narrative plus parables	47
NT epistles	19
NT apocalyptic	3

2007 and July 2009, and found that 31 percent of sermon texts were chosen from the Old Testament (OT) and 69 percent from the New Testament (NT) (see Table 16). This is not surprising given most Christians' preference for the NT, but it is surprising considering that about 70 percent of the Bible's content is in the OT.

The genre of passages chosen for preaching is also informative: 66 percent of sermon passages come from narrative, which is representative of the distribution of genres in the Bible—65 to 75 percent of the Bible is narrative. The preference for preaching on narrative passages is typical of people in preliterate societies, who are concrete thinkers and prefer to learn through narrative. Their common discourse style is narrative, as opposed to the complicated logic found in the epistles or the highly symbolic imagery of apocalyptic and prophecy.

While many ni-Vanuatu preachers employ a culturally appropriate pedagogical style (especially narrative and hortatory), it is important to note that the sermon itself has no cultural equivalent. A 20- to 30-minute monologue, especially an expository sermon with three points (even if it is based on a narrative passage) is out of place in any other social context in Vanuatu culture. Instead, a thoroughly enculturated pedagogy would involve very brief spurts of exhortation given by several "big men" in the church. Most churches have chosen to be countercultural in this case, and are unlikely to relinquish the sermon as a pedagogical medium. Others, like Deacon Nako, find the sermon time to be unnecessary or awkward, and have chosen to forgo the sermon most Sundays. The "John Frum, Christ, Unity" movement employs short sermons on Sunday, but on Wednesday the chiefs give brief spurts of hortatory incorporating the same themes of respect and love that they use in the *imarəm*.

FACTOR 8: INCORPORATES MATERIAL CULTURE (ART, DRESS, ARCHITECTURE, AND PEWS)

Incorporation of material culture is one of Moreau's aspects of "comprehensive contextualization" (2006, 333–335), because art, dress, and architecture must be culturally integrated if the worshipers are to be comfortable with their worship experience. Worshipers in a village setting are more comfortable with a simple church building than with an urban style building. However, the lines between foreign and indigenous art, dress, and architecture in church are becoming blurred.

"John Frum, Christ, Unity" is the only church movement on Tanna that uses entirely local architectural style. They meet in the shade, and dance in a clearing. All other churches have a "fuzzy" architecture—incorporating Western and indigenous architecture with their own modern Melanesian style. Western clothes are worn, but in a style particular to Melanesia. Local materials are used for church buildings, but the idea of a public meeting inside a building is an imported one.

The distinction between foreign and indigenous dress is also "fuzzy." Anyone who wears trousers or a dress instead of a penis sheath or bark skirt to church has adopted Western dress. However, the "Mother Hubbard" dress could hardly be considered Western, even though it was introduced by pioneer missionaries a century ago. Today, Mother

Hubbard dresses and flip-flops are a part of a unique Melanesian style of dress. While it is not kastom dress today, it is a culturally appropriate style. Locals make their own dresses, and these dresses are affordable in the markets. However, dress style can still be measured on a continuum of enculturation. Churches that require neckties and trousers on 90-degree days are less in tune with local patterns than churches that allow shorts and tank tops. Urban churches where women wear makeup, jewelry, and high heels are less connected with Vanuatu culture than the village churches are.

Church buildings show a similar mixture of old and new. They are usually constructed out of local materials. In the urban areas they are built according to local architecture, sometimes with the help of foreign funding. The church buildings made of local materials are obviously more culturally integrated than the cement ones constructed with foreign funds.

The seating arrangement, too, is an indication of enculturation. Any church that has people (especially women and children) sit on anything other than the floor is less in tune with cultural norms. Ironically, wooden benches more accurately reflect an archetypical ni-Vanuatu seat than a four leg chair does.

Material culture evolves—the churches have not particularly made conscious decisions to reflect indigenous culture nor to adopt foreign material culture. Churches with more outside influence typically incorporate more foreign material culture. But if a church desires to be culturally relevant, it must bear in mind the local material culture.

FACTOR 9: UTILIZES LOCAL METAPHORS AND SYMBOLS

The recent project of indigenous theologizing in Vanuatu has focused primarily on the use of local metaphors and symbols. A recent report from pastors suggested that early missionaries were aware of the richness of "talk pictures" in indigenous culture, but discouraged this genre because "such communication needs interpretation and can be very misleading or confusing" (Prior 2003, 13). Recently Randall Prior has encouraged ni-Vanuatu pastors to reclaim kastom images with Christian symbolism. Pastors have employed imagery of Jesus as the Great Healer, the High Chief, and our Uncle; they have also explored the Christian usage of indigenous metaphors such as the octopus, dolphin, yams, and the bow and arrow (Prior 2005). Banyan trees are another dominant symbol used for preaching in Vanuatu, representing leadership, respect, consensus, dance, and drunkenness. The Christian equivalent of the banyan would be the church building itself. In fact, the church building is a dominant metaphor in Vanuatu, symbolizing new patterns of leadership, new music style (and even dance), respect, and Western cargo.

Children's moments are the best time to find metaphors in church. The children's moment is often a kastom story—sometimes with a Christian twist. One Sunday, Lilian told the story of the bat:

> There was a woman and her husband. They had three kids, and they told them, "You stay here, but don't look in that basket. We're off to the garden." The kids stayed, and the younger looked in the basket. There was a bat in there that bit his hand. The two were over there gardening and heard the song:

Oh, daddy! It hurts.
Oh, daddy! It hurts.
It bit me!
It bit me!

"Hey, husband, is that our kids? I forbade them from looking in the basket. He has disobeyed my words and looked in the basket. The bat bit his hand. Listen, won't you, to the song he's singing!"

"Hey! That's our child whom we prohibited from touching the basket. And a bat bit his hand!"

The bat bit him and took off flying to his home. That's the end of my story. And the meaning is that if your parents tell you not to do something, you must obey them. Let's pray.

During another children's moment, an elder told the kastom story of a pig who would not stop following a boy. He tried all sorts of tricks to rid himself of the pest, to no avail. At last, the boy jumped into the fire and killed himself, and the pig did the same. Then the elder explained the story. "The pig is like a bad habit. You can't get rid of them. They'll end up killing you."

The Bislama Bible also incorporates local metaphors at times. For example, it speaks of a post in the house, rather than employing the Mediterranean image of a cornerstone (1 Pet 2). Tannese vernacular translations also occasionally employ local metaphors, including the one of the post in the house. In Acts 15:16, the vernacular speaks of King David's canoe (village, generation), rather than the tent (or kingdom). Canoes (or ships) and baskets are other rich local metaphors for the church. The church is a ship that brings "goodness," cargo, the gospel, and the light.

Churches also employ symbols for leadership. The primary symbol is dress: typically, the necktie introduced by the Scottish Presbyterians a hundred years ago. A ni-Vanuatu Presbyterian elder's "uniform" is a necktie, white shirt, and trousers. It would be as unusual for an elder to preach without a tie as it would be for a chief to refuse his chiefly symbol of kava. I have seen numerous elders skip church or pass the preaching duty on to someone else simply because they could not find a white shirt and tie. The elder also carries a Bible, which is also a symbol of his education and role. Increasingly, more young churchgoers are carrying Bibles as well. However, it would be highly unusual for nonelders to wear a tie, white long-sleeve shirt, and slacks.

Leadership titles are also symbolic. Just like the *yeni*, an elder or deacon's greatest asset as leader is his title. "Possession of a title [legitimates] a man's claim to authority" (White and Lindstrom 1997, 212). In Vanuatu, norms require referring to a church leader by his title in public. Many worshipers refer to God as "Big Man"—the title for chief. Although this potentially invites some undesirable imagery, God is envisioned as the greatest chief.

Finally, as a symbol of the church's defeat of kastom, a church in South Tanna has a flower garden constructed out of ancestral taboo stones! They use the kastom symbol, but have given it an entirely new meaning. The stones are ordinary—powerless; they are nothing compared to God.

FACTOR 10: METHOD FOR HEALING

Kastom-relinquishers cease spitting out demons to heal; they see prayer as a substitute for shamanism or divination in times of sickness. But what about the social functions of kastom healing? A culturally integrated church must have an answer for kastom healing rituals. If the church does not offer a Christian substitute, worshipers will continue doing what they are familiar with. Doug said:

> Some say that a *kleva* (diviner) is no good. If someone wants to see a *kleva*, he goes alone. The church does not know about it. It's just his choice. He just does it . . . The church does not talk about it, because the church only gives the straight talk of God. It does not talk about those things. That's a man's choice. If he wants to go to a *kleva*, he goes.

On the other hand, if prayer for the sick is considered efficacious, it will substitute (not augment) the services of diviners, sacrifice, or magical healing practices. When Pastor Perry prays for the sick, he tells them, "Don't turn around now and go to a shaman. Otherwise, you may not be healed." Turning to a shaman would be evidence of doubt or double-mindedness, which would render the prayer inefficacious (cf. Jas 1:6–8). For prayer to be efficacious, one must put his faith entirely in the Lord.

How can the church foster a healing ministry that is culturally relevant? Kastom healing practices are rich in community participation, discussion of sin, and symbols (Chapter 3). To be culturally relevant, the church should work out a theology of dreams, taboos, anger, and the local cosmology. These concepts may not seem to be significant to Westerners when discussing misfortune and the Bible, but they are central in tribal conceptualizations of cause and effect.[38]

Addressing Local Cosmology

At our sickness workshops, believers have spoken with confidence that Jesus is more powerful than local spirits; therefore, they understand that they should not employ shamanistic techniques for exorcism, such as "spitting out devils." On the other hand, some traditional herbal medicines may be efficacious, though this is difficult to determine, since very little research has been done to determine the medicinal effects of herbal medicines in Vanuatu (Bourdy 1992; Grace 2001).

Addressing Taboos

The breaking of taboos is another spiritual cause for sickness that the church must address. The observation of taboos and totems is a central value for the Tannese. The local church needs to discuss whether totemic foods are still off-limits, or whether all foods are "clean" (Rom 14:14–21). When people become Christians, do they still need to observe animistic taboos? What does it mean for a woman to be "unclean" (Lev 12; 15; Mark 5:21–30)?

---

[38] The following suggestions come from K. Nehrbass, "Dealing with Disaster: Critical Contextualization of Misfortune in an Animistic Setting," *Missiology* 39, no. 4 (2011) p. 459–471.

What about taboo places? What makes them taboo or holy (Gen 32:30; Ex 3:5; 1 Kgs 6)? Was it the presence of God? Can there be holy places today? Has the power of the cross nullified the power of all demonic taboo places?

The issue may not be easily settled, but it is important for the indigenous church to allow her new faith in the Bible to inform and challenge traditional views on all levels, lest she develop a "split-level Christianity" (Hiebert, Shaw, and Tienou 1999, 15). This other-wordly Christianity would potentially focus on issues like soteriology to the neglect of daily concerns such as illness, menstruation taboos, cleanliness, and gardening.

Addressing Dreams

In the traditional mind, dreams are a dangerous liminal period, because during sleep the body is neither alive nor dead. This is the time when spirits interact with people, causing sickness. I was confused when an elderly widower fell ill with an STD, but this did not cause cognitive dissonance for the Tannese. They explained that he contracted an illness by committing sexual sins in his dreams. The notion that people are responsible for sins committed in dreams needs to be addressed, offering hope that God is our protection from the demonic, even in sleep. Kastom requires that the victim of bad dreams strangle a chicken and let its blood run over kava; then the dreams will cease. However, Christians at our workshops generally consider this unacceptable, citing that "the blood of Jesus is enough."

Many Melanesian Christians maintain kastom understandings about dreams, believing that dreaming is a supernatural activity which may reveal the future, authenticate conversion experiences or a call to the ministry, and can be useful for divulging the source of sickness (usually the breaking of a taboo) and possible remedies (Hitchen, 2011, 24–41; cf Nehrbass, 2011b, 62). While this is certainly possible, the church must be mindful that dreaming about causes and cures for illness is more akin to kastom clairvoyance than to the apostles' methods for healing in the New Testament. In all cases, the church should remember the warnings about false oracles in Jeremiah 23 (43).

Addressing Anger

Since "bad insides," and especially anger, are deemed to be the root of many types of sickness, the church needs to give people tools for dealing with anger. Tannese believe a life free of anger, jealousy, and bitterness will also lead to a life without sickness or other types of misfortune. However, the Bible does not guarantee that righteous living will bring a life free of misfortune; in fact, it practically guarantees the righteous will face trouble (1 Thess 3:3). Tribal peoples have an earnest desire to live with shalom, and the church has an excellent opportunity to reach out with tools for Christian living that can help people live out shalom in their relationships.

Theology of Retribution Must be Contextualized

It has become apparent by this point that retribution or payback, *tain*, is a dominant theme in kastom as it is in most Melanesian religions (Trompf 1994). The theology of retribution which is so fundamental to traditional worldviews often bothers Western missionaries because, while divine retribution is a biblical principle (Deut 7:9–10), a full-fledged theology of retribution can be myopic, failing to recognize the beneficence and grace of God. True, at times, misfortune can be traced to sinful thoughts and actions. A theology of retribution has biblical support, but the church needs to contextualize this theology.

It became evident at the sickness workshops on Tanna that the church does not want to relinquish themes of retribution when dealing with misfortune; they see retribution as a significant motivator for behavior modification. They find that threats of future misfortune are effective in encouraging repentance and church attendance. Rather than entirely discounting this approach, I have encouraged the churches to consider the following five points.

1. God and following the rules

In light of animism's emphasis on keeping the rules to ensure prosperity, the tribal church must consider the nature of God's rules. Is God himself subject to those rules (are they more important than God?) If not, then God is more important than the rules; so what is their purpose? The "law" was meant for us to know God's holiness, our need for grace, and to lead us into a relationship with God (Gal 3:19–24). Unfortunately, many relationships in animistic cultures are based on reciprocity, which can cause confusion when we speak of a relationship with God. To "seek first the kingdom of God" is more about pursuing a relationship with him than following the rules, lest God "give back" our bad behavior (Halverson, 1998).

Additionally, in contrast to kastom's promise that following the rules will result in prosperity, churches need to consider whether one can really avoid catastrophe at all (2 Cor 5:6, 12:1–7; Phil 1:21–23). At our workshops, one elder who understood this principle suggested that misfortune *cannot* be avoided. "The banyan tree sheds its leaves several times a year. In the same way, we humans must get sick from time to time."

2. Holy lives and following taboos

The tribal church needs to address the relationship between God and kastom taboos. Are territorial spirits also engaged in regulation of cosmic rules, and do they punish those who break them? Does that mean that spirits of traditional religion are somehow in league with God–both enforcing cosmic rules? Why would these spirits be in league with God? Or, are these local spirits under God's sovereignty? Is it possible to please both local spirits and God by following kastom taboos, or are God's rules for holiness at odds with kastom taboos? The "divided house" parable (Matt 12:25–29) should be enlightening in this case, but we have had little success at communicating the logic of that parable in Vanuatu.

3. The nature of chastisement and God's mercy

There is biblical support for the argument that God disciplines sinners with sickness. Ananias and Sapphira is a poignant story in Acts 5:1–11, but also see King Herod's death because of pride in Acts 12:20–25 and Elymas the sorcerer's blindness in Acts 13:4–12. Also,

Paul advised the church in Corinth that they were sick because they were participating in the Lord's Supper while maintaining impure relationships with others (1 Cor 11:29–30). However, churches in animistic settings can only grasp the nature and purpose of chastisement after it has been established that God is above the rules, and that He ordained the rules as a pathway for us to have a relationship with Him. When the church sees God as above the rules—that the rules serve a purpose, then she can begin considering the extent to which the Law remains in effect, and the situations in which God chastises his children today.

Additionally, to imply that sickness or disaster is God's way of paying back sin is to cheapen the guilt that we as a human race carry. Mudslides and drought are not nearly severe enough of a payback for the rebellion that humans have repeatedly acted out toward God. If God truly chose to pay back our sin, he would punish us eternally in hell, which He has declared to be the only just recompense for our sin. Therefore, I have taken to explaining to the Melanesian church that sickness and disaster are not indicative of retribution for our sin, rather God's mercy. He is holding back (indeed, he has erased) the full measure of his wrath! Thank him that the worst we have to deal with is the temporal suffering on this earth.

4. When there is no misfortune

It is possible that, when a tribal church is enjoying a time of prosperity, she may use this as an opportunity to insist that her denomination is the best, to prove a certain doctrinal point or push an agenda, or as proof of righteous living. "Theology of retribution . . . argues that prosperity is a blessing from God and a sign that one has lived a good and moral life . . . [and] has tended to be propagated by those who benefit from systemic privilege" (Haddad, 2008, 81). Some Tannese have argued, "We are enjoying prosperity because we have done everything according to holiness."

While there is biblical support for such a claim (Psalm 24), it does not mean that whenever things are going well, the community is free of sin. The church needs to ask, "Are prosperity, peace, and health free gifts from a merciful God, or are they our just reward for following God's rules?" Even when the church seems to be free from suffering, she should continue to ask God to show where she has sinned (Ps 139:23); she should not assume that because she is free from misfortune she is free from sin. The wicked, in fact, prosper too (Ps 37:7, 73:3). In the NT, there are examples of churches prospering in spite of their sin (Corinth) and there were churches and individuals that were apparently pure but suffering or expecting suffering to come (Philippi, Smyrna).

Group Discussions about Misfortune Must Be Contextualized

Tannese church members inevitably experience cognitive dissonance when somebody is sick—especially when their pastor or missionary becomes ill. Did he commit a sin or break a taboo? Is he upset with the church, and are his "bad insides" making him sick? Did somebody perform sorcery on him? I once visited a village for several days and began vomiting. While I suffered inside the hut, the church sat outside considering all the possible scenarios. Ultimately, they apologized to me profusely, explaining that it was not sorcery, and it certainly was not a sin of mine, therefore it must be testing from God. On another occasion, I witnessed the local pastor strongly rebuking the congregation for making him sick. He threatened them that if they continued their sorcery, he would go pastor a church somewhere else. The point is, churches from animistic backgrounds inevitably feel a need to talk about misfortune, and especially misfortune causation.

Since sickness causation is group-oriented, the idea of workshops dealing with it is a way for the church to work out such misfortune in a group setting. There is a biblical basis for having sickness be the concern of the group at large. Paul encourages us to "bear one another's burdens" (Gal 6:2 NASB). If the church can use group discussions about misfortune as a way to extend compassion rather than condemnation (Eph 4:32), and to encourage one another in love and good deeds (Heb 10:24), these tribal discussions will meet this need and will be evidence of contextualized Christianity.

SUMMARY

Kastom-relinquishers differ from kastom-retainers in ten ways, which were discussed in Chapter 11. These ten factors make up the gospel-response continuum. But gospel response is only half of the contextualization model here. The other half requires that churches be culturally relevant. In this chapter I have suggested ten domains that form a cultural-integration continuum. When these two continua are juxtaposed, four ecclesiastical approaches toward kastom become apparent. These four approaches are discussed in the next chapter.

CHAPTER 13

Mixers, Transplanters, Contextualizers, and Separators

I HAVE discussed two religious systems in this book that are so different from each other that one almost wonders why they would appear together. On the one hand, I have paid close attention to the traditional religion of Tanna—a brand of animism that centers on the accumulation of power through ritual and sympathetic magic, and which perpetuates social alliances to ensure a system of economic exchange. On the other hand, I have recounted the history of Christian missions on Tanna and have performed in-depth interviews with twenty-five Christians about their beliefs. The reason, of course, for giving a treatment of both kastom and Christianity in this book is that many Tannese themselves experience both religious systems simultaneously.

I endeavored to discover why some Tannese relinquish traditional religious practices in order to become worshipers, while others continue to practice, inter alia, sacrifice, shamanism, divination, ancestor veneration, or totemism. What experiences have the kastom-relinquishers had that distinguish them from kastom-retainers? How are their churches different? What draws kastom-relinquishers to the churches that encourage relinquishing kastom? And what draws kastom-retainers to the churches that either neglect mentioning kastom or tacitly endorse it?

While I would not claim to have found a surefire formula for turning kastom-relinquishers into kastom-retainers, I have discovered ten factors that distinguish the former from the latter, and have highlighted ten factors that distinguish a culturally relevant church from a church that does not engage the culture. The ten domains on the gospel-response continuum and ten domains on the cultural-integration continuum allow us to plot an individual's attitude toward kastom on a gospel/culture model, which is presented here. The two-dimensional model makes four ecclesiastical approaches toward kastom evident: Mixers, Contextualizers, Separators, and Transplanters. Assuming that the goal of evangelical missions is to foster Contextualizers, we can use this model to measure the degree to which contextualization has been achieved.

MEASURING CONTEXTUALIZATION

In 1995 professor Doug Hayward challenged churches and mission organizations to measure the degree of contextualization in their fields. "Mission leadership should not take for granted that their church planting efforts are indeed the local expression of faith, but rather submit it to evaluation and scrutiny in light of . . . indicators for measuring contextualization" (1995, 135). Hayward listed more than a dozen indicators of a well-contextualized church. However, in order to actually attain his desired end—a tool for measuring contextualization—his challenge needed to be expanded in two ways. First, measuring implies some quantitative value; there needs to be a rubric for plotting how well churches are doing on each of the items that his article elucidated. Second, the components of contextualization that he mentioned all focused on one axis: the cultural integration of a church. A truly contextualized church must not only be culturally integrated, but must foster worldview transformation among the members. This chapter builds on Hayward's project for measuring contextualization by providing a tool for numeric measurement across both the gospel-response axis (discussed in Chapter 11) and the cultural-integration axis (discussed in Chapter 12). The method for measuring contextualization involves two steps: (1) rating individuals on the Gospel/Culture Assessment Tool, and (2) plotting them on the Gospel/Culture Grid.

Gospel/Culture Assessment Tool

The Gospel/Culture Assessment Tool (Table 17 and Appendix D) summarizes the ten gospel-response domains and ten cultural-integration domains that emerged from this study. This tool allows us to summarize what we know about the people's experiences of Christianity and animism based on the interview data.

Scores are given on a range from 0 (completely disagree) to 4 (completely agree). A score range is more suitable than binary oppositions (e.g., the congregant cites the Bible or not), because many people's attitudes and actions are not black and white. For example, some churchgoers articulate a vague conversion experience but know that becoming a "person of God" involves baptism. This partial answer receives a score in the middle of the range—2 points. Also, many cite the Bible, but some cite it incorrectly or only speak vaguely about the Bible. They will score 2 on that domain. No church on Tanna uses exclusively vernacular in liturgy or music, so they will not score a 4 on that item. Nor would any church score a 0 on the vernacular item, otherwise the worship service would be utterly meaningless to the members.

Gospel/Culture Grid

After interviewing each of the twenty-five participants, I rated them on the Gospel/Culture Assessment Tool. Once rated, they were plotted on the Gospel/Culture Grid, and appeared in one of the four quadrants: Mixers, Contextualizers, Separators, and Transplanters (see Figure 5). Those who have high scores on the gospel-response items end up on the right two quadrants. Those whose churches score high on cultural integration are plotted on the top two quadrants. Contextualizers have high scores on both axes and are in the upper right quadrant.

Note that there is no quadrant explicitly labeled "syncretizers." That is because, as Kraft pointed out, there are two types of syncretism: keeping the old, or blindly

Table 17a: Gospel/Culture Assessment Tool

GOSPEL-RESPONSE CONTINUUM	POINTS 0–4
Answer 0 to 4: strongly disagree 0; about halfway 2; strongly agree 4.	
Congregant discourages the practice of magic (for controlling natural phenomena such as rain, gardens, etc.), not only because he/she is afraid of it (i.e., they see it as risky), but because it competes with exclusive worship of God.	
Congregant articulates a theology of local cosmology (e.g., animistic gods are demons, Jesus is more powerful than local spirits).	
Congregant sees totemic system (e.g., annual harvest sacrifices) as ancestor worship or idolatry.	
Congregant articulates an experience of conversion to Christ.	
Congregant conceptualizes the church as a place for worship, evangelism, and teaching, not simply a place for meeting felt needs (of prosperity, development, health, etc.).	
Congregant conceptualizes salvation as atonement and restoration, not simply a way of avoiding earthly suffering.	
Congregant cites the Bible when talking about his/her faith.	
Congregant's church has stringent leadership selection (elders/pastors).	
Congregant sees divination, shamanism, sorcery, and religious use of drugs as sinful.	
Congregant evaluates plausibility of religious knowledge (i.e., myths and the Bible) in terms of historicity, feasibility, and logical consistency.	
Total Points on Gospel-Response Continuum:	

adopting the new (1998, 390). These two types of syncretism are different quadrants on the Gospel/Culture Grid. Churches that keep the old beliefs and practices are in the top left quadrant: Mixers. The ones that blindly adopt the new are in the bottom right quadrant: Transplanters.

Once individuals are plotted, the trend becomes obvious: kastom-retainers are found almost exclusively in Mixing or Separating churches, and kastom-relinquishers are found almost exclusively in Contextualizing or Transplanted churches. This suggests that if

Table 17b: Gospel/Culture Assessment Tool

CULTURAL-INTEGRATION CONTINUUM	POINTS 0–4
Answer 0 to 4: strongly disagree 0; about halfway 2; strongly agree 4.	
Congregant's church is independent (not dependent on foreign funds or foreign governance).	
Congregant's church has a functional substitute for meeting social obligations to in-laws (regarding, e.g., clan-division exchanges, marriage obligations, and other rites of passage) and a way to honor (dead) ancestors.	
Congregant's church utilizes indigenous models of leadership (power, succession, and authority).	
Congregant's church uses a local musical style with local instruments.	
Congregant's church uses liturgy (including prayer and preaching) in the vernacular.	
Congregant's church's pedagogy reflects local style (hortatory, narrative, harangue, dialogue, and propositions).	
Congregant's church utilizes local material culture (art, architecture, pews, and style of dressing).	
Congregant's church uses local metaphors.	
Congregant's church has a functional substitute for dealing with sickness (e.g., deals with possible transgressions, is public, and uses local symbols).	
Total Points on Cultural-Integration Continuum:	

churches wish to bring people out of animism on their journey toward Christ, they must emphasize a full gospel response described by the ten items on the gospel-response axis. It also shows that, even in a homogeneous animistic society, a gospel-adhering church can indeed be culturally relevant. In fact, the prevalence of kastom-relinquishing Christians on the chart suggests that a culturally relevant church that is strong on the gospel is the most effective way to help people change their allegiances from kastom to Christ.

PLOTTING DENOMINATIONS

Individual responses are not indicative of denominational approaches toward kastom.

However, when a number of respondents from the same denomination are plotted on the Gospel/Culture Grid, it may become apparent that they uniformly fit into a certain region. This would suggest a general denominational tendency (see Figure 6). It can also reveal the uniformity of response. The SDAs and PRCs are rather homogeneous in their response, all tightly in the Contextualizing quadrant, whereas the Presbyterians are spread across the top two quadrants. The Baptist response is unpredictable, ranging from Mixers to Transplanters.

Denominational leaders may use this assessment tool to see where they are excelling and what domains they wish to work on more. If they are strong on cultural integration but weak on the gospel response, they will wish to see which parts of the gospel response

---

Figure 5: Individuals plotted on the Gospel/Culture Grid

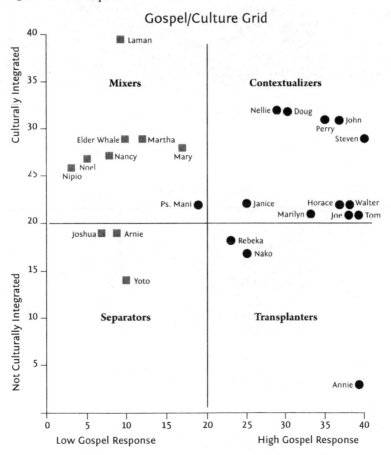

- ▓ = kastom retainers
- ● = kastom relinquishers

remain to be emphasized. Do they need to accentuate conversion more? Are they using the Bible as a basis for the evaluation of truth? Do they have an answer to local cosmology? Have they given church members tools for fulfilling social obligations without practicing magic or idolatry?

Alternately, if denominational leaders or church planters discover that they are excelling at fostering a full gospel response, but are not careful to engage the culture, they will want to see what areas still need to be addressed. Are they using local material culture? What style of pedagogy are they using? Do they address obligations to in-laws and ancestors, or are they leaving church members to practice split-level Christianity?

Figure 6: Churches plotted on the Gospel-Culture Grid

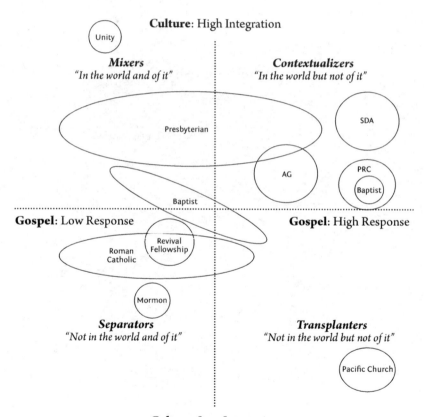

FOUR APPROACHES TOWARD ANIMISM

A two-dimensional model delineates four quadrants. By synthesizing the data from my interviews, I found that there are four different approaches toward kastom: Mixers, Transplanters, Contextualizers, and Separators. I have found it intriguing to interview people from each of these groups to see what makes them tick. Below, I describe each of these four approaches.

Mixers

Low gospel response + high cultural integration = mixed Christianity.

"Mixing" is the type of syncretism that Western missionaries fear, and therefore try to avoid. It is the scenario where local churches are excellent at being culturally relevant, but they project their animistic beliefs onto the church, resulting in nonorthodox beliefs about the purpose of church, the nature of salvation, and the exclusive worship of God. They are in the world and of it. Their beliefs and practices reflect their animistic background.

Mixers are those who see church as a place to meet felt needs; they do not regularly quote Scripture; they conceptualize salvation as freedom from suffering rather than atonement from sin. They are low on the gospel-response continuum, but they attend churches that use vernacular liturgy, train their own leaders locally, and are independent.

Elder Whale is an archetypical Mixer. His denomination is a rapidly expanding charismatic movement that is entirely independent in Vanuatu. Churches in his denomination are easily accepted by the community because the leaders are chosen locally and speak the vernacular. They expand rapidly because they do not depend on foreign funding and do not require extensive training for their leaders. They construct new churches with bamboo walls and thatch, so a church can be established in a new village in a matter of weeks. Their leaders, once appointed, typically receive little training. In fact, Elder Whale did not receive any training before he became the preacher of his local church.

For Elder Whale, the church is an extension of kastom. It is an additional place to teach respect and love, and it is an additional route for bringing healing and material prosperity. His church and the *imarəm* have a harmonious relationship.

Laman is another quintessential Mixer. His movement, "John Frum, Christ, Unity," uses sermons and chiefly speeches, sings songs about local history and geography, is entirely independent and multiplying, and has an amiable attitude toward the church.

The strength of the Mixers is that they are culturally relevant. Their weakness is that they have not emphasized a full gospel response as outlined in Chapter 11. To move into the upper right quadrant, Mixers need to emphasize that conversion is a change of allegiance from local powers to Christ. They need to emphasize that Christians relinquish sacrifice, magic, and divination not because it is merely dangerous, but because it dishonors Christ. They should cite the Bible as an authority, and they should be careful to give more training to their leaders.

Eight people were plotted as Mixers. They are probably the most common type of churchgoer on Tanna. Only culturally relevant movements can thrive in a village setting, so Transplanters are few on the outer islands of Vanuatu. This raises the question: if the village setting is so amenable to enculturated churches, why was nobody plotted above 33 on the cultural-integration axis? This is because the church is relatively new to Melanesia. In South America, where the church has been established for five hundred years, there is indigenous music, national training institutions, material culture, and an indigenous preaching style. It takes generations for a church to become enculturated to that point. In Melanesia, even well-enculturated denominations still utilize foreign music, and even rely on foreign training institutions.

Transplanters

High gospel response + low cultural integration = transplanted Christianity.

Transplanting is syncretism in the other direction. Rather than local church communities projecting kastom onto the church, Transplanters mimic foreign norms for church. They may have orthodox teachings, but their praxis can be somewhat culturally irrelevant. If church leaders cannot be trained locally; if the liturgy is in foreign languages; if the church depends on foreign money to expand; and if the church architecture, schedule, or dress reflects middle-class urban patterns rather than local norms—the church's effectiveness in reaching its own people will be diminished.

Transplanting is an urban phenomenon, not a village one. Village churches must be culturally relevant to thrive, so Transplanting churches in the village setting will either die or become Mixers before long. Transplanted churches thrive in urban areas because of heterogeneity. Pastors cannot preach in vernacular in a city where more than a hundred languages are spoken. Social obligations are less relevant when the in-laws live in a village one hundred miles away. Also, foreign funds and influence reach the urban areas more quickly, making Transplants more viable there.

Three of the people I interviewed are Transplanters. The quintessential one is Annie. She grew up on Tanna, but has spent most of her life in the capital city, or overseas. As a child on Tanna, she received an evangelical faith from her father, who did not participate in *tupunas* or *tamafa*. She is aware of relatives on Tanna who kill chickens or pigs to "release" sickness and who practice *tamafa*, but her knowledge of kastom is limited. She married an Australian and has spent a few years in Australia. Now she attends an English-speaking church in the capital city led by an Australian church planter. The church has ni-Vanuatu members, including some Tannese. But the church does not address Vanuatu cosmologies, nor does it offer functional substitutes for social obligations. The preaching is propositional, and in English. The expatriate praise band sings current English praise songs, with the lyrics projected onto a screen. The building is clean and attractive; you almost forget you are in Vanuatu. That is probably why a large expatriate group attends the church—they get a little bit of Australia each Sunday.

Obviously, Annie's church relies on foreign funding and leadership. While she has experienced a thorough gospel response, her church offers little Christian response to her own culture and animistic background. Nor, then, does it offer tools for reaching her family and transforming their allegiance from animism to Christ. Her church is not of the world, but is not in it, either. It would be a contextualized church in Brisbane, but not in Vanuatu.

Can Transplanted churches in urban areas realistically move into the upper quadrant? Can they preach in the vernacular of such a diverse audience? Vanuatu has 106 people groups—can an urban church address such varied customs, local cosmologies, and social frameworks? Indeed, it is more difficult to enculturate a church in such a diverse urban setting; however, many churches in Port Vila are in the upper right quadrant. Kejio's SDA church uses Bislama and the songs that people are singing in their villages on the "outer islands," but does not rely on foreign money. Its building is made of cinder blocks, but it is not as sterile as Annie's Transplanted church. Annie's church will need to address the areas where it scored low on the cultural-integration continuum in order to move up into the upper right quadrant.

Contextualizers

Thorough gospel response + high cultural integration = contextualized Christianity.

Contextualizers' faith allows them to be thoroughly involved in the community and yet true to the gospel. They are in the world, but not of it. Like Mixers, their churches are independent and self-multiplying. They appreciate the vernacular; they use local metaphors; and they incorporate local leadership patterns, local hymnody, and local art forms. Rather than ignoring felt needs, they address them head on. They have a Christian answer for meeting obligations to in-laws and honoring ancestors. Since their substitute for magic and animistic ritual meets the underlying need for maintaining family relationships, Contextualizers are not compelled to practice both the Christian substitute and the kastom ritual. Since their Christian healing practices are public in nature, address the problem of sin, are rich in symbol, and claim the power of Christ over local deities, Contextualizers are not compelled to visit diviners, sorcerers, or clairvoyants, or to perform sacrifice in times of sickness or disaster.

For Contextualizers, conversion is a change of allegiances: from local deities to Jesus Christ; from pleasing self to pleasing God; from trusting in good works to trusting in the atonement through Christ. Contextualizers cite the Bible and conceptualize salvation as atonement from sin.

Steven is a Contextualizer. He does not ignore local deities, but refuses to let them have power over him. He does not participate in totemism, but fulfills his social obligations. He cites the Bible as an authority, and his plausibility structure is based on truthfulness. He sings songs in his heart language and reads Scripture in the trade language of Vanuatu (Bislama).

Evangelical church planters endeavor to end up in the upper right quadrant of the Gospel/Culture Grid. Much of evangelical missiological literature in the past three decades has been devoted to understanding the key to nurturing churches that end up in that quadrant. My findings indicate that churches that are careful to emphasize the ten factors on the gospel-response continuum and the ten factors of the cultural-integration continuum are likely to be Contextualizers.

Eleven of the people I interviewed were plotted as Contextualizers. It is encouraging to see that the Contextualizers come from a variety of denominations, and that they are numerous on Tanna.

Separators

Low gospel response + low cultural integration = a separated movement.

The Separators are neither culturally relevant nor strong on the gospel. They are not in the world, but they are of it. They do not address healing practices, so the members go to kastom for healing. They do not have an answer for meeting social obligations during marriage ceremonies, or rites of passage, so the members continue on in kastom. Three people were plotted as Separators. Joshua's Catholic church is a deliberate Separating movement. The lack of functional substitutes is deliberate. He encourages members to participate in kastom and does not expect the church to have substitutes. The church is not meant to address day-to-day issues. Its existence is more for political motives than to meet felt needs.

"Separator" is a fitting description of Pastor Arnie. He believes in a separation of church and kastom, whereas Mixers enthusiastically wish to join the two. Pastor Arnie essentially has a denominational church plant that was transplanted from Papua New Guinea. As a transplant, it has no infrastructure for training leaders or multiplying. Further, it is too new in the country to have worked out functional substitutes; it does not offer an answer to local cosmology. The pastor wants to experience speaking in tongues and Christian liturgy, especially Bible reading, on Sundays, but wants to engage fully in kastom life.

In some cases, Separators are foreign religious movements, or cults, which have not yet mastered the art of enculturation. The Mormons, for instance, do not incorporate the vernacular into liturgy or printed material, and their church polity requires that to become a full (male) member, one must seal his marriage in a temple, which would require a trip to New Zealand, Australia, or perhaps Salt Lake City. Additionally, full members must wear "temple garments" daily, which cannot be purchased within Vanuatu. Mormons use an English hymnal and heavily rely on foreign missionaries for multiplication. Because of these limitations, the movement's ability to be culturally integrated is diminished. And because of their doctrine, their score on gospel response is moderate at best. Yoto is a kastom-retaining Separator. He enthusiastically participates in his local Latter Day Saints (LDS) church, but he also retains kastom. His church life has done little to engage or transform his kastom worldview.

An educated businessman in the commercial center who neither worships nor participates in kastom would also be a Separator. His belief system is neither Christian nor culturally integrated. He is too busy to bother with *nier* or *nakur* ceremonies. He is too Westernized to participate in *tupunas* or shamanism. However, the secular businessman is not given much attention in this study, because the gospel/culture model specifically focuses on four ecclesiastical approaches toward kastom.

SUMMARY

Four ecclesiastical approaches to animism have emerged from this study: Mixers, Separators, Transplanters, and Contextualizers. Each of these approaches is idiosyncratic in the way it deals with the animistic worldview, conversion, functional substitutes, worship music, and felt needs (see Figure 7).

When the Gospel/Culture Grid is used in conjunction with the Gospel/Culture Assessment Tool, individuals can be plotted on one of the four quadrants. And when numerous people from a church or denomination are plotted, a church trend becomes obvious—highlighting where the church has been successful at contextualization and where it falls short. Therefore, the goal of finding a way to measure contextualization within the animistic setting has been realized. What remains is for church leaders in animistic contexts to begin testing the model to see how well it addresses their local situations.

Figure 7: Characteristics of four types of ecclesastical approaches

Culture: High Integration

MIXED	**CONTEXTUALIZED**
☐ Animistic beliefs mixed with the church life	☐ Break from animism
☐ Unclear conversion	☐ Conversion + depth
☐ Does not observe functional substitutes	☐ Understands functional substitutes
☐ Appreciates vernacular	☐ Appreciates vernacular
☐ Uses local songs	☐ Uses local songs
☐ Felt-needs overemphasized	☐ Felt-needs addressed

Gospel: Low Response   **Gospel**: High Response

SEPARATED	**TRANSPLANTED**
☐ Animistic beliefs not addressed	☐ Relies on foreign money and leadership
☐ Conversion not emphasized	☐ Conversion w/o depth
☐ Does not observe functional substitutes	☐ Little understanding of the "why" behind functional substitutes
☐ Relies on foreign language for liturgy and doctrine	☐ King James only
☐ Felt-needs ignored	☐ Singing English hymns only
	☐ Felt-needs ignored

Culture: Low Integration

APPLYING THE GOSPEL/CULTURE MODEL

After researching Tannese attitudes about kastom, I began sharing the results with church leaders in Vanuatu. One elder responded, "Ken, now I understand that it's a good idea for us to begin evaluating the belief of churchgoers. We should see, when we baptize them, 'Do they really believe, or not?'" A church planter told me, "Ken, now I think about the work I did planting that church—I raised up elders too quickly." The research has pointed out ecclesiastical tendencies toward mixing Christianity and animism, or separating, or transplanting. It has also given suggestions for how to foster contextualized churches. I agree with the elder and church planter: prebaptismal training and adequate training of elders are necessary for fostering contextualized churches.

Many pastors see the dual practice of kastom and Christianity as primarily a problem with dividing people's allegiances between the church (or God) and false gods or the village. One pastor summed it up, "It'd be good for people to leave kastom nowadays, because it takes them away from the work of the church." Other more evangelical pastors spoke about the issue in terms of idolatry.

After completing this study, I reported my findings to a national assembly of pastors in Port Vila, Vanuatu. Some of the pastors were threatened by the idea of a "kastom-relinquisher" as if that meant relinquishing their culture at large—throwing the baby out with the bathwater. They wondered, "How can you separate traditional religion from traditional values, dress, food, music, and art?" The Gospel/Culture Assessment Tool presented in this book is meant to help pastors and missionaries answer just that sort of question. It is meant to help the church foster a full gospel response and still be thoroughly culturally relevant.

Surprisingly, it does not go without saying that churches should aim for the contextualizing quadrant. When I taught on the material in this book at a Bible college in Vanuatu, several students (pastors themselves) challenged my a priori that we would want to turn mixing churches into contextualizing ones. One student, Lucy, asked me, "Why is a contextualizing church more desirable than a mixing one? Aren't mixing ones okay too?" I explained to the class, "We want to move into the contextualizing quadrant because that's where we can experience the fullness of the Christian life. Only in that quadrant do we trust in God for our needs, experience meaningful worship, and truly understand what it means to call Jesus our Savior and Lord." Later, I led a discussion on Gospel and Culture at an assembly of expatriate missionaries in Vanuatu, and I asked them how they would respond to Lucy's question. They, too, indicated that it is only in the contextualizing quadrant that people can become mature disciples of Christ.

Missionaries in fields throughout the globe have also tested the gospel/culture model. Many of them, especially those working in Melanesia, have found that the model addresses important issues of animism and contextualization in their field. Most, if not all, of the ten aspects on the Gospel and Culture axes were relevant to those mission fields, and they were able to plot individuals in one of the four quadrants and could identify Mixers, Transplanters, Separators, and Contextualizers in their congregations.

However, some missionaries have reported that they are not familiar enough with the worldview of the people with whom they work to complete the Gospel/Culture Assessment Tool. I hope this book encourages missionaries to familiarize themselves with the local worldview. In the spirit of Hiebert's (1984) project of "critical contextualization," I hope I have given a gentle exhortation for missionaries in animistic contexts to begin with questions, rather than answers. Strategizing begins with an in-depth study of the culture. Only after missionaries have a good grasp of kastom from an emic perspective can they begin helping the host church to be self-critical about how to handle the interaction between their Christian faith and traditional religion.

REFERENCES

A. M. B. n.d. *John G. Paton: The four years on Tanna*. Melbourne: Brown, Prior & Co.

Adams, R. 1975. *Energy and structure: A theory of social power*. Austin: University of Texas.

——. 1984. *In the land of strangers: A century of European contact with Tanna 1774–1874*. Canberra: Australian National University.

Allen, J. [1905?] *The story of a noble life: John G. Paton: His early days and his work in the New Hebrides*. Sydney: Keir Murray.

Allen, M., ed. 1981. *Vanuatu: Politics, economics and ritual in island Melanesia*. Sydney: Academic Press.

Armstrong, W. D. 1909. The struggle of the soul. *Regions Beyond* (February): 28–29, 172, 198–99.

Barker, J., ed. 1990. *Christianity in Oceania*. Lanham, MD: University Press.

Berger, A. 1999. *Signs in contemporary culture: An introduction to semiotics*, 2nd ed. Salem, WI: Sheffield.

Bieniek, J., and G. Trompf. 2000. The millennium, not the cargo? *Ethnohistory* 47, no. 1: 113–32.

Bonnemaison, J. 1991. Magic gardens in Tanna. *Pacific Studies* 14, no. 4: 71–89.

——. 1994. *The tree and the canoe: History and ethnogeography of Tanna*. Honolulu: University of Hawaii.

Bosch, D. 1991. *Transforming mission*. New York: Orbis.

Bourdy, G. 1992. Maternity and medicinal plants in Vanuatu. *Journal of Ethnopharmacology* 37: 179–96.

Brown, R. 2006. Contextualization without syncretism. *International Journal of Frontier Missions* 23, no. 3: 127–33.

Brunton, R. 1979. Kava and the daily dissolution of society on Tanna, New Hebrides. *Mankind* 12, no. 2: 93–103.

——. 1989. *The abandoned narcotic: Kava and cultural instability in Melanesia*. New York: Cambridge University Press.

Burnett, D. 1988. *Unearthly powers: A Christian's handbook on primal and folk religions*. Nashville: Thomas Nelson.

Callaway, H. 1868. *Nursery tales: Traditions and histories of the Zulus*. Westport, CT: Negro Universities Press.

Calvert, K. 1978. Cargo cult mentality and development in the New Hebrides today. In *Paradise postponed: Essays on research and development in the South Pacific*, eds. A. Mamak and G. McCall, 209–24. Rushcutters, Australia: Pergamon.

Campbell, F. 1873. *A year in the New Hebrides, Loyalty Islands, and New Caledonia*.

Geelong, Australia: Mercer.

Capell, A. 1938. The stratification of afterworld beliefs in the New Hebrides. *Folklore* 49, no. 1: 51–85.

Codrington, R. 1891. *The Melanesians: Their anthropology and folk-lore*. Oxford: Clarendon.

Corduan, W. 1998. *Neighboring faith: A Christian introduction to world religions*. Grand Rapids: InterVarsity.

Cromarty, J. 1997. *King of the cannibals*. Darlington, UK: Evangelical Press.

Crowley, D. J., and M. L. Crowley. 1996. Religion and politics in the John Frum Festival, Tanna Island, Vanuatu. *Journal of Folklore Research* 33, no. 2: 155–64.

D'Arcy, A. 2003. *Tanna Island kastom law*. Tasmania, Australia: D'Arcy.

D'Souza, D. 2007. *What's so great about Christianity?* Washington, DC: Regnary.

Douglas, B. 1989. Autonomous and controlled spirits: Traditional ritual and early interpretations of Christianity on Tanna, Aneityum and the Isle of Pines in comparative perspective. *Journal of the Polynesian Society* 98: 7–48.

Durkheim, E. 1915. *The elementary forms of the religious life*. New York: Free Press.

Evans-Pritchard, E. 1965. *Theories of primitive religion*. Oxford: University Press.

Ferguson, J. 1918. *A bibliography of the New Hebrides and a history of the Mission Press*. Sydney: Ferguson.

Finnegan, R. 1996. Oral tradition. In *Encyclopedia of cultural anthropology*, vol. 3, eds. D. Levinson and M. Ember, 887–91. New York: Henry Holt.

Flemming, B. 1980. *Contextualization of theology: An evangelical assessment*. Pasadena: William Carey Library.

Flemming, D. 2005. *Contextualization in the New Testament: Patterns for theology and mission*. Downer's Grove, IL: InterVarsity.

Fraser, D. 1911. *The future of Africa*. Westport, CT: Negro Universities Press.

———. 1914. *Winning a primitive people: Sixteen years work among the warlike tribe of the Ngoni and the Senga and Tumbuka peoples of Central Africa*. London: Seeley, Servicet & Co.

Frazer, J. 1922. *The golden bough: A study in magic and religion*. New York: Macmillan.

Freud, S. 1950. *Totem and taboo*, trans. J. Strachey. New York: Norton.

Friesen, J. S. 1996. *Missionary responses to tribal religions at Edinburgh, 1910*. New York: Lang.

Gardissat, P. 2005. *Nabanga*. Port Vila, Vanuatu: Vanuatu Cultural Center.

Grace, R. 2001. Anticholinergic poisoning secondary to custom medicine in Vanuatu. *Journal of Ethnopharmacology* 77: 2–3.

Green, J. 2007. "JESUS" video tools and prints. Campus Crusade for Christ International. https://give.ccci.org/give?Action=ViewDetail&Desig=2777600&SeqNo=736.

Gregory, J. E. 1982. *Structural determinants of education and socialization on Tanna, Vanuatu*. PhD diss, University of North Carolina.

Gregory, R. J. 1984. John Frum: An indigenous strategy of reaction to mission rule and the colonial order. *Pacific Studies*, 7: 68–90.

———. 2003. An early history of land on Tanna, Vanuatu. *Anthropologist* 5, no. 2: 67–74.

J. Gregory, and J. Peck. 1981. Kava and prohibition in Tanna, Vanuatu. *Addiction* 76, no. 3: 299–313.

Guiart, J. 1956. Culture, contact, and the 'John Frum' movement on Tanna, New Hebrides. *Southwestern Journal of Anthropology* 12: 105–16.

Halverson, D. 1998. Animism: The religion of the tribal world. *International Journal of Frontier Missions* 15, no. 2: 59–67.

Harris, W. T., and E. G. Parrinder. 1960. *The Christian approach to the animist.* London: Edinburgh House.

Harvey, G. 2006. *Animism.* New York: Columbia University Press.

Hayward, D. 1995. Measuring contextualization in church and missions. *International Journal of Frontier Missions* 12, no. 3: 135–38.

———. 1997. The evangelization of animists: Power, truth or love encounter? *International Journal of Frontier Missions* 14, no. 4: 155–59.

Hiebert, P. 1982. The flaw of the excluded middle. *Missiology: An International Review* 10, no. 1: 35–47.

———. 1984. Critical contextualization. *Missiology: An International Review* 12, no. 3: 287–96.

———. 2008. *Transforming worldviews.* Grand Rapids: Baker.

———, R. D. Shaw, and T. Tienou, T. 1999. *Understanding folk religion.* Grand Rapids: Baker.

Hitchen, J. 2011. Dreams in traditional thought and in the encounter with Christianity in Melanesia. *Pacific Journal of Theology,* 27(2), 5–53.

Hook, M. n.d. *A mission among murders: Early Adventism in Vanuatu.* Wahroonga, NSW, Australia: South Pacific Division, Department of Education of the Seventh Day Adventist Church. http://www.google.com/#q=southern+islands +presbyterian+bible+college+tanna&hl=en&prmd=imvnsb&ei=Q-3RTo7I4nw8 QPth3DDBg&start=20&sa=N&bav=on.2,or.r_gc.r_pw.,cf.osb&fp=e9de948b95aa5 75a&biw=1280&bih=622. Accessed Nov. 28, 2011.

Hopkins, E. W. 1918. The background of totemism. *Journal of the American Oriental Society* 38: 145–59.

Howells, W. W. 1948. *The heathens: Primitive man and his religions.* Garden City, NY: Doubleday.

Humphreys, C. 1926. *The southern New Hebrides.* New York: Cambridge.

Inglis, J. 1887. *In the New Hebrides: Reminiscences of missionary life and work.* London: Nelson & Sons, Paternoster Row.

Jebens, H., ed. 2004. *Cargo, cult and culture critique.* Honolulu, HI: University of Hawaii.

Jersey, S. C. 1978. *Letters, New Hebrides Islands.* Paper presented at the Forty-fourth American Philatelic Congress.

Keesing, R. 1984. Rethinking mana. *Journal of Anthropological Research* 40, no. 1: 137–56.

Keller, J., and T. Kuautonga. 2007. *Nokonofo kitea: We keep on living this way; Myths and music of Futuna, Vanuatu.* Honolulu: University of Hawaii Press.

Kelley, R. 1992. *The power of followership: How to create leaders people want to follow and followers who lead themselves.* New York: Doubleday.

Killingbeck, R. 1978. *Tabu fire*. Puyallup, WA: Valley Press.
Kraft, C. 1978. The contextualization of theology. *Evangelical Missions Quarterly* 14: 31–36.
———. 1998. Culture, worldview and contextualization. In *Perspectives on the world Christian movement*, eds. R. Winter and S. Hawthorne, 384–91. Pasadena: William Carey Library.
———. 2005. The development of contextualization theory. In *Appropriate Christianity*, ed. C. Kraft, 15–34. Pasadena: William Carey Library.
Lange, R. 2005. *Island ministers: Indigenous leaders in nineteenth century Pacific Islands Christianity*. Canberra: Pandanus Books.
Langridge, A. 1934. *The conquest of cannibal Tanna: A brief record of Christian persistency in the New Hebrides Islands*. London: Hodder & Stoughton.
Larson, L. 1997. *The Spirit in paradise: History of the Assemblies of God of Fiji and its ministries*. St. Louis: Plus Communications.
Lebot, V., and L. Lindstrom. 1997. *Kava: The Pacific elixir*. Rochester, VT: Healing Arts Press.
Lessard, M. 2003. A life changing book. *The Covenant Companion*, February.
Leuba, J. 1909. On three types of behavior: The mechanical, the coercitive (magic) and the anthropopathic (including religion). *American Journal of Psychology* 20, no. 1: 107–19.
Levi-Strauss, C. 1963a. *Structural anthropology*. Garden City, NY: Anchor.
———. 1963b. Totemism. Boston: Beacon Press.
Lindstrom, L. 1979. Americans on Tanna: An essay from the field. *Canberra Anthropology* 2, no. 2: 36–45.
———. 1981. *Achieving wisdom: Knowledge and politics on Tanna (Vanuatu)*. PhD diss., University of California, Berkeley.
———. 1990a. Big men as ancestors: Inspiration and copyrights on Tanna (Vanuatu). *Ethnology* 29, no. 4: 313–26.
———. 1990b. *Knowledge and power in a South Pacific society*. Washington, DC: Smithsonian.
———. 1991. Kava, cash, and custom in Vanuatu. *Cultural Survival Quarterly* 15, no. 2: 28–31.
———. 2004. History, folklore, traditional and current uses of kava. In *Kava: From ethnology to pharmacology*, ed. Y. Singh 10–28. Boca Raton: CRC Press.
Lingenfelter, S., and M. Mayers. 1986. *Ministering cross-culturally*. Grand Rapids: Baker.
Lowie, R. 1948. *Primitive religion*. New York: Live Right.
MacClancy, J. 1980. *To kill a bird with two stones*. Port Vila, Vanuatu: Vanuatu Cultural Center.
Malinowski, B. 1935. *Coral gardens and their magic: A study of the methods of tilling the soil and of agricultural rites in the Trobriand Islands*, vol. 2. New York: American Book.
Marett, R. 1900. *Pre-animistic religion*. Folklore 11, no. 2: 162–84.
Mauss, Marcel. 1990. *The gift: The form and reason for exchange in archaic societies*. New York: W. W. Norton.

Mayne, B. 2006. *A remarkable man: Letters from a doctor/missionary in the South Seas to his mother c1900*. Oxford: Trafford.

McDermott, G. 2007. *God's rivals: Why has God allowed different religions?* Grand Rapids: IVP Academic.

Miller, J. G. 1978. *Live! A history of church planting in the New Hebrides*, vol. 1. Sydney: Committees on Christian Education and Overseas Missions, General Assembly of the Presbyterian Church of Australia.

———. 1981. *Live! A history of church planting in the republic of Vanuatu*, vol. 2. Sydney: Committees on Christian Education and Overseas Missions, General Assembly of the Presbyterian Church of Australia.

———. 1986. *Live! A history of church planting in the republic of Vanuatu*, vol. 4. Sydney: Committees on Christian Education and Overseas Missions, General Assembly of the Presbyterian Church of Australia.

Miller, R. S. 1975. *Misi Gete*. Tasmania, Australia: Presbyterian Church of Tasmania.

Moreau, A. S. 2006. Contextualization that is comprehensive. *Missiology: An International Review* 34, no. 3: 325–35.

Nassau, R. 1904. *Fetichism in West Africa: Forty years' observation of native customs and superstitions*. New York: Charles Scribner's Sons.

Nehrbass, K. 2010. *Animism and Christianity in a South Pacific society: Four ecclesiastical approaches toward "kastom."* PhD diss., Biola University.

———. Dealing with disaster: Critical contextualization of misfortune in an animistic setting. *Missiology* 39, no. 3. 459–71.

———. 2011b. Formal Theological Education in Vanuatu: Hopes, challenges and solutions. *Melanesian Journal of Theology*, 27(2), 54–72.

Nida, E. 1954. *Customs and cultures*. Pasadena: William Carey Library.

———. 1959. *Introducing animism*. New York: Friendship Press.

Niebuhr, H. R. 1956. *Christ and culture*. New York: Harper & Brothers.

Paton, F. 1903. *Lomai of Lenakel: A hero of the New Hebrides; A fresh chapter in the triumph of the gospel*. New York: American Tract Society.

Paton, J. 1889. *John G. Paton, missionary to the New Hebrides: An autobiography*, vol. 1. New York: Carter.

Paton, M. W. 1894. *Letters and sketches from the New Hebrides*. London: Hodder & Stoughton.

Patterson, G. 1864. *Memoirs of the Rev. S. F. Johnston, the Rev. J. W. Matheson, and Mrs. Mary Johnston Matheson: Missionaries on Tanna; With selections from their diaries and correspondence, and notices of the New Hebrides, their inhabitants and missionary work among them*. Philadelphia: Martien.

Patterson, M. 2002. Moving histories: An analysis of the dynamics of place in North Ambrym, Vanuatu. *Australian Journal of Anthropology* 13, no. 2: 200–218.

Piper, J. 2010. *Let the nations be glad: The supremacy of God in missions*, 3rd ed. Grand Rapids: Baker.

Prior, R. 2003. *Gospel and culture in Vanuatu 3: The voice of the local church*. Wattle Park, Australia: Gospel Vanuatu Books.

————. 2005. *Gospel and culture in Vanuatu 4: Local voices on Jesus Christ and mission.*
    Wattle Park, Australia: Gospel Vanuatu Books.
————. 2006a. *Gospel and culture in Vanuatu 5: Women in culture and church and other
    issues.* Wattle Park, Australia: Gospel Vanuatu Books.
————. 2006b. *Gospel and culture in Vanuatu: An experiment in Pacific theology.* Canberra:
    2nd ANU Missionary History Conference, Asia-Pacific Missionaries.
Proctor, J. H. 1999. Scottish missionaries and the governance of the New Hebrides.
    Journal of Church and State (March 22).
Radin, P. 1957. *Primitive religion.* New York: Dover.
Rice, E. 1974. *John Frum he come: A polemic work about black tragedy.* Garden City, NY:
    Doubleday.
Richardson, D. 1981. *Eternity in their hearts.* Ventura, CA: Regal.
Rivers, W. H. R. 1926. *Psychology and ethnology.* New York: Routledge.
Rush, J. 1997. *The man with the bird on his head: The amazing fulfillment of a mysterious
    island prophecy.* Seattle: YWAM.
Sapiro, W. 1991. Claude Levi-Strauss meets Alexander Goldenweiser: Boasian
    anthropology and the study of totemism. *American Anthropologist* 93, no. 3:
    599–610.
Schmidt, W. 1931. *The origin and growth of religion: Facts and theories.* London: Methuen.
Shears, R. 2006. Prince Philip a god. *Sunday Mail*, November 6.
Shenk, W. 1977. Henry Venn's instructions to missionaries. *Missiology* 5, no. 4: 467–85.
Sire, J. 2004. *Naming the elephant: Worldview as a concept.* Grand Rapids: InterVarsity.
Spriggs, M. 1986. *Landscape, land use and political transformation in southern Melanesia.* In
    Island societies: Archaeological approaches to evolution and transformation, ed. P. V.
    Kirch, 6–18. New York: Cambridge University Press.
Stanner, W. E. H. 1966. *On Aboriginal religion.* Sydney: University of Sydney.
Stapleton, E. 2008. *The Nafe New Testament: Demonstrating the need for a new translation.*
    MA thesis, Graduate Institute of Applied Linguistics.
Steel, R. 1880. *The New Hebrides and Christian missions with a sketch of the labor traffic.*
    London: James Nisbet.
Steffen, T. 1997. *Passing the baton,* revised ed. Pasadena: Center for Organization and
    Ministry.
Strathern, M. 1984. Marriage Exchanges: A Melanesian Comment. *Annual Review of
    Anthropology,* 13, 41–73.
Strelan, J. 1977. *The search for salvation: Studies in the history and theology of cargo cults.*
    Adelaide, Australia: Lutheran Publishing House.
Tabani, M. 2009. *Dreams of unity, traditions of division.* Paideuma 55: 1–17.
Tippett, A. 1967. *Solomon Islands Christianity.* Pasadena: William Carey Library.
————. 1968. Anthropology: Luxury or necessity for missions? *Evangelical Missions
    Quarterly* 5, no. 1: 7–19.
————. 1975. The evangelisation of animists. In *Let the earth hear his voice,* ed. J. D.
    Douglas, 844–57. Minneapolis: World Wide Publications.
————. 1987. *Introduction to missiology.* Pasadena: William Carey Library.

Tomlinson, M. 2006. *Retheorizing mana: Bible translation and discourse of loss in Fiji.* Oceania 76, no. 2: 173–85.

———. 2009. *In God's image: The metaculture of Fijian Christianity.* Berkeley: University of California Press.

Tonkinson, R. 1982. National identity and the problem of kastom in Vanuatu. *Mankind* 13: 306–15.

Trompf, G. 1990. *Cargo cults and millenarian movements: Transoceanic comparisons of new religious movements.* Berlin Mouton de Gruyter.

———. 1994. *Payback: The logic of retribution in Melanesian religions.* New York: Cambridge University Press Turner, G. 1861. *Nineteen years in Polynesia: Life, travels, and researches in the islands of the Pacific.* London: John Snow, Patternoster Row.

Turner, V. 1967. *The forest of symbols: Aspects of Ndembu ritual.* Ithaca, NY: Cornell University Press.

Tylor, E. 1891. *Primitive culture: Researches into the development of mythology, philosophy, religion, language, art, and custom,* vol. 2. London: Murray.

———. 1892. On the limits of savage religion. *Journal of the Anthropological Institute of Great Britain and Ireland* 21: 283–301.

Van Rheenen, G. 1991. *Communicating Christ in animistic contexts.* Grand Rapids: Baker.

Walls, A. 2002. *The cross-cultural process in Christian history.* Maryknoll, NY: Clark.

Warneck, J. 1954. *The living Christ and dying heathenism: The experiences of a missionary in animistic heathendom.* Grand Rapids: Baker.

Watt, A. 1896. *Twenty-five years' mission life on Tanna.* London: Parlane.

Watt, W. 1895. Cannibalism, as practiced on Tanna, New Hebrides. *Journal of the Polynesian Society* 4, no. 4: 226–30.

Westropp, Hodder. 1880. Notes on fetichism. *Journal of the Anthropological Institute of Great Britain and Ireland* 9:304–311.

White, G., and L. Lindstrom. 1997. *Chiefs today: Traditional Pacific leadership and the postcolonial state.* Stanford: Stanford University Press.

Whiteman, D. 1983. *Melanesians and missionaries: An ethnohistorical study of social and religious change in the Southwest Pacific.* Pasadena: William Carey Library.

———. 1997. Contextualization: The theory, the gap, the challenge. *International Bulletin of Missionary Research* (January): 2–7.

Zocca, F. 2006. Vanuatu. In *Globalization and the re-shaping of Christianity in the Pacific*

———, ed. 2009. *Sanguma in Paradise: sorcery, witchcraft and Christianity in Papua New Guinea.* Goroka, PNG: Melanesian Institute.

Glossary of Frequently Used Terms in the Southwest Tanna Language

imarəm	sacred dancing place
kəjiə	harvest festival
kivɨr	magical stone(s)
kleva	clairvoyant, diviner
natuakəmien	laws, fasts
nauta	property, cargo
netik	poison, black magic
nɪgɨs	coconut bark strainer
nɨvo	cottonwood (Hibiscus tiliaceus)
nohunu	food prepared for the kava libation
rao	canoe, generation, village
tamafa	kava libation
tupunas	magical stones, one who works them
yeni	chief (spokesman)

History of Resident Missions on Tanna

MARTYRS 1800–1857	PIONEERS 1858–1899	MAINTAINERS 1900–1935	RECESSION 1936–1969	PARTNERS 1970–PRESENT
John Williams, James Harris martyred 1839 on Erromango	John G. Paton, 1858–1862, Whitesands	Thomson Mac-Millan, Annie Robertson, and later, Elsie Stocks Yarkei, 1900–1936	John Frum cargo cult and other cults become dominant	Father Bordiga, 1970–? (Imaki), Father Stephainis
Turner and Nisbet, 1842, (not martyred, but driven off after 7 months)	Mary and John William Matheson, 1858–1862, Kwamera	Alex Gillies, 1897–1901, Kwamera	Henry Martin (and Daphne Green-shields) Bell, 1936–1942, Whitesands	LDS, AG, NTM, Missionary Baptists
Samoans: Lalolangi, Salamea, Mose, Pomare, Vaiofanga, Vasa, and Upokumano	Betsy and Samuel Fulton Johnston, 1860	Houlton Forlong, 1894–1900, North Tanna	Marjorie Mitchell, 1938–1940, Lenakel Father Roman Martin (Catholic), 1938–1955, Ikiti	Ken and Ann Calvert, 1967–1979, Whitesands
	Joseph Copeland, 1859, Kwamera	William Anderson, 1902–1903, Lenakel	Effie Nicholson, 1944–1947, Lenakel	Vili Railau, AG, 1970s

MARTYRS 1800–1857	PIONEERS 1858–1899	MAINTAINERS 1900–1935	RECESSION 1936–1969	PARTNERS 1970–PRESENT
	William Gray, Waisisi, 1882–1894	J. Campbell Nicholson, Isabel Campbell, 1903–1917, Lenakel	Sister Janet Brown, 1944–1947	Foursquare, independent Pentecostals
	William and Agnes Watt, and later, Jessie Paterson, 1869–1910, Kwamera	Ernest Robertson, 1910, Lenakel	Charles McLeod and wife, 1945–1953, Whitesands	Hugh Proctor, 1972, Lenakel
	Thomas (and Lucy Geddie) Neilson, 1868–1882/3	J. Campbell Rae and wife, 1918–1922, Lenakel	Sister Elizabeth Edgar, 1946, Lenakel	SIL begins 1985
			Father Pierre Massard (Catholic), 1953–1960	
			Father Albert Sacco (Catholic), 1954–1981	
	Frank Paton, 1896–1900, Lenakel	Catholics, 1925–present	Stanley and Joan Cooper, 1954–1962, Whitesands	
	Frank Hume, 1896–1900, Lenakel	Dr. F. J. Williams, 1923–1924, Lenakel	Nancy Robb, 1956–1960, Lenakel	
		Dr. William Armstrong, 1925–1927, 1938–1956, intermittently until 1969, Lenakel	Neil and Mary Brisbane, 1959–1961, Whitesands	

MARTYRS 1800–1857	PIONEERS 1858–1899	MAINTAIN-ERS 1900–1935	RECESSION 1936–1969	PARTNERS 1970– PRESENT
		SDA churches, ca. 1930– present	Dorothy Dy-all, 1961–1965	
		Dr. Daniel Macleod and wife, 1930–1936, Lenakel	Alexander Peerman, Heather Keep, 1961–1965, Lenakel	
		Father Pierre Bochu (Catholic), 1933–1938, Loanatom	Caroline Weaver, 1963–1964, Lenakel/ Whitesands	
			Walter and Mary Stratford, 1964–1966, Whitesands	
			Fred and Bev-erly Jungwirth, 1966–1970, Lenakel	
			Walter and Rosemary Zurrer, 1969–1970, Lenakel	
			David and Lynley McFarlands, Lenakel (date unknown)	

Gospel/Culture Assessment Tool

GOSPEL-RESPONSE CONTINUUM	POINTS 0–4
Answer 0 to 4: strongly disagree 0; about halfway 2; strongly agree 4.	
Congregant discourages the practice of magic (for controlling natural phenomena such as rain, gardens, etc.), not only because he/she is afraid of it (i.e., they see it as risky), but because it competes with exclusive worship of God.	
Congregant articulates a theology of local cosmology (e.g., animistic gods are demons, Jesus is more powerful than local spirits).	
Congregant sees totemic system (e.g., annual harvest sacrifices) as ancestor worship or idolatry.	
Congregant articulates an experience of conversion to Christ.	
Congregant conceptualizes the church as a place for worship, evangelism, and teaching, not simply a place for meeting felt needs (of prosperity, development, health, etc.).	
Congregant conceptualizes salvation as atonement and restoration, not simply a way of avoiding earthly suffering.	
Congregant cites the Bible when talking about his/her faith.	
Congregant's church has stringent leadership selection (elders/pastors).	
Congregant sees divination, shamanism, sorcery, and religious use of drugs as sinful.	
Congregant evaluates plausibility of religious knowledge (i.e., myths and the Bible) in terms of historicity, feasibility, and logical consistency.	
Total Points on Gospel-Response Continuum:	

CULTURAL-INTEGRATION CONTINUUM   POINTS 0–4

Answer 0 to 4: strongly disagree 0; about halfway 2; strongly agree 4.

Congregant's church is independent (not dependent on foreign funds or foreign governance).

Congregant's church has a functional substitute for meeting social obligations to in-laws (regarding, e.g., clan-division exchanges, marriage obligations, and other rites of passage) and a way to honor (dead) ancestors.

Congregant's church utilizes indigenous models of leadership (power, succession, and authority).

Congregant's church uses a local musical style with local instruments.

Congregant's church uses liturgy (including prayer and preaching) in the vernacular.

Congregant's church's pedagogy reflects local style (hortatory, narrative, harangue, dialogue, and propositions).

Congregant's church utilizes local material culture (art, architecture, pews, and style of dressing).

Congregant's church uses local metaphors.

Congregant's church has a functional substitute for dealing with sickness (e.g., deals with possible transgressions, is public, and uses local symbols).

Total Points on Cultural-Integration Continuum:

Gospel/Culture Grid

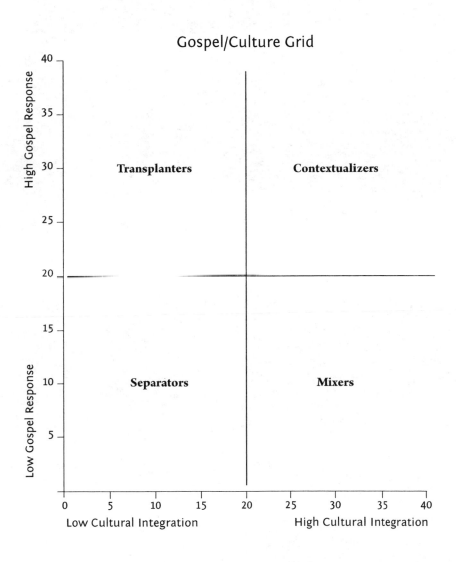

Gospel/Culture Grid

INDEX

A